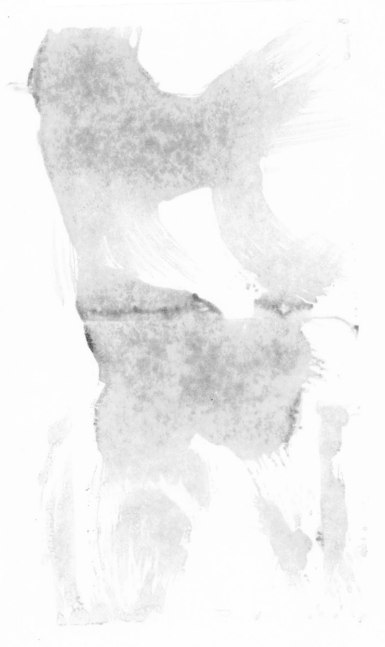

# Also by Ken Hom

# Easy Family Recipes from a Chinese-American Childhood

# EASY FAMILY CHINESE=

*With illustrations by Emily Lisker*

# RECIPES from a AMERICAN CHILDHOOD

## by KEN HOM

Alfred A. Knopf    New York    1997

THIS IS A BORZOI BOOK
PUBLISHED BY ALFRED A. KNOPF, INC.

Copyright © 1997 by TAUROM Incorporated
Illustrations copyright © 1997 by Emily Lisker

http://www.randomhouse.com/

Library of Congress Cataloging-in-Publication Data
Hom, Ken.
Easy family recipes from a Chinese-American childhood /
by Ken Hom. — 1st ed.
p.   cm. — (Knopf cooks American ; 16)
Includes bibliographical references and index.
ISBN 0-394-58758-8
1. Cookery, Chinese.   2. Cookery, American.   I. Title.
II. Series.
TX724.5.C5H586   1997
641.5951—dc21          96-51917
CIP

Manufactured in the United States of America
First Edition

*This book is for Daniel Taurines*

# Contents

# Acknowledgments

This book would not have happened without the long patience, persistence, and encouragement of Judith Jones, my editor at Knopf, who guided me through this very personal project. I am thankful for the professional experience of working with her and her assistant, Ken Schneider.

There are many voices of my Chinese-American friends in this book. They were kind enough to spend time sharing their most intimate experiences with me. I am most grateful to Gordon Wing, who spent countless hours doing research and assisting me in testing all the recipes, and to Amy Tan, Steve Wong, Donald Wong, Ming Tsai, Lillian Chou, Lillian Robyn, Tim Mar, and Kent Wong.

Gerry Cavanaugh deserves my gratitude for his research and editorial assistance in helping me shape the text, as does Drew Smith, who checked the recipes as well as the text.

And, finally, to Martha Casselman, who always believed I would finish this book: thank you.

# Easy Family Recipes from a Chinese-American Childhood

# Introduction

## Chinese Lessons

My earliest memories, ones that to this day still recur in my dreams, are of pleasant days filled with warm gentle winds, brightly colored festive ribbons, and cloudy humid skies, punctuated by tropical rains. Having grown up in Chicago, whose virtues emphatically do not include much pleasant weather, I often wondered where these memories came from. One day, as an adult, it hit me. I was remembering Tucson, Arizona, where I was born, and recalling as well my mother's warm recollections of her own birthplace, Canton, in South China, which I had absorbed even before I understood what her words meant. These earliest memories remain deep in my consciousness.

Comforting, pervasive aromas and delightful tastes were part of everyday life. My mother was a superlative cook, and our home was always filled with the smells of the seasonings, spices, and sauces that characterize Cantonese cooking: ginger, scallions, soy sauce, garlic, hoisin sauce, and the oils—peanut and sesame. When she and I moved to Chicago after my father's sudden death in 1950, the tastes and aromas of home were joined by those emanating from my uncle's restaurant, which my mother and I frequented.

Of course, at the time I was not aware that my senses were absorbing "Chinese lessons." I do know that I loved these aromas, tastes, and textures and that they signified, as they do to this day, sustenance laced with the love and warmth of a close family and friends. These lessons were reinforced when I was apprenticed at an early age to my uncle's restaurant—like today's precocious female tennis players, I turned professional before I was a teenager.

Living in Chicago, America's most multicultural city, I might as well have been in Canton, because Chicago is also our most ethnically segregated city. Chicago's Chinatown was my turf, my familiar neighborhood. Beyond its boundaries, all was exotic and, according to my mother, dangerous as well. My mother spoke little English; I spoke only Cantonese until I started public school. We lived in a small apartment in a complex that had formerly consisted of commercial offices. That meant that most of the ten-

*With my mother*

ants shared the common bathroom down the hall. Our apartment was located above a Chinese restaurant. A distant relative of my mother lived across the hall from us. He had his own bathroom, including a tub, which he graciously allowed my mother and me to use. We thought it quite a luxury.

This relative—I called him "uncle"—left a lasting impression on me. I learned later that he was a bookie and a runner for a local Chinese gambling house. I remember seeing him hurrying about the neighborhood, and he would sometimes let me peek into the small bag of money he always had with him. My mother never spoke to me about his trade, but she treated me to many lectures on the evils of gambling.

More important in terms of my "Chinese lessons," this uncle had a passion for food. He made his own Chinese sausages and cured his own dried beef and pork. His small apartment exuded the smells of five-spice powder and rice wine used in the curing process. He would hang strings of fatty Chinese sausages and Chinese cured bacon in the bathroom; they would be removed temporarily while I took my Saturday-night bath or if my mother had laundry to be dried. Sheets of cured meats were often draped about his apartment. My uncle would slice the meats thin and rub them with spices and sugar, then air-dry them on metal sheets. The meats would keep forever, like beef jerky.

It impressed me that this "man about Chinatown," with money to spare and with status in the community, was so lovingly and deliciously involved with food. I ate many small pieces of the treats he prepared, sometimes without his permission. And I still relish their taste.

Life with my mother in this Chinese microcosm revolved around home, food, and the neighborhood. My mother worked with other Chinese women in a Chinese-owned food-canning factory. We went only to Chinese-language movies; we read only Chinese magazines and newspapers; we ate foods prepared only in Chinese style. This was the common experience of most Chinese-Americans at that time.

The Chinatowns of America, which were "ghettos," were both forced upon the Chinese—in the San Francisco Chinatown of the nineteenth century, any Chinese man who ventured forth was liable to verbal and physical assault—and formed as a matter of choice. All immigrant groups tend to seek out their common culture and thus settle close together. However, as with African-Americans, the physical characteristics of Chinese-Americans perpetuated their ghettoization long after the legal and social barriers to assimilation had been lowered.

Thus, the Chinese formed their own world, called Chinatown. It was complete with doctors, teachers, bankers, grocers, tailors, shoemakers, launderers, and, of course, restaurateurs. We had no supermarkets. We shopped at the local specialty-food stores that offered the traditional foods of Chinese cookery. These nearby corner stores were gathering points where people came to gossip and exchange news from the homeland as well as to shop. When I was a child, there were still professional letter writers around, and they frequented the shops; I remember seeing people dictate to them, and have them read the return letters from home.

The singular fresh and pungent aromas of these stores must have had a pleasant and soothing influence on the shoppers, reminding them at a barely conscious level of home, friends, comfort, and love. Nothing evokes such good feelings more than the sight and smell of favorite foods. The familiar vegetables and fruits, the strings of Chinese sausage and bacon, the dried cured duck, and the roasting pig—all of these delighted the eyes and nose of the shopper. Occasionally, fresh water chestnuts would be flown in from San Francisco, and their arrival always sparked, quite literally, a run on the market.

I particularly recall the glistening skin and spicy smell of the whole pig roasting away, held over the coals by thick iron hooks, slowly browning away to perfection. Another "uncle" of mine was a specialist cook. He often stayed up all night to attend to a roasting pig. He was known affectionately around Chinatown as "Roast Pig Lei." His clothes were redolent of roast pig and the oils and spices he used in the process. On Chinese festival days, all of these shops would be brightly decorated, mainly with "good-luck red ribbons," and the meat shops would feature roast suckling pig, which would make my mouth water.

Almost every afternoon, after school and work, my mother and I would go to the Wentworth Avenue or Cermak Road shops to buy the essentials for our evening meal. I recall vividly receiving special treats from shopkeepers, bits of savory barbecued pork or candied or salted sour plums. When my mother was distracted, I managed to wheedle sticks of Wrigley's chewing gum as well: my mother did not want me to have anything artificially sugared. She would pinch and squeeze the Chinese melons, sniff the dried meats, eye carefully the roasted prepared meats, shake the fresh bean curd (tofu), and carefully choose from the array of dried peppercorns. As I grew up, I absorbed without knowing it at the time many essential lessons in the Chinese approach to the freshness, variety, balance, relationships, and medicinal qualities of food. "We are what we eat" is true of all of us, but perhaps even more so of the Chinese.

These shopping tours were vastly entertaining to me as well as educational. I know that my mother enjoyed the outings, as she does to this day: she has never moved away from that neighborhood.

My mother and I had our own separate family rites as well. On Sundays, her one day off, we almost always went to the local Chinese-language movie house, the "Sing Sing" theater, near Harvey Park. The films were from Hong Kong—mainland China was sealed off by then—and in the Cantonese dialect. There were subtitles in the written characters that can be read by anyone, no matter what Chinese dialect he or she may speak. The films were usually reruns, and the audiences were very familiar with the plots, the actors, the actresses, and the forms of dialogue. They would comment on the performers, hoot at the villains, shout warnings to the heroes, sob with the desperate heroines, and laugh as all turned out well in the end. If the film was a Chinese opera, everyone sang along, in a mixture of dialects.

One of my favorite characters was Wong Fai Hung, the original kung-fu master. Every week I could count on him to vanquish at least twenty or more opponents in remarkably agile hand-to-hand and foot-to-face combat. It looked absolutely real to my young eyes, and even the adults thought he was a superman. Along with the films there was food, of course. Because we sat through each showing at least twice, my mother would bring sacks of salted and dried plums, sugared lotus roots, and candied chestnuts. This was the only time I was allowed anything sweet.

In my perception as a child, Chinatown seemed a vast place. As an adult, I learned how small it really is. But that congested eight-block area, bounded by Cermak and Wentworth Avenues, held at that time an entire world for me, and it was a Chinese world. This diversity was most particularly true in the matter of food. Practically every traditional ingredient of several styles of

South Chinese cuisine was available. In the summer, Chinese vegetables abounded: bok choy (Chinese cabbage), Chinese celery cabbage, the various Chinese mustard greens, okra, Chinese silk squash, Chinese chives, Chinese parsley or fresh coriander, and radishes.

I later found out that Chinese residents of the area supplied most of these ingredients from tiny neighborhood gardens, some of them quite literally window boxes. Others were flown in from San Francisco and other parts of California. In the summer, we would get produce from Chinese farmers in upstate New York and other parts of the East.

There were also cans and jars of plum sauce, hoisin sauce, five-spice powder, chili peppers and paste, Chinese pickles and pickled vegetables, dried lily stems and lotus leaves. These were imported from Taiwan and Hong Kong—imports from mainland China were unavailable until the 1970s. The one traditional food we rarely found was fresh bamboo shoots, a deficiency so enormous in my mother's eyes that it almost made her regret she had ever left China. We had to rely on canned shoots, which are never as good as the fresh. Somehow we survived.

Bountiful America provided our two-person household with all the other foods my mother required: pork, often; fresh fish or seafood, almost daily; beef, only occasionally (it was too expensive and my mother disliked its taste).

Rice, of course, was abundant. I was soon old enough to haul fifty-pound sacks of the staple up the stairs to our apartment. I remember savoring the yeasty smell of fresh noodles in some stores and the pungent odor of soy in others, as well as the sweet fragrance of fresh litchi nuts—a brief pleasure, because their season was only two weeks long. The litchi nuts came from Hawaii, and my mother compared them unfavorably with the

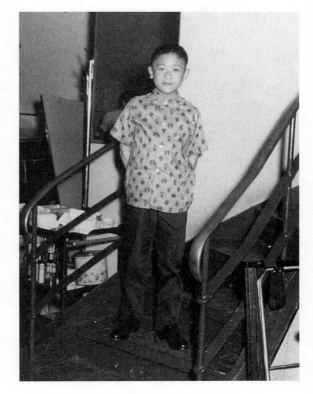

*As a young boy at a Chinese wedding banquet*

ones from South China: the Hawaiian ones, she said, had seeds that were much too big, they had too little meat, and they were not as sweet-tasting as those she remembered from her childhood. However, to me every litchi nut was delicious.

The tiny Chinese market that sold them was just down the street and even as a little boy I loved going there to examine its produce. My mother and I would carry home bags of dried mushrooms, vinegars, sesame seeds, and different kinds of oil. I don't know how these all fit into our little apartment, but my mother went shopping every day, so I imagine that, aside from the staples, we kept a low inventory.

Poor as we were, I never experienced a sense of deprivation. My mother's skill in the kitchen provided more than physical sustenance. It gave me a sense of security, and it has left me with a stockpile of memories more enduring than any material possessions. These memories are intimately joined to the fragrances of my mother's cooking: for example, the sharp, refreshing gingery smell of a platter of freshly steamed pike, piled high with fresh scallions and doused with hot peanut and sesame oil, immediately transports me back to family gatherings on special occasions. I remember other family banquets attended by "uncles" whose names I did not know but whose numbers I recall. The smell of braised tender spareribs, laden with black beans and garlic, brings back the family banquet celebrating "Fifth" Uncle's becoming an American citizen.

My mother's herbal wine was a special case. She would concoct this heady, healthful brew from a variety of Chinese medicinal herbs and roots. On special occasions, or when someone was under the weather, my mother would carefully administer the appropriate potion. I can still see that enormous glass crock she stored it in. I think it was an old pickle jar that she obtained from some store. It sat in our hallway, and every time I passed by I smelled its odor, neither pleasant nor unpleasant, but most distinct. There is nothing else quite like it. Even now, as an adult, every once in a while when I combine certain herbs in a recipe, I suddenly see that white vat of medicinal wine.

# Food and Family

In Chinese culture one can never say enough about food. We love talking about what we have eaten, what we dream about eating, and what we hope to eat the next moment.

In contrast to others, Chinese people actually spend more on food as a percentage of total income as they become wealthier. Such a practice violates the so-called Engel's Law of food consumption, which maintains that the proportion so spent goes down as income rises.

This Chinese exception to the rule is most glaring in Hong Kong, where food serves as the great social cement, and where, as the scholar E. N. Anderson writes, "even the most trivial matters are occasions for a feast." But the phenomenon is also seen, if to a lesser degree, in Taiwan and Singapore and other overseas Chinese communities. And until the recent relaxation of the government's hold over mainland China, the most vigorous resistance of the people to the state's enforcement of ascetic puritanism was not in regard to sex, or corruption, or family limitation, but in regard to banquets. Despite the government's best efforts to discourage what was considered extravagance or overindulgence, people from all walks of life persisted in throwing huge banquets whenever they could.

Amy Tan captures this characteristic approach to food in her imaginative re-creation of Chinese-American life, *The Joy Luck Club.* Mother Suyuan Woo recalls that in China she and her friends put on banquets even as the Japanese Army surrounded her city and food supplies had dwindled. "People thought we were wrong to serve banquets every week while many people in the city were starving [but] each week one of us would host a party to raise our spirits. The hostess had to serve dyansyin foods to bring good fortune of all kinds—dumplings shaped like silver money ingots, long rice noodles for long life, boiled peanuts for conceiving sons, many good-luck oranges for a plentiful, sweet life. . . . We knew we were the lucky ones."

"This use of food," Anderson writes, "as social lubricator, stimulus, and marker, is traceable to the very dawn of Chinese civilization—and beyond."

Countless food metaphors are embedded in the Chinese language. Again, this is not unique to the Chinese. But the richness and naturalness of the usages are without comparison. Everything, for example, from desire ("to eat ice cream with the eyes"), to envy ("to eat vinegar"), to unemployment ("his wok is broken"), to real-estate speculation ("to stir-fry the land"), to rebukes ("dead shrimp head"), finds an appropriate and very telling food metaphor. My mother was not above so addressing me by this last, quite unflattering term whenever I did something of which she especially disapproved.

My favorite of these metaphors is the familiar Chinese greeting *Chi fan le mei you.* The phrase is close to the English "How are you?" and also implies a wish for health and happiness. But the literal meaning of the words is "Have you eaten yet?" A whole world of meaning rests within this commonplace greeting.

Within every Chinese family, in whatever country the family may be, food is a matter of central concern. All Chinese know the importance of the various tastes, textures, and colors of so many different foods; the techniques of their preparation; the richly symbolic and metaphorical significance of food in general; and the quite specific virtues, ritual uses, and medicinal value of a vast array of edibles. In no other culture, with the possible exception of French and Italian, are the preparation and serving of food of such central importance in daily life.

Around the dinner table, whether it was only my mother and I or our extended Chicago family, the occasion was not simply a meal but a time to catch up on family and homeland news, to reinforce traditional values, to reiterate the crucial precepts of Chinese culture, and to observe the rules of

proper behavior, especially table etiquette. It was a time to engage in a discussion of the favorite subject, food: where a particular ingredient was purchased, how it was prepared, what were our favorite dishes and combinations, what would be the proper menu for the time of year or for an upcoming holiday. The family table is where I imbibed the fundamental lore and meaning of Chinese cuisine.

My mother had grown up in China with maidservants in the household. These servants did all of the onerous and time-consuming food preparations for the household, but my grandmother and my

*My maternal grandfather, Canton, China*

mother and her sister closely supervised everything. Indeed, my maternal grandmother was a splendid cook, renowned among her family and friends. When I visited the ancestral home in 1989, I was surprised by the number of people who still recalled her prowess as a master cook.

My mother grew up relatively well-off, at least until the Japanese invasion reached her region in 1941. Her grandfather had immigrated to America, where by dint of some luck and very hard work he managed to build a profitable business. His remittances to his son in China allowed for the purchase of land and other investments, which raised my mother's family to the level of the local elite. My mother's father was an enlightened man who rejected the still-prevalent customs of foot-binding and seclusion for his daughters. Having attended the University of Beijing, he valued learning and saw that his daughters were educated. Often away on official business in Beijing and Shanghai—he was a high-level functionary in the government salt monopoly, in those days a very important agency—he left the running of the household to his wife and daughters. And thus my mother and her sister grew up sharing the supervision of the domestic economy under their mother's direction.

My mother never had to prepare foods from start to finish until she came to America, where to her shock she discovered that no maidservants were available. After my father's untimely death, her lack of money meant she could afford even less help. But because she had always watched her mother cook, my mother quickly flowered as a superb cook and homemaker. Relying on all she had observed and on her natural technical skill, she evolved an impressive repertory of delicious home-cooked meals.

A delicate balance of tastes, textures, and colors was her ideal. She always knew the precise amount of seasoning to add to a dish. She never used recipes, drawing instead upon her memory and her intimacy with the fundamentals of Chinese cooking. She stuck close to the Cantonese approach (none better!) and never attempted other Chinese regional styles. She would, however, try dishes she had enjoyed at friends' homes or in restaurants, re-creating them in her own style.

I grew up believing that every mother went to the market very early on Sunday and returned with a live chicken for lunch or dinner. Just before my mother dispatched the bird, its squawking would wake me up. My mother was an expert at defeathering chickens, and, in the Chinese fashion, very few parts of the bird were wasted. She would catch the chicken blood and mix it with salt, producing a blood pudding that would be steamed

*When my mother and I returned home to Kaiping, we made offerings and paid homage to our ancestors at the family shrine.*

and served with certain soups. This mixture, my mother assured me, was very good for my health. The breast meat of the chicken would be velveted (that is, mixed with cornstarch, salt, and egg white) and stir-fried with vegetables or noodles; the thigh meat would be braised in either a black bean sauce or a spicy ginger sauce. The bones were carefully saved to make chicken stock. And, yes, my mother saved the feet as well, and when she had collected enough of them she made a braised chicken-feet dish that was quite delectable.

In traditional Chinese fashion, my mother would dry and preserve all sorts of vegetables and meats. I remember chicken and duck gizzards and giblets drying on metal racks set on our fire escape, and scallops spread out on trays to dry in the sunlight. My mother also pickled all sorts of vegetables. In our kitchen there were enormous glass jars filled with mustard greens, bought in season at low prices and then pickled. She would rub the greens with salt and pickle them in a vinegar-and-sugar mixture. Besides serving as a vegetable during the long Chicago winter, these pickled greens made tasty and refreshing snacks—the way good kosher pickles are enjoyed.

On April 4, during Ching Ming, my mother would prepare a special food offering in memory of my deceased father and all of our ancestors. I remember these occasions vividly because of the evocation of my lost father and also because the food was so delicious. Steeped chicken, an array of savory dim-sum pastries, slices of roast suckling pig, pieces of duck or barbecued pork—these were the main attractions. My father was buried in Arizona and our ancestors slept in China, so we could not pay our respects to them at the cemetery, as the custom requires. But we had a small shrine in our kitchen dedicated to their memories. We burned our joss sticks, bowed three times toward the shrine, and then began to feast in their honor. Many years later, my mother and I performed the same ritual in her ancestral village. It was a very moving event that linked me to my heritage.

I have discovered that my experiences in growing up are quite similar to those of almost every other Chinese-American I know. Social isolation tempered by extended-family ties, the tenacity of tradition, the central importance of traditional foods and family gatherings—these are part of the common ground shared by all Chinese in America.

# Growing Up Chinese=American and Chinese=American Cuisine

To understand fully the experiences of Chinese-Americans, and to see why the "extended family" and Chinese food were so important to them in America, one must bear in mind the legal and social difficulties they faced when they arrived in America and for many decades thereafter.

The first Chinese in America—among whom was my maternal great-grandfather—were drawn by the promise of better economic conditions and pushed by the often miserable conditions in China. From the beginning, however, the Chinese immigrants, who were at the start almost entirely males, encountered racial prejudice. To be sure, with the exception of the so-called invisible immigrants, the English and Scotch-Irish, all immigrant groups have suffered more or less from the general prejudice against those who are racially, religiously, or ethnically "different." But the Chinese encountered prejudice whose virulence and chronic violence were surpassed only by that inflicted upon African-Americans and American Indians.

The majority of the first Chinese in America came from the Cantonese region, a relatively cosmopolitan trading area with a long tradition of overseas contacts and migration. Indeed, between 1850 and 1900, millions of Southern Chinese left the homeland for Australia, South America, South Africa, East Asia, and other places. This mass migration has been called the "Chinese diaspora."

Only a small minority of these Chinese emigrants came to North America. Almost everyone went to California after 1851 as prospectors to work in the booming gold fields of the "forty-niners" and then, after 1865, as laborers on the construction of the transcontinental railroad (for more about those frontier days, see box on page 179).

As gold miners, the Chinese evoked hostility because they were deemed "foreigners who had no right to extract wealth from the land belonging to the native born." As laborers they were blamed for lowering the wage scale of white workers. As laundrymen, restaurant operators, tailors, and "coolies" they were cast as stereotypes of all Chinese. Only as truck farmers—isolated, productive, and not in competition with other powerful or threatened groups—did the Chinese escape the worst effects of racial prejudice.

The informal restrictions against the Chinese in America were strengthened by the Chinese Exclusion Act of 1882 and by subsequent federal and state laws. Such laws prohibited or penalized the further immigration of Chinese men and blocked the immigration of Chinese women. Most of these restrictions were not lifted until 1965.

The "exclusion" had an awful effect on Chinese family life everywhere in America. Most Chinese men were forced to remain bachelors; even those legally married could not bring their wives into the country. There were very few Chinese women available for marriage. And we should not forget that "antimiscegenation" laws prohibited Asians as well as African-Americans from marrying white women. These laws, too, were not abolished until the 1960s.

In a culture like the Chinese, where the family is so strong an institution—for many the only institution they had known—the laws inflicted cruel and unusual punishment. The deprivation they caused explains why the idea of the extended family was so fiercely embraced. Any Chinese, no matter how remotely related, and often only fictitiously related, would be taken in as part of the family.

I remember from my mother's and my own experience the way "bachelor uncles" usually lived together in dormitory-style apartments, four or more to a bedroom. Their narrow existence consisted of hard work, gambling, an occasional visit to a prostitute (Chinese or otherwise), loneliness, and homesickness. Conditions of life in China had never held out any promise of improvement, so these men accepted their fate with an outward appearance of stoic or, rather, Confucian resignation.

But at "family" gatherings, their stoicism gave way to feelings of joy that reflected their deeply hidden longings. The "family" seized upon any opportunity to celebrate, to "share rice together," to relieve tedium, and to reward hard work. Chinese holidays, "family" anniversaries, the rare weddings, any significant and not so significant event was a chance to bring people together. And these gatherings all were, in my memory, extraordinarily festive.

On the major holidays, like New Year's or the Autumn Moon Festival, red crepe would be attached to the rafters or the ceiling, along with bright strips printed with Chinese characters, to assure all of the family guests long lives and prosperity. When I was a child, bright-red decorations meant to me that a fabulous meal and many sweet treats were on their way, along with the arrival of many of my "uncles" around the table. For the bachelors, the banquets were the brightest moments of their existence; these meant, for them and for everyone else, a joyful, sometimes boisterous time, but, above all, a time when family bonds and a sense of belonging were reinforced.

I remember listening carefully as the adults related news of other family members, in America or back in China—who had married, who had died, who had had children, who was ill, who was attending what school, how the children were faring. I know now that I was a late bloomer and made slow progress when I first attended school. I remember my mother uncharacteristically making excuses for me when the "family" asked about my scholarly progress. Years later, I read Timothy Mo's brilliant re-creation of Chinese life in contemporary Britain, *Sour Sweet*. The mother in that story had a baby son whose head was inordinately large for his age, and the poor mother was constantly either denying or rationalizing the condition. When I read those passages, I was reminded of my mother explaining away my own inadequacies, afraid that she and I would be the subject of demeaning gossip. But invidious gossip, too, is part of family life.

The richest and most delightful aspect of this family life, however, was centered around the wonderful array (or procession) of dishes, especially at banquets, funerals, birthdays. Almost any occasion was a special event to celebrate with food. Nothing is more reassuring or comforting than to be able to partake of familiar foods in foreign lands, amidst alien corn, as it were, especially when food is invested with so much social, religious, and symbolic meaning, as it is in Chinese culture. So the Chinese did everything possible to maintain, to re-create, to imaginatively reorder their ancient cuisine in the new world called America.

# Chinese=American Cuisine

Perhaps the central defining idea my mother inculcated in me about how I was to distinguish Chinese-Americans from all the other Americans, hyphenated or not, was that the Chinese knew about food whereas the others did not. Chinese cooking was good; theirs was not. Our food was healthy, aromatic, colorful, tasty, and inventive; theirs was the antithesis of all these qualities: it looked, smelled, and tasted bizarre. Our identity is entwined with our food; theirs is not. We know how to enjoy food and live to eat; they pay little heed to what or how to eat and merely eat to live.

I carried these prejudices with me when I went off to grade school at age six, my first real interaction with the non-Chinese world. Fortunately, with the flexibility of a child, I saw that not everything was so bad outside of Chinatown. My mother would pack me a hot lunch in a thermos—Chinese do not really like cold foods—such as hot rice with Chinese sausages. But I soon learned how to trade my ethnic lunches for someone else's sandwiches of cold bologna on thick slices of real rye or pumpernickel bread with mustard.

I also learned to enjoy corn and mashed potatoes. Later, as a young man, I traveled to Europe and discovered and entered fully into the wonderful worlds of French and Italian cooking. So my ethnic food prejudices were not written in concrete. On the other hand, I drew the line at roast turkey, which I found incredibly dry and tasteless. And I never could understand my non-Chinese classmates' aversion to fresh vegetables. My school cafeteria offered the most lifeless, tasteless foods—stodgy, overcooked, without color or imagination.

The question then arises: given this cultural difference in regard to food, how did Chinese cuisine become such a favorite among Americans of every background? The short answer is that the Chinese restaurateurs were smart businessmen who gave the customers what they wanted. But that is only part of the answer.

From the beginning of the Chinese immigration into California and elsewhere, Chinese restaurants sprang up. There was an immediate demand among the Chinese gold miners and railroad workers for the traditional foods. So there was an opportunity for immigrants who found the gold mines too risky and railroad labor too onerous to open restaurants to cater to this ready-made clientele. It also presented a challenge: how could one get hold of the fresh ingredients that make Chinese cookery so unique?

The problem was partially solved by the rapid emergence of Chinese-American truck farmers, many of whom converted their mining claims into vegetable gardens. Rice, tea, and other staples were available as imports from China and Hawaii. With the fan (rice) and the tsai (green leaves and vegetables) in hand, an acceptable menu could be offered. Not being professional cooks, and usually simply recalling what their mothers had done in the old country, these "chefs" created but a facsimile of the real thing: the unglamorous but hearty peasant favorites of their region: dishes like chow mein and, of course, chop suey.

To the Chinese restaurateurs' good fortune, their offerings were immediately accepted by Chinese and Anglo-Americans alike. In retrospect, one can understand why. The vast majority of the first Chinese immigrants were from the Canton region. Centuries of necessity, inventiveness, and relative openness to the world had made Cantonese cuisine into the most versatile, nondogmatic, experimental cuisine in all China, virtues that became even greater strengths in America. Forced to rely upon what was available to them, but retaining the theory and practice of Cantonese style—that

*My family at a San Diego Chinese restaurant*

is, freshness of ingredients, balance of contrasting tastes and colors, an emphasis on vegetables, and an avoidance of overcooking—the proprietors put out foods that at once gratified their Chinese compatriots and satisfied their American customers. Later on, as the restaurateurs learned more about their Anglo clientele, they offered the Anglos what they demanded: heavy stuffed egg rolls, sticky sweet-and-sour pork, stir-fried beef dishes, and plenty of soy sauce. Exotic in appearance and taste, these dishes are nothing like authentic Cantonese food. As one historian puts it, the early restaurants, "capable of producing their succulent native fare, [corrupted it] into a distinctive species billed as 'Chinese-American' food to suit the lo fan ('barbarians')." Popular as these corruptions were, they effectively hid the true Cantonese cuisine from Americans until well into the twentieth century.

Nevertheless, the system worked. By the beginning of the twentieth century, Chinese-American restaurants could be found in almost every city and region in the country. Today, there are more restaurants specializing in Chinese cuisine than in any other ethnic cuisine, a full 30 percent of all the ethnic and regional cuisines in America. The current geographic distribution of Chinese restaurants in America shows that they are virtually universal. (They are also to be found in practically every country in the world.) The popularity of these restaurants in America is even more striking when one considers that Chinese-Americans make up only about .3 percent of our population. Today, some of the best-loved restaurants in America are those that offer the authentic foods of the Chinese canon.

But that was not always the case, as my experience in my uncle's restaurant taught me. I was eleven years old when I was apprenticed to my uncle. From three to six every day after school and all day Saturday and on Sunday, I washed dishes, rinsing them with a long powerful spray hose, stacking them on plastic trays, and then pushing them through the drying machine. It was hard, hot work. I was taught how to "prep" foods: to devein shrimp, clean sea snails, peel garlic, chop ginger, shell ginkgo nuts. After only a few months, I was actually cooking short orders—I still remember my first production, a beef-tomato dish. And I was not the only preteen in the kitchen. Child-labor laws did not impinge on the sanctity of the family, even if the family was both quite extended and even fictitious.

I was soon promoted enough to put up those take-out orders that consisted mainly of the stereotypical "Chinese" food that most Americans preferred: fried rice; sweet-and-sour pork (much more sweet than sour, and artificially crimson red); and the old standby, chow mein. The demand for these dishes never slackened, rain or shine, summer or winter. But they were never eaten by the Chinese-Americans.

It is no longer a secret that every Chinese restaurant in those days had two separate menus, one for the Chinese customers, another for the Americans, of whatever ethnic background. The same was true in other countries. A character in Timothy Mo's *Sour Sweet,* set in England, refers to "the tourist menu listing rubbish, total *lopsup,* fit only for foreign devils." So clearly marked was the distinction that most restaurants had two separate refrigerators, to avoid an accidental confusion of the ingredients to be used.

The Americans stuck to the familiar exotic and gooey dishes—chop suey, chow mein, egg drop soup—that so beguiled their palates. Chinese customers would order such dishes as crispy-skin squab, Peking duck, steamed lobster with ginger, duck and mushroom casserole. All of these were richer and more expensive to prepare than my mother's meals. In flavor and subtlety of color and balance, however, they were of a piece: excellent Cantonese-style cooking.

Today, the secret menus are gone. Now Americans are ordering and en-

*American and Chinese menus at King Wah Chinese Restaurant in Chicago, where I worked*

joying to their heart's content the entire repertory of Chinese cuisine. In 1965, the strict prohibitions against Chinese immigration were dropped. Chinese from all of the various regions of China have since entered America, bringing with them their regional cuisines. Cantonese cookery has been joined by many other styles—Sichuan, Hunan, Fuxian, Shanghai, Peking—all elaborating variations on the great themes of Chinese cuisine. This new influx happened at a time when Americans were opening up more to new foods that had hitherto been looked upon as foreign or exotic. They were eager to experience the authentic tastes of different cultures and to incorporate into their own kitchens some of the flavorings and cooking styles they were exposed to. Soy sauce soon became a standard item in the kitchen cupboard, and stir-frying entered our culinary vocabulary. Chinese cuisine had become a naturalized member of American culture.

However, I feel that today fewer home cooks in America are experimenting with Chinese cooking. The books as well as the special utensils and ingredients they bought are moldering on the shelf, because the weary cook got tired, I believe, of recipes that required so much preparation, such a variety of exotic ingredients, and split-second timing in the execution of a dish. The trouble was that the kinds of recipes they were attempting were too often restaurant dishes that were overly demanding for average home cooks; furthermore, the cookbooks would recommend that at least two or three dishes be prepared simultaneously to represent an authentic Chinese meal.

But the recipes that I have put together here are typical of the simple, easy home cooking that I, as well as many of my Chinese-American friends, enjoyed every day. Our families used ingredients readily available and cooked with simple techniques.

You will find in these recipes that the same basic seasonings are called for again and again—light and dark soy sauce, rice wine, sesame oil, oyster sauce, fermented black beans, garlic, ginger, scallions. I have made a list of these essentials, and you should have them at hand in your cupboard so that you can come home at the end of a working day and prepare a home-style Chinese supper as readily as my mother always did. It is no harder than whipping up a meal of pasta—often easier, in fact.

Some of the Chinese cutting techniques may be unfamiliar and take a little time to master, but the more often you do Chinese cooking the easier it becomes. After all, to cook Western style one had to learn to chop an onion and julienne a carrot, and Chinese techniques are not so different. But the right preparation of the ingredients has an important part in the proper cooking of the dish, so it is worth looking at the illustrated guide to slicing, shredding, roll-cutting, etc., to get the hang of these techniques. Once the preparation is done, the cooking is usually fast—except for slow simmering dishes, and they need no tending.

I hope that, in reading about the kind of cooking I grew up on, as you experience vicariously the wonderful tastes and aromas of the comfort foods I knew as a child, you will be tempted to make Chinese cooking an integral part of your repertoire. And you can vary the dishes with what is in season or what may be in your refrigerator. Nothing is written in stone. We adapted to America. You add your own adaptations. That's what American cooking is all about.

# Techniques

Rapid cooking presupposes that every ingredient in a dish has been properly prepared beforehand. Foods that have been chopped into smallish, well-shaped pieces can be cooked for a minimum of time, ensuring that they retain their natural texture and taste. Careful cutting also enhances the visual appeal of a dish. For these reasons, Chinese cooks are very specific about cutting techniques, particularly where vegetables are concerned. The Chinese always use a cleaver to cut and chop, wielding it with skill and dexterity. But if you are more comfortable with a large sharp knife, by all means use it.

## Slicing

Hold the food firmly on the chopping board with one hand and cut straight down to make very thin slices. Meat is always sliced across the grain to break up the fibers, so it will be more tender when cooked. If you are using a cleaver, hold it, as illustrated, grasping the handle with your thumb and index finger on either side, close to the blade. Always keep the fingers of the hand holding the food tucked under for safety. Your knuckles should act as a guide for the blade.

## Horizontal or Flat Slicing

The cleaver with its wide blade is particularly suitable for splitting an ingredient into two thinner pieces while retaining its overall shape. Hold the blade of the cleaver or knife parallel to the chopping board. Place your free hand on top of the piece of food to keep it steady. Using a gentle cutting motion, slice sideways into the food. Depending on the recipe, you may need to repeat this process, cutting the two halves into even thinner flat pieces.

## Diagonal Slicing

Used for cutting vegetables such as asparagus, carrots, or scallions, diagonal slicing is designed to expose more of the surface of the vegetable for quicker cooking. Angle the knife or cleaver at a slant and cut evenly.

## Roll=Cutting

Rather like diagonal slicing, roll-cutting is used for larger vegetables such as zucchini, large carrots, eggplant, and Chinese white radish (daikon). The technique allows more of the surface of the vegetable to be exposed to the heat, thereby speeding up the cooking time. Begin by making one diagonal slice at one end of the vegetable. Then turn it 180 degrees and make the next diagonal slice. Continue in this way until you have chopped the entire vegetable into evenly sized, diamond-shaped chunks.

## Shredding

Like the French julienne technique, shredding means to cut into thin, fine, matchsticklike pieces. First cut the food into slices, then pile several slices on top of each other and cut them *lengthwise* into fine strips. Some foods, par-

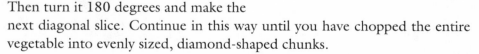

23

ticularly meat and chicken breasts, are easier to shred if they are first stiffened slightly in the freezer for about twenty minutes.

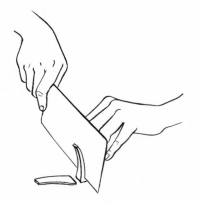 

## Dicing

First cut the food into slices, then stack the slices and cut them *length-wise* into sticks, just as you would for shredding (above). Stack the strips or sticks and cut *crosswise* into evenly sized cubes or dice.

## Mincing

Chefs use two cleavers to mince, rapidly chopping with them in unison for fast results. One cleaver or knife is easier for the less experienced, although the process will of course take a little longer. First slice the food and then, using a sharp knife or cleaver, rapidly chop the food, letting it spread out over the chopping board. Scrape it into a pile and chop again. Continue chopping until the ingredient is minced. You may find it easier to hold the knife or cleaver with two

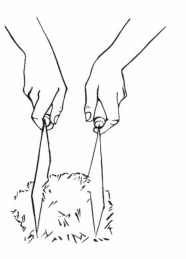

hands by the top of the blade (rather than by the handle), as though you were chopping parsley. A food processor may also be used to mince, but be careful not to overmince the food or you will lose out on texture and taste. I found using the pulsing button on the food processor more effective in mincing for Chinese food.

## Chopping

Put the food on a firm cutting surface and bring the cleaver or knife down on it, using a straight, sharp motion. To chop through bones, hit down with the blade and then finish off the blow with the flat of your other hand on the top edge of the cleaver or knife. A heavy-duty cleaver or knife is best for these tasks.

## Scoring

Piercing the surface of certain foods helps them to cook faster and more evenly. It also gives them an attractive appearance. Using a cleaver or a sharp knife, make cuts into the food at a slight angle to a depth of about an eighth of an inch. Take care not to cut all the way through. Make cuts all over the surface of the food, cutting crisscross to give a wide diamond-shaped pattern.

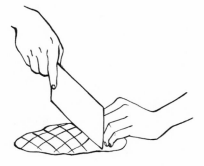

# Cooking with a Wok

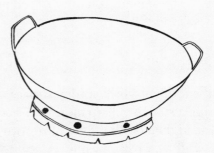

A most useful and versatile piece of equipment, the wok, now widely available, is the best utensil for stir-frying, blanching, deep-frying, and steaming foods. Its shape, with deep sides and either a tapered or a slightly flattened or round bottom, allows for fuel-efficient, quick, and even heating and cooking. When used for stir-frying, its deep sides prevent the food and oils from spilling over; when used for deep-frying, much less oil is required, because the shape of the wok concentrates the heat and ingredients at its base.

There are two basic wok types: the traditional Cantonese version, with short rounded handles on either side of the edge or lip of the wok; and the pau or Peking wok, which has one long handle, from twelve to fourteen inches long. The long-handled wok keeps you more safely distanced from possible splashing hot oils or water.

The round-bottomed wok is best for gas stoves and is used with a wok ring to stabilize the round bottom. More practical are woks now available with flatter bottoms; though these are designed especially for electric stoves, they work well with all modern American stoves of all types. This shape really defeats the purpose of the traditional design, which is to concentrate intense heat at the center, but it does have the advantage of deeper sides than ordinary frying pans. I highly recommend this type of wok.

## Choosing a Wok

Choose a larger wok—preferably about twelve to fourteen inches in diameter, with deep sides. It is easier, and safer, to cook a small batch of food in a large wok than a large quantity in a small one. Be aware that some modernized woks are too shallow or too flat-bottomed and thus no better than frying pans. A heavier wok, preferably made of carbon steel, is superior to the lighter stainless-steel or aluminum type, which cannot take very high heat and tends to blacken and scorch the food. There are now on the market good nonstick carbon-steel woks that maintain the heat without sticking. However, these woks need special care to prevent scratching. In recent years, the nonstick technology has improved vastly, so they can now be safely recommended. They are especially useful when cooking foods that have a high acid level, such as lemons. The wok can also be used as a steamer: simply pour two inches of hot water into the wok, then place either a bamboo steamer or a rack inside the wok (it must be set so as to allow the domed cover to fit snugly). Put the food to be steamed on a heatproof plate, place the plate on the steamer or rack, cover, and steam according to the recipe instructions. The ring of a tuna fish can—that is, with top and bottom removed—may also be used to support the heatproof plate.

## Seasoning a Wok

All woks (except nonstick ones) need to be seasoned. Many need to be scrubbed first as well, to remove the machine oil applied to the surface by the manufacturer to protect it in transit. This is the only time you will ever scrub your wok—unless you let it rust up. Scrub it with cleanser and water to remove as much of the machine oil as possible. Then dry it and put it on the stove over low heat. Add two tablespoons of vegetable cooking oil and, using paper towels, rub the oil over the inside of the wok until the entire surface is lightly coated with oil. Heat the wok slowly for ten or fifteen minutes and then wipe it thoroughly with more paper towel. The paper towel will become blackened. Repeat this process of coating, heating, and wiping until the paper towel comes clean. Your wok will darken and become well seasoned with use, which is a good sign.

Once the wok is seasoned, you must then use the proper cooking procedure, which means heating the wok *first* and getting it hot before you add the oil. The technique acts as a sealant to the porous carbon-steel wok and ensures heating the oil to the high temperature that is necessary for successful wok cooking.

## Cleaning a Wok

Once your wok has been seasoned, it should never be scrubbed with soap or water. Plain clear water is all that is needed. The wok should be thoroughly dried after each use. Putting the cleaned wok over low heat for a minute or two should do the trick. If by chance it does rust a bit, then it must be scrubbed with cleanser and reseasoned as per instructions above.

When stir-frying, it is important to first heat the wok or frying pan until it is very hot *before* adding the oil. It should be so hot that if you toss in a few drops of water, it will immediately evaporate. When you add the oil, it should begin to smoke slightly. That is the signal to you that the wok is ready. You must get your wok or pan hot enough for successful stir-frying. The resulting dish will have nuances of smoky, rich flavor—the hallmark of proper stir-frying.

# The Chinese Larder

Today, practically every ingredient called for in this book can be readily obtained not only in Chinese groceries but often in local supermarkets. If you have certain basic ingredients on your shelf, you can make almost all of the delicious recipes in this book, stopping to shop for only the one or two fresh items. Here, then, is a short list of essentials you should have on hand:

## Light Soy Sauce

As the name implies, this soy sauce is light in color, but it is full of flavor and saltier than dark soy sauce. The best one to use for marinating and cooking, it is known in Chinese markets as Superior Soy. It keeps indefinitely in the cupboard.

## Dark Soy Sauce

This sauce is aged for much longer than light soy sauce, hence its darker, almost black color. Known in Chinese markets as Soy Superior Sauce, it is slightly thicker and stronger than light soy sauce and is more suitable for stews. Although it is used less than light soy, it is important to have some on hand. It keeps indefinitely in the cupboard.

## Asian Sesame Oil

Toasted Asian sesame oil (not to be confused with the flavorless light sesame oil used in Middle Eastern cooking) is highly regarded as a flavoring used, sparingly, in marinades or as a final seasoning. It is also favored in many cold dishes, as part of a dressing or as a condiment in dipping sauces.

A native of India and one of the world's oldest spices and oil-seed crops, sesame seeds produce an aromatic oil that is golden or dark brown in color, thick, rich, and strong-flavored. It is not used as a cooking oil.

Buy sesame oil only in glass bottles. The purest and best I have found is the Japanese Kadoya. It has a clean, fresh aromatic flavor. Brands from China, Hong Kong, and Taiwan can be very good, but occasionally you can stumble upon a bottle that may be rancid because it has been stored too long or its shipment delayed. Avoid *any* of the sesame oil that comes in a plastic bottle, which increases the chances of its turning rancid.

Sesame oil can also be a wonderful aromatic addition to Western-style marinades and salad dressings. Stored in a cool place and tightly sealed, it should last for many months.

## Shaoxing Rice Wine

Rice wine has been an integral part of Chinese cuisine for over two thousand years. At banquets and special feasts it is an essential element. It is made from a blend of glutinous rice, millet, yeast, and spring water.

Shaoxing rice wine is China's most famous wine. It is known in Chinese as *hua tiao,* or "carved flower," from the name given to the pattern carved on the urns in which the wine is stored. The wine is kept in cellars until it matures, usually for ten years, although some have been aged for as long as one hundred years. With its amber color, bouquet, and alcohol content, it resembles sherry more than grape wine.

Rice wine is an indispensable ingredient in many recipes, imparting a rich flavor and aroma to all sorts of dishes. It is also used in marinades and sauces.

Kept tightly corked at room temperature, it will last indefinitely.

Do not confuse Shaoxing rice wine with Japanese sake, which is a Japanese version of rice wine and quite different. Nor should one confuse it with Chinese rice *vinegar.*

A good-quality pale dry sherry can be substituted but will not equal its rich, mellow taste. Western grape wines are not an adequate substitute.

## Oyster Sauce

This very popular and versatile South Chinese sauce, widely used in Chinese-American cooking, is a thick, brown, richly flavored concoction, one of the most ancient sauces in the culinary canon. Fresh oysters are boiled in large vats, seasoned with soy sauce, salt, spices, and seasonings.

The salty taste of oyster sauce largely dissipates during the cooking process; it doesn't even taste "fishy" after it has been cooked, but retains its rich and distinctive savory flavor.

It is usually sold in bottles and can be bought in Chinese markets and some supermarkets. Search out the most expensive ones; they tend to be less salty, have more flavor, and have less cornstarch—their higher quality is worth the price. Cheaper oyster sauces tend to contain MSG, as well as other additives, to make up for fewer oysters. Get the best you can afford.

Once the bottle has been opened, oyster sauce is best kept in the refrigerator, where it will last indefinitely.

## Black Beans (Fermented Black Beans, Salted Beans, Preserved Beans)

These small black soybeans have a distinctive salty taste and a pleasantly rich aroma and are often used as a seasoning, usually in conjunction with garlic or fresh ginger or chilies. They are preserved by being cooked and fermented with salt and spices, resulting in pungent soft black beans. Black beans are especially good in steamed, braised, and stir-fried dishes, imparting a rich flavor to every dish. They should not be confused with the dried black beans used in Western cooking.

The beans will keep indefinitely if stored in the refrigerator or in some other cool place. Take the beans from the package and transfer them to a cleaned covered jar. Store away from light and heat.

Although some recipes say to rinse them before using, I find this unnecessary; the salt adds to the flavor of the dish without overpowering the other flavors.

## Chinese Dried Black Mushrooms

These "black" mushrooms actually range from light brown to dark brown in color. The most popular are the larger-sized, light-brown ones with a highly cracked surface. They are, predictably, the most expensive ones. But all versions and grades of this mushroom add a very desirable flavor and aroma to Chinese recipes. It is interesting to note that these mushrooms grow on fallen, decaying trees; the Chinese have been gathering them for over a thousand years. The Japanese cultivate them by growing them on the *shii* tree; hence the familiar fresh shiitake mushrooms.

However, the Chinese rarely eat them fresh, but prefer them dried: dehydrating them concentrates their smoky flavors and robust taste and allows them to absorb sauces and spices, which gives the mushrooms an even more succulent texture. As a result, they are most appropriate for use as seasonings, finely chopped and combined with meats, fish, or poultry, though they are sometimes used whole.

Depending on your budget, the lighter and more expensive grade is the best to buy. These should be reserved for special occasions. However, for normal everyday fare, a moderately priced good-quality mushroom is fine. A little goes a long way.

Stored in an airtight container, they will keep for many months in a cool dry place. If they are not to be used often, it is a good idea to store them in the freezer to maintain their fragrant aroma and taste.

To use Chinese dried mushrooms: Soak the mushrooms in a bowl of warm water for about twenty minutes, or until they are soft and pliable. Squeeze out the excess water and cut off and discard the woody stems. Only the caps are used.

The soaking water can be saved and used in soups, rice-cooking water, a vegetarian stock, and sauces or braised dishes. Strain through a fine sieve to eliminate any sand or residue from the dried mushrooms.

## Bean Thread (Transparent or Cellophane) Noodles

These noodles are not made from a grain flour but from ground mung beans; mung beans also give us the familiar bean sprouts. Freshly made noodles can sometimes be seen in China, fluttering in the breeze on lines like long thread-like fabric. They are available dried, and are very fine and white. Easy to recognize, packed in their neat, plastic-wrapped bundles, they are stocked by most Chinese markets and some supermarkets. They are never served on their own, but always added to soups or braised dishes, or deep-fried and used as a garnish. Once they have been soaked, they become soft and slippery, springy and translucent. Since they are a vegetable product, they are popularly used in vegetarian dishes. When fried, they puff up immediately and become very white and crispy.

There are only a few brands available, and I recommend all of them. They come in packages from one ounce to one pound. I prefer the smaller, one- or two-ounce packages, since these are easier to handle as well as to measure. The ones most widely available are from China and are quite inexpensive.

Store the noodles in a dry place; they will last indefinitely.

The noodles should be soaked in hot water for about five minutes before use. Because they are rather long, you might find it easier to cut them into shorter lengths after soaking. If you are frying them, omit the soaking but be sure to separate them first. A good technique for separating the strands is to put them into a large paper bag, then reach in to pull them apart; this prevents them from flying all over the place.

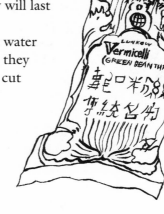

## Hoisin Sauce

Used in South China as a condiment and as a glaze for roasted meats, hoisin sauce is part of the bean sauce family. It is a rich, thick, dark-brownish-red sauce made from soybean paste, garlic, vinegar, sugar, spices, and other flavorings. It is at once sweet and spicy, with a texture ranging from creamy-thick to thin. In the West, it is often used as a sauce (mixed with sesame oil) for Peking duck instead of the traditional bean sauce. Hoisin sauce is sold in cans and jars. Store in the refrigerator, where it will keep indefinitely.

## Five-Spice Powder

This ancient spice formula harmonizes star anise, Sichuan peppercorns, fennel, clove, and cinnamon or the stronger-scented cassia.

Whatever the exact combination, this spice is pungent, fragrant, hot, mild, and slightly sweet—all at once. Its distinct fragrance and unique flavor make the most prosaic dish something special. Stored in a glass jar tightly sealed in a cool place, it will keep indefinitely.

## Lily Buds

Also known as tiger-lily buds, golden needles, or lily stems, dried lily buds are the unopened flowers, not buds, of a type of day lily. About two inches in length, they have a slightly chewy texture and an earthy fragrance that is special. The buds serve well as an ingredient in muxi (mu shu) dishes, a stir-fried pork dish with cloud ears, and hot-and-sour soup, providing texture as well as additional dimension to dishes.

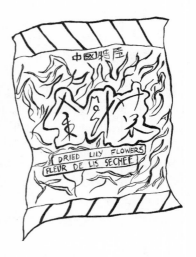

Buy lily buds that are bright golden yellow in color. Avoid dark, brittle ones, for these are too old. Available in plastic or cellophane bags from Chinese grocers or supermarkets, they are very inexpensive. Store them tightly sealed in a glass jar, where they will keep indefinitely.

## Rice Vinegar

Vinegars used in Chinese cooking are usually made from fermented rice and grains such as wheat, millet, and sorghum. They should not be confused with Western wine vinegars, which are much more acidic. Vinegar is one of the oldest seasonings used in Asian cuisine; its name appears in documents from the twelfth century B.C. Vinegar is used directly as a seasoning in dishes or in dipping sauces. There are several main types. Western-style wine vinegars cannot serve as a substitute. Nor should rice vinegar be confused with Shaoxing rice wine—which is a wine, not a vinegar. Vinegar, remember, is from the French for "sour wine."

### Black rice vinegar:
Black rice vinegar is very dark in color with a rich but mild taste and an appealing depth of flavor, similar to Italian balsamic vinegar. It is usually made from glutinous rice, which imparts its mildness and taste. Really good black rice vinegar has a rich, impressive complexity of flavors and aromas. In North Chinese cooking it is used for braised dishes, noodles, and sauces.

### Red rice vinegar:
Red rice vinegar is a clear pale-red vinegar. It has a delicate, tart, slightly sweet and salty taste and is usually used as a dipping sauce for seafood or shark's fin soup.

White rice vinegar:    White rice vinegar is clear and mild in flavor. It has a faint taste of glutinous rice and is used for sweet-and-sour dishes. Western cider vinegar can be substituted.

Sweet rice vinegar:    This vinegar is a brownish black and thicker than plain rice vinegar, looking a bit like dark soy sauce. It is processed with sugar and star anise, and the result is an aromatic, caramel taste. Unlike other vinegars, it has very little tartness. It is used in large quantities for braised pork dishes.

# Commonly Used Fresh Ingredients

Many once-exotic Chinese ingredients are now regularly available in most supermarkets. Many are now as American as apple pie.

## Bean Curd

Bean curd, which is also known by its Chinese name, *doufu,* or by its Japanese name, *tofu,* has played an important part in Chinese cookery since it was discovered during the Han Dynasty (206 B.C.–220 A.D.). It became known as "meat without bones," because it is highly nutritious and rich in protein, and works well with other foods. It is also low in saturated fats and cholesterol, easy to digest, and inexpensive. Bean curd has a distinctive smooth, light, almost creamy texture but a bland taste. However, it is extremely versatile and lends itself to all types of cooking. It is made from yellow soybeans which are soaked, ground, mixed with water, and then cooked briefly before being solidified. It is usually sold in two forms: in firm, small blocks, or in soft custardlike blocks; it is also available in several dried forms and in a fermented version. The soft bean curd (sometimes called silken tofu) is used for soups and braised dishes, whereas the solid, firm bean curd blocks, white in color, are used for stir-frying, braising, and deep-frying. Both are packed in water in plastic containers.

If possible, purchase bean curd fresh from a Chinese market or grocer. Many commercial forms of bean curd available in supermarkets and health-food stores, though nutritious, are ordinarily without the subtle distinctive flavor prized by bean-curd lovers in China.

Fresh bean curd once opened may be kept in the refrigerator for up to five days, provided that the covering water is changed daily. It is best, however, to use the bean curd within two or three days of purchase.

## Coriander, Fresh (Chinese Parsley, Cilantro)

Fresh coriander, one of the relatively few food herbs in the Chinese culinary lexicon, is a standard in South China and has been used in China since 200 B.C. It looks like flat parsley, but its pungent, musky, citruslike character gives it an unmistakable flavor. Its feathery leaves make it appealing as a garnish; or it is chopped and then mixed into sauces and stuffings. Its strong, earthy, fresh flavors help moderate rich flavors. It is widely used as a garnish as well as in recipes.

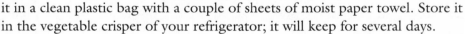

When buying fresh coriander, look for deep-green, fresh-looking leaves. Yellow and limp leaves indicate age and should be avoided.

If you buy fresh coriander with roots, stand the coriander in water. Otherwise, to store fresh coriander, wash it in cold water, drain it thoroughly or spin-dry in a salad spinner, and put it in a clean plastic bag with a couple of sheets of moist paper towel. Store it in the vegetable crisper of your refrigerator; it will keep for several days.

## Garlic

The Chinese have been cultivating garlic since at least 3000 B.C., and Chinese cuisine is inconceivable without its distinct sweet, pungent, aromatic contribution. Cooks often drop a smashed clove of garlic into hot cooking oil to "sweeten" it and give it a bracing aroma. Once the essence of the garlic is captured by the oil, the garlic husk is removed and discarded. Garlic, whether whole, chopped, minced, crushed, pickled, boiled, or smoked, in flavored oils and spicy sauces, by itself, or with other robust ingredients such as black beans, curry, shrimp paste, scallions, or ginger, is an essential and revered element in the Chinese culinary tradition.

## Ginger

Ginger is one of the five "ancient" spices of Chinese cookery, along with red pepper, scallions, garlic, and cinnamon. The Chinese have been exploiting its virtues since 600 B.C., both as a spice and as a medicinal food. In its latter role, ginger is believed to soothe one's intestines, ward off the common cold, and do wonders for one's sexual and gustatorial appetites.

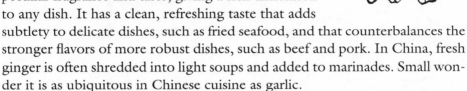

Ginger is a root, golden beige in color, with a thin dry skin. Whether whole, sliced, or ground into a powder, or pickled or candied, ginger preserves its peculiar fragrance and taste, giving a rich dimension to any dish. It has a clean, refreshing taste that adds subtlety to delicate dishes, such as fried seafood, and that counterbalances the stronger flavors of more robust dishes, such as beef and pork. In China, fresh ginger is often shredded into light soups and added to marinades. Small wonder it is as ubiquitous in Chinese cuisine as garlic.

Fortunately, fresh ginger is now widely available even in supermarkets. Older, more shriveled ginger is used for medicinal broths. However, for most culinary purposes, you want to look for the firmest ginger, not shriveled, but solidly heavy and clear-skinned.

Very young, almost pale-yellow ginger should be used within two days of purchase, whereas ordinary ginger, if wrapped in a paper towel, and then in plastic wrap, will keep in the refrigerator for up to two weeks. Peeled ginger covered with rice wine or dry sherry refrigerated in a glass jar will last for several months. This method has the added benefit of producing a flavored wine that can be substituted in recipes. Ginger should *never* be frozen.

## Chinese White Cabbage (Bok Choy)

Chinese white cabbage, popularly known as bok choy or pak choi, is a nutritious and versatile vegetable with a long smooth milky-white stem and large crinkly dark-green leaves. Found today in many supermarkets, bok choy has a light, fresh, slightly mustardy taste and requires little cooking. In China, bok choy is used in soup, stir-fried with meats, or simply blanched. When cooked, the leaves have a robust, almost spinachlike flavor, and the stalks are sweet and mild with a refreshing taste. Bok choy is often said to resemble

Swiss chard in taste; in fact, however, it is not only milder but juicier than chard.

Look for firm, crisp stalks and unblemished leaves. The size of the plant indicates how tender it is—the smaller the better, especially in the summer, when the hot weather toughens the stalks. Look at the bottom of the stalk; if it has a hole, this means the bok choy is old and fibrous, and best avoided.

Store bok choy wrapped tightly in paper towels in the vegetable crisper of your refrigerator and it will keep for up to one week.

The best way to rinse bok choy is to cut it according to the recipe, then rinse in at least two or three changes of cold water. Drain thoroughly before cooking.

# Other Special Ingredients

## Bitter Melon

This unusual, uncommon vegetable, which ranges in size from as small as baby zucchini to as large as cucumbers, is very much an acquired taste. It has as many detractors as it has fans, even among the Chinese, but those who love it insist it is worth the effort to appreciate its taste. Bitter melon has a bumpy dark-to-pale-green skin, and a slightly bitter quinine flavor that has a cooling effect in one's mouth. Not surprisingly, it was originally prized for its supposed medicinal qualities: something so bitter *had* to be good medicine. Used unpeeled, this tropical vegetable has a fibrous seed core, which is usually cut away, leaving a thin ring of flesh. It is used in soups, stir-fried, steamed, or quick-braised. A popular preparation, which reduces its bitterness, is to stuff it with seasoned pork and steam it. It is often paired with strong, pungent ingredients, such as black beans, garlic, or chili, whose flavors also tone down the melon's bitterness. In some parts of China it is often dried and used as a medicine. It is also thought to purify the blood and to cool the digestive system. The greener the melon, the more bitter its taste; most cooks wisely look for the milder yellow-green varieties.

Buy only the freshest variety, which can be found at Chinese markets or grocers. Again, the greener, firmer bitter melons tend to be stronger, the yellowish varieties milder.

Store in the bottom of your refrigerator in a loose plastic or paper bag. It can keep there for three to five days, depending on how fresh it was when you got it.

## Preserved Mustard Greens or Cabbage

Mustard greens are known in Chinese as "greens heart," because only the heart of the plant is eaten—that is, the stem, buds, and young leaves. Unrelated to and quite unlike the mustard greens of the American South, these greens are a vital part of the Chinese diet, being rich in vitamins and minerals and easy to cultivate. As such, they are enjoyed year-round, either fresh or preserved. The leaves are pickled with salt, water, vinegar, and sugar, making a true sweet-and-sour food that is used as a vegetable or as a flavoring ingredient, especially in soups. The preserve can be served as a snack or in stir-fries with meats, poultry, or fish.

The best preserved mustard greens are to be found in large crocks in Chinese markets, which usually means they have been locally made. The next best alternative is the ones available in small crocks or cans labeled "Preserved Vegetable" from Hong Kong, Taiwan, or China. All are recommended.

## Peking Cabbage (Napa Cabbage)

All types of cabbages cultivated in China are more nutritious than the common European varieties. They all have a mild taste, but Peking cabbages are the mildest. They have been cultivated for over fifteen hundred years, because they are very rich in vitamins, minerals, and fiber, and provide a few calories as well. In these vitally important nutritional ways, they are much more like broccoli than the green cabbages that we know. Peking cabbages

39

have delightfully crisp, fibrous leaves, leading people to call them "celery cabbages."

Because of the regional and climatic differences, these cabbages come in various shapes and sizes, from long, barrel-shaped specimens to fat, squat types. Their leaves are firm and tightly packed, and pale green or yellowish in color (because the leaves are hidden from the sun). They look a lot like our romaine lettuce.

This versatile vegetable is used in soups and in stir-fried meat dishes. Its leaves readily absorb flavors, and its sweet, pleasant taste makes it a good match for foods that have rich flavors. It is also enjoyed pickled with salt and chili.

Look for a fresh cabbage that is not wilted. It should have a crisp look with no yellow or brown spots.

## Sugar

Sugar has been used, sparingly, in the cooking of savory dishes in China for a thousand years. Excessive sugar destroys the palate, but when it is properly employed, sugar helps balance the various flavors of sauces and other dishes. There are two types of sugar used:

Rock or yellow lump sugar:   I particularly like to use rock sugar, which I find to have a richer, more subtle flavor than that of refined granulated sugar. It also gives a good luster or glaze to braised "red-cooked" Chinese dishes. It imparts translucence to glazes and sauces. You may need to break the lumps into smaller pieces with a wooden mallet or rolling pin.

Brown sugar slabs:   This type of sugar is layered and semi-refined, having been compressed into flat slabs and cut to resemble caramel candy. It has the flavor of good brown sugar.

# SOUPS

Iceberg Lettuce–Egg Drop Soup

Mrs. Wong's Savory Oxtail Soup

Peppery Watercress Soup

Classic Wonton Soup

Ambrosial Abalone and Squab
Soup

Silky Bean Curd Soup

Chinese-Cabbage Soup

Chinese–Mustard Greens Soup

Subgum Chicken Soup

Double-Steamed Squab and Ham
Soup

Chicken-Cucumber Soup

Sizzling Rice Soup

Chinese Chicken Stock

# Iceberg Lettuce–Egg Drop Soup

*This recipe is from my friend Steve Wong's family. His people, like so many other Chinese-Americans, grew up poor and cut off from their homeland, so they gradually adapted American produce into South Chinese cuisine. The ingredients they used were usually dictated by cost. Iceberg lettuce, a California staple, was inexpensive and filling. Its light, sweet flavor, faint green color, and versatility make it a perfect foil to Chinese cookery. Here it is combined with eggs to make a simple and quick soup, useful for a working family. The soup is known in this country as "egg drop soup" because the mixed egg mixture is slowly dropped in a steady stream into the hot soup. The result is a gentle, fragile soup that is tasty and delicious.*

*I have altered the original recipe by adding the lettuce at the last minute to preserve its crispy texture. The heat of the soup is enough to cook the lettuce to perfection.*

Serves 4

4 cups homemade chicken stock (page 60) or reduced-salt
  canned broth
1 egg
2 teaspoons Asian sesame oil
1 teaspoon sugar
1 teaspoon salt
1/4 teaspoon freshly ground white pepper
1 tablespoon light soy sauce
3 tablespoons finely chopped scallions or green onions,
  white part only
1/2 pound iceberg lettuce, finely shredded (about 2 cups)

## Garnish

3 tablespoons finely chopped green scallion tops

Pour the chicken stock into a pot and bring it to a simmer.
Lightly beat the egg and then mix with the sesame oil in a small bowl.
Toss the sugar, salt, pepper, and soy sauce into the simmering stock, and

give it several good stirs. Next toss in the scallions, and then drizzle in the egg mixture in a very slow, thin stream. Using a chopstick or fork, pull the egg slowly into strands. (I have found that stirring the egg in a figure eight works quite well.)

Remove the soup from the heat and toss in the shredded lettuce, stirring all the while. Garnish with the finely chopped scallion tops and serve at once.

*A Chinese wedding celebration in Berkeley in 1948*

# Mrs. Wong's Savory Oxtail Soup

*There is sometimes a fine line between a soup and a stew. In general, the Chinese use soups as a beverage to be consumed in the course of the meal. So, if it can be drunk, it is a soup; if you need chopsticks or a spoon, it is a stew. My friend Steve Wong told me that his mother's oxtail dish was a hyphenated soup-stew, and when I tried it, I could see he was right. Mrs. Wong, a true Chinese-American, has in fact blended Chinese touches into American oxtail soup, making it a bit thicker than usual and adding such exotics as star anise to enliven it. Like all good cooks, Mrs. Wong knows how to take inexpensive cuts of meat and bring out their virtues while artfully compensating for any of their deficiencies.*

*Mrs. Wong worked outside the home, so she often made meals in advance. This soup-stew reheats very well and, as with most such dishes, is even better the day after it is prepared.*

*Serves 4*

3 pounds oxtails
10 cups homemade chicken stock (page 60) or
    reduced-salt canned broth
1 tablespoon salt
8 star anise
2 tablespoons light soy sauce
1 tablespoon dark soy sauce
10 small white potatoes, peeled
5 carrots, peeled
1 small celery heart, cut in half
6 whole scallions, roots trimmed

Blanch the oxtails in salted boiling water for 15 minutes. Remove them with a slotted spoon and drain them well in a colander.

In a large pot, bring the stock to a simmer. Toss in the salt, star anise, soy sauces, and oxtails. Continue simmering gently for 20 minutes, uncovered, skimming several times. Cover tightly and continue to simmer for 3 hours, or until the oxtails are tender. Skim any excess fat from the surface.

Now add the vegetables, cover, and continue to simmer for another 25 minutes, or until all the vegetables are tender. Leave the vegetables whole.

Ladle into a large soup tureen or individual soup bowls and serve at once.

# Peppery Watercress Soup

*This most refreshing soup appeared often at my family table as
well as those of my Chinese-American friends. Steve Wong's family
used to pick the watercress on the banks of the Sacramento River.
It was fresh and cheap. My mother liked making it because she
could come home from work and literally have it on the table in
minutes. She would make the stock the night before and simply
reheat it and toss in the watercress leaves.*

*Serves 4*

4 cups homemade chicken stock (page 60) or reduced-salt
   canned broth
1 teaspoon salt
1/2 teaspoon freshly ground black pepper
2 cups loosely packed watercress leaves
2 teaspoons Asian sesame oil

Bring the stock to a simmer, sprinkle in the salt and pepper, and continue to simmer for 2 minutes uncovered. Remove the soup from the heat,
stir in the watercress leaves, and continue stirring for 1 minute. Drizzle the
sesame oil on top of the soup and serve at once.

# Classic Wonton Soup

*This dish, so familiar to American patrons of
Chinese restaurants, is an authentic Chinese
classic that somehow managed to avoid being corrupted
beyond recognition. Why this is so is unclear. Of course, wontons
are small dumplings, and dumplings in any form, whether fried,
poached, or steamed, are universally popular. Perhaps it is simply
that they sell themselves as they are, and Chinese-American chefs
wisely stayed with the original.*

 *At their best, wontons are filled with savory meats, vegeta-
bles, and seasonings. The light, sheer dough that serves as a
wrapper can be easily purchased in Chinese groceries and sometimes in general supermarkets. Gently poached and floating in a
rich clear chicken stock, they make a dish that is at once exotic and
familiar to Americans. And the soup is delicious. Poaching, incidentally, removes excess starch, which would tend to cloud the
chicken stock. Those who prefer their wontons fried are making a
mistake.*

 *The Chinese compulsion to make sense of the world in its food
metaphors is well represented here. "Wonton" derives from "hun-
tun," E. N. Anderson writes, "the original cosmic chaos when the
universe was 'without form and void.' " Out of something akin to
this splendid soup, one imagines, arose the balance and harmony
of all the elements that make life possible and enjoyable. Americans were instinctively wise to take wonton soup as it is.*

*Serves 4*

## Wonton Filling

½ pound shrimp, peeled, deveined, and chopped
½ pound fatty ground pork
6 ounces fresh peeled and chopped water chestnuts or 3
 ounces canned water chestnuts
1 teaspoon salt
½ teaspoon freshly ground black pepper
3 tablespoons finely chopped scallions
1 tablespoon finely chopped ginger
1 tablespoon light soy sauce
1 teaspoon dark soy sauce
2 teaspoons Shaoxing rice wine
1 teaspoon sugar
2 teaspoons Asian sesame oil
1 lightly beaten egg white

1 package wonton skins
4 cups homemade chicken stock (page 60) or reduced-salt
 canned broth

1 tablespoon light soy sauce
1 teaspoon Asian sesame oil

## Garnish

3 tablespoons chopped scallions, white and green parts
2 tablespoons fresh coriander leaves

Put all the wonton filling ingredients together in a large bowl and mix well. Allow to marinate for about 20 minutes.

Place about 1 tablespoon of filling in the center of a wonton skin. Dampen the edges with water and bring the sides of the dough up around the filling. Pinch the edges together at the top to seal; it will look like a small sack. Continue to fill the dough until you have used up all the filling.

When the wontons are filled, bring the stock to a simmer, stirring in the soy sauce and sesame oil.

In another pot, bring salted water to a boil and poach the wontons for 1 minute. Remove them with a strainer and put them into the simmering stock. Continue to simmer for 2 minutes. Ladle the wontons and soup into a large soup tureen or individual bowls. Garnish with scallions and coriander leaves and serve at once.

# Ambrosial Abalone and Squab Soup

*Banquets are, by definition, special occasions. To me, as a child, they represented good times, great food, special treats, lots of joyful people, games, tipsy men, and much hilarity. Everyone looked forward to these family gatherings and anticipated the procession of platters of food that we never experienced at home: abalone and squab soup never emerged from my mother's kitchen to serve as the family dinner!*

*Banquets meant extraordinary things, like 7-Up and ginger ale for the children, cognac and whiskey for the adults. And the oohs and aahs as the food was paraded to the table. The adults would critique each dish—there were at least ten courses— comparing it with the one they had enjoyed in the homeland, relating anecdotes, and making judgments about the taste and significance of the various foods.*

*If a dish was deemed wanting, the blame was always placed on the inadequacy of American supplies. People accepted this deficiency stoically and proceeded to devour every scrap. Any exceptionally good dish was a tribute to the genius of the cook, who had to overcome the American lack of interest in good food and proper ingredients.*

*After several hours of eating and drinking, adults and children would play various games of skill and chance, jovially and with much horseplay. I remember thinking that it was strange but nice to see these normally quite restrained and quiet adults having so much fun.*

*Ambrosial Abalone and Squab Soup is a dish I especially remember from these family banquets. Abalone and squab blended together make a broth fit indeed for the gods. It is rich in flavor, and the chewy texture of the abalone bits provides just the right body to the soup. The long, gentle steaming process coaxes the flavors from each ingredient. It is easy to make: all it needs is tender loving care, patience, and some time.*

*Serves 4*

2 small squabs
1 12-ounce can abalone
4 cups homemade chicken stock (page 60) or reduced-salt
   canned broth
1 tablespoon Shaoxing rice wine
2 teaspoons light soy sauce
2 teaspoons salt
1/2 teaspoon freshly ground black pepper

Blanch the squabs for 5 minutes in a large pot of boiling water. Remove and rinse under cold running water. Cut the squabs in half.

Cut the abalone crosswise into 1/2-inch slices.

Bring the chicken stock to a boil in a large pot. Pour the stock into a heatproof soup tureen and add the rest of the ingredients.

Cover the tureen and set it on a rack inside a large steamer or an old turkey roaster.* Pour 2 inches of water into the steamer. Place the cover on the steamer, and keep tightly covered. It is a tureen within a steamer. Steam continuously for 3 hours, replenishing the hot water from time to time as necessary.

When the soup is done, skim off any excess fat and adjust the seasoning with salt to taste. Cut the squabs into small pieces, discarding the bones or returning them to the soup. Serve at once, distributing equal amounts of abalone and bits of squab among the soup bowls.

* I find the old turkey roaster perfect for this technique.

# Silky Bean Curd Soup

When I was a child, few things made me feel more Chinese than eating bean curd or tofu, as it is now popularly known. In Chicago at the time, bean curd was found only in Chinatown. My American friends would look at it in a strange way: "Is it cheese?" they would ask.

It is rather bland and flavorless, but to my Chinese palate, its subtle, slightly chalky taste was most appealing, especially when it was fresh. Even then I knew it was as nutritious but much less expensive than meat and lighter.

At home, my mother prepared fried, stuffed, and braised bean curd, but I much enjoyed it when she simply added it to soup. Bean curd very congenially absorbs the nicest flavors. The silky texture of the bean curd would gently swirl inside my mouth as I savored this delicate and much-prized food.

Serves 4

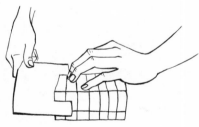

4 cups homemade chicken stock
    (page 60) or reduced-salt canned
    broth
1 teaspoon salt
1/2 teaspoon freshly ground black
    pepper
1/2 pound silky soft bean curd
2 cups bok choy leaves and stems cut
    into 1-inch pieces
2 teaspoons light soy sauce
2 teaspoons Asian sesame oil

Bring the stock to a simmer, sprinkle in the salt and pepper, and continue to simmer for 2 minutes uncovered. Cut the bean curd into bite-size cubes and gently slide them into the simmering stock. Dump in the bok choy and allow the soup to simmer for 2 minutes. Drizzle the soy sauce and sesame oil on top of the soup, mix, and serve at once.

# Chinese=Cabbage Soup

*Growing up Chinese-American in Chicago—not famous for its long growing season—meant that the variety of Chinese vegetables and other traditional ingredients was extremely limited. The Cold War economic blockade against China and the distance between the United States and Taiwan/Hong Kong prevented us from enjoying the full possibilities of Chinese cooking.*

*However, we were able to grow some Chinese vegetables. I remember our Chinese neighbors in Chicago's Chinatown culti- vating a variety of cabbages, turnips, even bitter melon, in their small garden plots. These they very often shared with us, and then, for example, my mother would make a simple bok choy soup that was refreshing and delicious. She would add an egg to enrich the whole mixture. Today, bok choy is readily available in supermar- kets everywhere.*

*Serves 4*

4 cups homemade chicken stock (page 60) or
    reduced-salt canned broth
1/2 pound bok choy (1 cup cut-up)
1 egg
2 teaspoons Asian sesame oil
1 teaspoon sugar
1 teaspoon salt
1/4 teaspoon freshly ground white pepper
1 tablespoon light soy sauce
3 tablespoons finely chopped scallions, white part only
1 cup shredded iceberg lettuce

Garnish

3 tablespoons finely chopped green scallion tops

Put the chicken stock in a pot and bring it to a simmer.

Prepare the bok choy: Separate the leaves and stalks, and cut the leaves into 2-inch pieces. Peel the stems, cut them into diagonal slices, and wash them well in several changes of water.

Lightly beat the egg and then mix with the sesame oil in a small bowl.

Toss the sugar into the simmering stock, taste, then add salt, pepper, and soy sauce and give the stock several good stirs. Next toss in the bok choy and scallions and then drizzle in the egg mixture in a very slow, thin stream. Using a chopstick or fork, pull the egg slowly into strands. (I have found that stirring the egg in a figure eight works quite well.)

Remove the soup from the heat and toss in the shredded lettuce, stirring all the while. Garnish with the finely chopped scallion tops and serve at once.

# Chinese—Mustard Greens Soup

*Chinese mustard greens have been a favorite vegetable of mine since I was a child. They have a strong, pungent aroma and a mustard bite with a slightly bitter edge. (You can tell that my childhood palate was not ruined by too much sugar and too many Cokes!)*

*Now, as then, I find them refreshing, whether combined with meat in a simple stir-fry or when they add zest to a refreshing soup, as in this recipe. All hyphenated American adults are sure to enjoy it.*

Serves 4

1/2 pound Chinese mustard greens
1/2 pound lean pork
4 teaspoons light soy sauce
1 teaspoon Shaoxing rice wine or dry sherry
1 teaspoon Asian sesame oil

1 teaspoon cornstarch

2 teaspoons peanut oil

4 cups homemade chicken stock (page 60) or reduced-salt
   canned broth

1 teaspoon sugar

1 teaspoon salt

1/4 teaspoon freshly ground white pepper

3 tablespoons finely chopped scallions,
   white part only

### Garnish

3 tablespoons finely chopped green scallion tops

Prepare the mustard greens: Separate the leaves and stalks, and cut the
leaves into 2-inch pieces. Peel the stems, cut them into diagonal slices, and
wash them well in several changes of water.

Cut the pork into thin strips and mix it with 2 teaspoons of soy sauce,
the rice wine, sesame oil, and cornstarch.

Heat a wok or large frying pan over high heat until it is hot. Swirl in the
peanut oil, and when it is very hot and slightly smoking, toss in the pork and
stir-fry for 1 minute. Remove and set aside.

Put the chicken stock in a pot and bring it to a simmer.

Sprinkle the sugar into the simmering stock, taste, and add salt, pepper,
and remaining 2 teaspoons of soy sauce, and give it several good stirs. Next
toss in the mustard greens and scallions.

Remove the soup from the heat and toss in the stir-fried pork, stirring
all the while. Garnish with the finely chopped scallion tops and serve at once.

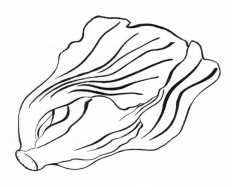

# Subgum Chicken Soup

*This popular soup is almost certainly an ad hoc Chinese-American creation. Many of the ingredients are distinctly American. But they are fine ingredients, so we may happily enter it into the Chinese-American canon of satisfying and wholesome foods for the American taste.*

*With the addition of bok choy, we transform the soup into a Chinese-American gem that still may be found on many Chinese restaurant menus. It is a satisfying and hearty soup.*

Serves 4

1/2 pound bok choy
1/4 cup peeled, seeded, and chopped tomatoes
1/4 cup seeded and chopped green pepper
1/4 cup chopped celery
1/4 cup peeled and chopped fresh water chestnuts, or canned
1/4 cup chopped fresh mushrooms
4 cups homemade chicken stock (page 60) or
  reduced-salt canned broth
1 teaspoon sugar
1/2 teaspoon salt
1/4 teaspoon freshly ground white pepper
1 tablespoon light soy sauce
1/4 cup chopped cooked chicken meat
3 tablespoons finely chopped scallions, white part only
2 teaspoons Asian sesame oil

## Garnish

3 tablespoons finely chopped green scallion tops

Prepare the bok choy: Separate the leaves and stalks, and cut the leaves into 2-inch pieces. Peel the stems, cut them into diagonal slices, and wash them well in several changes of water.

Put the chicken stock in a pot and bring it to a simmer.

Sprinkle the sugar into the simmering stock; taste; add salt, pepper, and soy sauce; give it several good stirs. Next toss in the bok choy and the rest of the vegetables and cook for 5 minutes.

Remove the soup from the heat and toss in the cooked chicken and the scallions, stirring all the while. Finally, drizzle on the sesame oil and stir once. Garnish with the finely chopped scallion tops and serve immediately.

# Double=Steamed Squab and Ham Soup

*Once my mother was awarded a small amount of money in back pay, and she immediately splurged by purchasing some expensive food items. She bought some delicate Smithfield ham, because it was the closest thing to the Chinese ham she had known as a child. She finished off her windfall with the purchase of a couple of squabs. Then she combined them, using the following unusual technique for making soup.*

*It is called double-steaming, a process in which rich ingredients are steamed for hours in a covered casserole filled with soup. The technique extracts all the flavors from the ingredients, and is often used for making the classic shark's fin and bird's nest soups. The result is a distinctive soup, clear and rich but also light. You may know that in Chinese cuisine soups serve as a beverage, and therefore the broth or consommé style is the norm. But this soup may be served as a separate course.*

*To make the soup extra wholesome, my mother would add a few pieces of ginseng, a medicinal as well as a flavorful ingredient. However, I have omitted it from this recipe. For easy planning, I would make it in advance and freeze it, for it reheats well.*

*Serves 4*

2 squabs, about 1 pound each
1/4 pound slice Smithfield ham
4 cups homemade chicken stock (page 60) or reduced-salt
  canned broth
4 slices fresh ginger, 2 inches by 1/8 inch
4 whole scallions
2 tablespoons Shaoxing rice wine or dry sherry
1/2 teaspoon salt
1/4 teaspoon freshly ground white pepper

Using a sharp heavy knife or cleaver, cut the squabs in half. Bring a pot of water to the boil, turn the heat down, and toss in the squabs and the slice of ham. Simmer them in the water for 10 minutes. Remove them with a slotted spoon and discard the water.

Set up a steamer, or put a rack into a wok or deep pan, and fill it with 2 inches of water. Bring the water to the boil over high heat.

Meanwhile, bring the stock to the boil in another large pot and then pour it into a heatproof china casserole. Add the squab, ham, ginger, scallions, Shaoxing rice wine or dry sherry, salt, and pepper to the casserole and cover it with a lid or foil. Put the casserole on the rack and cover the wok or deep pan tightly with a lid or foil. You now have a casserole within a steamer; hence the name "double-steaming." Turn the heat down and steam gently for 2 hours, replenishing the hot water from time to time.

When the soup is cooked, remove all the ingredients with a slotted spoon and discard the scallions and ginger. Cut the ham and squab into bite-size pieces and put them on a platter. Serve the soup alongside the squab and ham. The soup can be served immediately or, if made ahead, cooled and stored in the refrigerator or freezer to be reheated just before serving.

# Chicken=Cucumber Soup

*Chicago's Chinatown was never exactly the center of the great
Chinese empire. We had a small Chinese community, perhaps a
few thousand people. But as I grew up, I was always surprised at
the diversity and variety of Chinese ingredients and foods available within that narrow circle.*

*For example, we were delighted when fresh water chestnuts
were available. They came from Hong Kong via San Francisco.
We acted like deprived refugees or exiles, happy to see the abundant and well-remembered fruits of the homeland. Everyone
rushed to buy whatever authentic ingredients had arrived, even
at exorbitant prices. People were willing to pay for that taste of
China, which made them feel closer to the homeland.*

*One popular vegetable that made rare appearances at our
dinner table was fuzzy or hairy melon. As a child, I loved to play
with the melon before my mother would peel it for soup. In season,
it had a wonderful refreshing texture and taste. Because the
melon was not always available, my mother would often substitute
cucumber in this unusual chicken soup. It did not taste the same
to my mother as the fuzzy-melon version of her childhood, but,
then, we weren't living in China either. However, if you are able
to find fuzzy melon, you can use the same proportion as in this
recipe.*

*Serves 4*

1/2 pound boneless, skinless chicken breasts
1 egg white
1 1/2 teaspoons salt
1 teaspoon cornstarch
1 pound (2 medium-sized) cucumbers
4 cups homemade chicken stock (page 60) or reduced-salt
   canned broth
2 tablespoons light soy sauce
1 tablespoon Shaoxing rice wine or dry sherry
2 teaspoons Asian sesame oil
2 teaspoons sugar
2 tablespoons finely chopped scallions

Cut the chicken into thin slices about 2 inches long and ⅛ inch wide and toss them with the egg white, ½ teaspoon of salt, and cornstarch. Let sit in the refrigerator for about 20 minutes.

Peel the cucumbers, halve them, and remove the seeds with a teaspoon. Cut the cucumber into 1-inch cubes, sprinkle with the remaining 1 teaspoon of salt, and put them in a colander to drain for 20 minutes. This removes the excess moisture from the cucumber. Next rinse the cucumber cubes in cold running water and blot them dry with paper towels.

In a pot of boiling water, blanch the chicken slices for 2 minutes, until they are slightly firm and white. Drain the chicken and set aside.

Just before you are ready to eat, bring the chicken stock to a simmer and season it with the soy sauce, rice wine, sesame oil, and sugar. Toss in the cucumber and simmer for 3 minutes, then finally toss in the chicken. Bring the soup back to simmering point, add the scallions, and serve at once.

# Sizzling Rice Soup

*One of the most popular foods in our home was not an expensive item but, rather, an imaginative dish made of leftovers. My mother would cook rice the Chinese way, then leave the rice to cook longer and allow a crisp brown crust to form on the bottom.*

*We all lusted after the crust; it was so toasty and crunchy, almost like popcorn. Sometimes we would have it with just hot water, which would make a crackling porridge dish that was quite dramatic and exciting. In fact, my mother liked the crust so much that sometimes she would cook the rice, scrape it out, and eat the crust before I got home. She would then smilingly say that there was no crust. I always knew better, because I could smell the aromatic rice as soon as I walked in. On occasion, my mother would fry the rice and toss it into a simple soup, adding something like frozen peas. The soup would sizzle or sing, as my mother poetically put it.*

*The rice crust keeps well in a dry area, but not in the refrigerator, where it is moist. Once the crust is made, the rest of the soup can be assembled easily. I'm sure you will find this as delicious as I did growing up.*

### Rice

2 cups long-grain white rice
3¹/₂ cups water

Put the rice and water in a large, wide, heavy pot. Bring the water to a boil over high heat. Then turn the heat down as low as possible, cover, and let the rice cook for about 45 minutes. The rice should form a heavy crust on the bottom. Remove all the loose rice to eat with your meal or to make fried rice, leaving the heavy crust.

Allow the crust to cook over a very low heat for 15 minutes, enough time to dry out the crust so that it should lift off easily. If it is still sticky, continue to cook over very low heat for another 5 minutes or so. It doesn't matter if the crust breaks. Put the crust on a plate until it is ready for use. Once it has been cooked, it can be left out at room temperature for several days. Do not cover or refrigerate it, or moisture will form and make the cake moldy or soggy.

### Soup

4 cups homemade chicken stock (page 60) or reduced-salt
 canned broth
¹/₂ cup frozen peas
2 tablespoons finely shredded scallions
1 tablespoon light soy sauce
1 tablespoon Shaoxing rice wine
¹/₂ teaspoon salt
¹/₄ teaspoon freshly ground black pepper
1 teaspoon Asian sesame oil
2 cups peanut oil, for deep-frying

Bring the stock to a simmer in a large pot. Toss in the peas and scallions. Pour in the soy sauce and rice wine, then sprinkle in the salt and pepper. Allow to simmer another 5 minutes. Turn the soup into a large soup tureen. Swirl in the sesame oil.

Heat a wok or large frying pan over high heat until it is hot. Pour in the peanut oil, and when it is very hot and slightly smoking, deep-fry the pieces of rice crust until they puff up and brown slightly. Remove immediately and drain on paper towels. Then quickly drop the hot rice crust into the soup. Serve at once.

Note: The oil, once cooled, should be drained and reused. It will have a toasty aroma.

To shred scallions, first cut them into 3-inch lengths. Cut these pieces in half lengthwise and then into fine julienne shreds.

# Chinese Chicken Stock

*Although my mother worked at a full-time job, she always had time to make the all-important chicken stock. It was the foundation for all her soups and sauces. The chief ingredient is inexpensive; the stock is light and delicious, and it marries well with other foods, enhancing and sustaining them. The usual Chinese chicken stock is precisely that: the essence of chicken, with complements of ginger and scallions often added. Combined with the condiments that give Chinese food its distinctive flavor, good stock captures the essential taste of China. Many of the most famous recipes in the repertory require such stock.*

*Often at family meals and banquets, stock was prepared so that it could also be used as a clear soup. We drank it as a bever-*

age as we sampled all the different dishes. This simple and fairly easy-to-make recipe for stock reflects what I believe works best for any Chinese dish.

There are commercially prepared canned or cubed (dried) stocks, but many of them are of inferior quality, either too salty or containing additives and colorings that adversely affect your health as well as the natural taste of good foods. However, I have found low-sodium canned broth acceptable as a convenient substitute. Stock does take time to prepare, but it is not difficult or complex—and it is best when homemade. You can make a big batch and freeze it for your own use when needed. Here are several important points to keep in mind when making stock:

◆ Good stock requires meat to give it richness and flavor. It is therefore necessary to use at least some chicken meat, if not a whole bird.

◆ The stock should never boil. If it does it will be undesirably cloudy and the fat will be incorporated into the liquid. Flavors and digestibility come with a clear stock.

◆ Use a tall, heavy pot, so the liquid covers all the solids and evaporation is slow.

◆ Simmer slowly and skim the stock regularly. Be patient; you will reap the rewards each time you prepare a Chinese dish.

◆ Strain the finished stock well through several layers of cheesecloth or a fine mesh strainer.

◆ Let the stock cool thoroughly, refrigerate, and remove any fat before freezing it.

The classic Chinese method to ensure a clear stock is to blanch the meat and bones before simmering. I find this unnecessary. My method of careful skimming achieves the same result with far less work. Remember to save all your uncooked chicken bones and carcasses for stock. They can be frozen until you are ready to prepare it.

Makes about 1 gallon

4½ pounds uncooked chicken bones, such as backs, feet, or
   wings
1½ pounds chicken parts, such as wings, thighs, or
   drumsticks
1 gallon cold water
3 slices fresh ginger, 3 inches by ¼ inch
6 whole scallions
6 whole garlic cloves, unpeeled
1 teaspoon salt
2 teaspoons whole black peppercorns

Put the chicken bones and chicken pieces into a very large pot. (The bones can be put in either frozen or defrosted.) Cover them with the cold water and bring it to a simmer. Meanwhile, cut the ginger into diagonal slices, 2 inches by ½ inch. Trim and clean the scallions. Lightly crush the garlic cloves, leaving the skins on.

Using a large, flat spoon, skim off the scum as it rises from the bones. Watch the heat—the stock should never boil, only simmer. Keep skimming until the stock looks clear. This can take from 20 to 40 minutes. Do not stir or disturb the stock.

Now turn the heat down to a lower simmer. Toss in the ginger, scallions, garlic cloves, salt, and peppercorns. Simmer the stock on a very low heat for 4 hours, skimming any fat off the top at least twice during this time. The stock should be rich and full-bodied; simmering it for such a long time gives it (and any soup you make with it) plenty of taste.

Strain the stock through several layers of dampened cheesecloth or through a very fine mesh strainer, and then let it cool thoroughly. Refrigerate. Remove any fat that has risen to the top. It is now ready to be used, or transferred to containers and frozen for future use.

Note: If you find the quantity too large for your needs, cut the recipe in half.

# FISH and SHELLFISH

*Steamed Halibut with Ginger and Scallions*

*Traditional Steamed Whole Pike*

*Tender Home-Style Fish Cakes with Bean Sprouts*

*Crispy Fish with Pan-Fried Bean Curd*

*Crunchy Fish with Tender Eggplant*

*Steamed Trout with Fried Garlic*

*Crispy Fried Five-Spice Trout*

*Crispy Fish Roll*

*Crispy Butterflied Shrimp*

*Tasty Shrimp Toast*

*Easy Shrimp with Crispy Snow Peas*

*Classic Shrimp with Lobster Sauce*

*Curried Shrimp with Vegetables*

*Home-Style Stir-Fried Scallops with Fragrant Shrimp Paste*

*Savory Black Bean Clams*

*Easy Steamed Fresh Oysters*

*Smoky Dried Oysters with Vegetables*

*Stir-Fried Fresh Crabs*

*Steamed Lobster with Duck Eggs*

*Mussels in Curry Sauce*

*Stir-Fried Crunchy Conch*

*Aromatic Garlic Squid*

# Steamed Halibut with Ginger and Scallions

*I remember this dish from my childhood with great fondness. It is quite unpretentious, simple but really delicious, and I always felt it was one of my mother's favorites. Halibut was relatively inexpensive in the 1950s and '60s, so we enjoyed it whenever it was in season and most fresh. The steaming technique kept its firm flesh moist and tender—steaming is usually the best fish-cooking technique—and the addition of ginger and scallions infused the fish with perfectly harmonious flavors.*

*This is a fine example of South Chinese home cooking at its best: simple ingredients blended carefully and respectfully.*

Serves 4

1 pound halibut fillets
2 teaspoons kosher salt
2 tablespoons Shaoxing rice wine or dry sherry
1/4 cup homemade chicken stock (page 60) or reduced-salt
   canned broth
8 thin slices ginger
5 scallions, cut into 3-inch pieces

Cut the halibut fillets into 2-inch chunks. Place the fish in a heatproof bowl and toss well with the salt. Drizzle in the rice wine and stock, then scatter the ginger and scallions around the fish.

Next set up a steamer, or put a rack into a wok or deep pan, and fill it with 2 inches of water. Bring the water to a boil over a high heat. Carefully lower the bowl onto the rack. Turn the heat to low and cover the wok or pan tightly. Steam gently for 15 minutes, or until the fish is cooked. When it is cooked, the fish should be firm to the touch.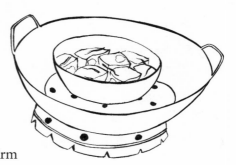

Remove from the steamer and serve at once with rice.

*Variation:* This recipe is just as delicious with salmon fillets or any firm white fish fillets, such as sea bass.

# Traditional Steamed Whole Pike

*This was always a special culinary treat, and pike remains one of my favorite fish today. The fish's sweet, firm, and slightly flaky flesh makes it perfect for steaming. We enjoyed it simply steamed, so that its fresh, natural flavor could shine. Then we quickly doused it with a shower of freshly shredded scallions, a touch of light soy sauce, and hot, smoking oil that was ladled on as a last-minute touch like butter in American cooking. We served the pike whole in my uncle's restaurant, and it appeared frequently at the family table on special occasions. I remember how other restaurant patrons would look on curiously when the fish came to the table, whole and steaming. After we enjoyed the delicate pike, there was always a struggle to see who got to enjoy the fish head, which contains the highly prized cheek meat. I was taught as a young child to extract the cheeks with my chopstick and to place them dutifully in my mother's bowl as my filial gift to her. Every adult at the table would then nod with approval, and I knew that I was on the right path.*

*Serves 4*

3 pounds cleaned and gutted whole pike or whole
    firm white fish, such as cod or sea bass
1 tablespoon salt
6 finely shredded scallions, white and green parts
2 tablespoons light soy sauce
3 tablespoons peanut oil

Rub the fish evenly inside and outside with the salt and set it on a heat-proof platter.

Set up a steamer, or put a rack into a wok or deep pan, and fill it with 2 inches of water. Bring the water to a boil over high heat. Carefully lower the platter onto the rack. Turn the heat to low and cover the wok or pan tightly. Steam gently for 15 minutes, or until the fish is cooked. When it is cooked, the fish should be firm to the touch.

Remove the fish and pour off any excess liquid. Scatter the scallions and soy sauce evenly over the fish. Heat the peanut oil in a wok until it is very hot and smoking. Pour the hot oil over the scallions and fish and serve at once.

Note: A large turkey roaster is perfect for steaming a large whole fish.

# Tender Home=Style Fish Cakes with Bean Sprouts

*This popular South Chinese treat demonstrates how Chinese cooks are masters at creating something marvelous out of (apparently) almost nothing. In this case, leftover fish fillets are minced to a soft fish puree, and seasonings and egg whites are added. The mixture is then quick fried and sliced; or it is rolled into round cakes and poached. The cake can be made ahead of time and then stir-fried with vegetables or sliced into pieces and added to soups.*

*It is not surprising to see that these favorites were common foods in Chinese-American homes. Fish cakes were available in our local Chinese groceries, but my mother always made her own. It was cheaper to do so and avoided the MSG that the store-bought versions sometimes contained. She would pan-fry the fish cakes, slice them thinly, and then stir-fry them with fresh bean sprouts. It made a light and delicious dish at our dinner table.*

Serves 4

## Fish Mixture

1 pound boneless white fish fillets, such as sea bass, rockfish, red snapper, or cod
1 egg white
2 teaspoons cornstarch

2 tablespoons finely chopped scallions
2 teaspoons finely chopped ginger
1 teaspoon salt
1/4 teaspoon freshly ground white pepper
2 teaspoons Shaoxing rice wine or dry sherry
2 tablespoons cold water

1 cup peanut oil
1 1/2 tablespoons finely sliced garlic
1 tablespoon finely shredded ginger
1 cup finely sliced red onions
2 cups cleaned bean sprouts
3 tablespoons chicken stock or water

## The Sauce

2 teaspoons oyster sauce
1 tablespoon light soy sauce
1 teaspoon sugar
1 tablespoon Shaoxing rice wine or dry sherry
1/4 cup homemade chicken stock (page 60) or reduced-salt
  canned broth
1 teaspoon cornstarch mixed with 2 teaspoons water

Remove any skin from the fish fillets and cut them into small pieces.
Blend all the ingredients for the fish mixture in a food processor until you
have a fine paste.

Heat a wok or large skillet until it is hot and pour in the oil. Form the
paste into 1/2-inch by 5-inch patties and deep-fry them for 5 minutes, or until
they are golden brown. Remove them with a slotted spoon and drain on
paper towels. Pour off most of the oil, leaving 2 tablespoons. When the fish
cakes are cool, slice them into bite-size pieces.

Reheat the wok with the oil, and when it is hot, toss in the garlic, ginger, and onions and stir-fry for 1 minute. Then toss in the bean sprouts and
3 tablespoons of chicken stock and continue to stir-fry for another 2 minutes.
Pour in the sauce ingredients and continue to cook for 1 minute. Return the
fish cake pieces to the sauce, mix gently, and heat through. Serve at once.

# Crispy Fish with Pan=Fried Bean Curd

*This delectable dish is typical of what one would find at my mother's dinner table. It is a winning combination of firm, crispy fish and silky-soft bean curd: nutritious, delicious, and easy to make. For a working mother, such as my own mother was, recipes like this are a godsend.*

*With the rice already cooking, my mother would quickly chop, dice, and slice vegetables, cut up and marinate the fish, combine the essential garlic, ginger, and scallions. Finally, sauces were mixed in bowls. Once these steps were accomplished, the actual cooking took literally ten minutes. I was always amazed how, within half an hour, we sat down to a four-course meal (often reheated dishes she had made the night before or leftovers) almost every night.*

*When I recall her kitchen style, I remember my mother's quiet efficiency, the flowing smoothness of her techniques, and the economy of effort. She rarely showed anything but composure as she worked her magic.*

*Serve this with a vegetable dish and soup for a complete meal; for a true feast, add a meat dish to the menu.*

Serves 4

1 pound fillets of red snapper, rockfish, sea bass, or any firm
    white-fleshed fish
2 teaspoons salt
Cornstarch, for dusting
1 pound soft bean curd
1/2 cup peanut oil
1 tablespoon finely chopped garlic
1 tablespoon finely chopped fresh ginger
1 tablespoon finely shredded fresh red chili

## Sauce

2 teaspoons yellow bean sauce
2 teaspoons light soy sauce

2 teaspoons dark soy sauce
1 teaspoon sugar
1 teaspoon Chinese black vinegar
2 teaspoons Shaoxing rice wine or dry sherry

## Garnish

2 tablespoons finely chopped scallions

Cut the fish into bite-size pieces. Blot completely dry with a paper towel. Evenly sprinkle the salt over all the pieces and dust them with cornstarch, shaking off any excess. Gently cut the bean curd into bite-size pieces and set them aside to drain on paper towels. Heat a wok or large frying pan over high heat until it is hot. Pour in the oil, and when it is very hot and slightly smoking, pan-fry half of the fish pieces for 2 minutes on each side, until they are brown and slightly crispy. Fry the remaining half of the fish. Remove and drain well on paper towels. Pour off all but 1½ tablespoons of oil from the wok.

Reheat the wok; toss in the garlic, ginger, and chili; and stir-fry for 1 minute. Next, gently layer in the bean curd pieces. Pour in the sauce ingredients and bring to a boil, return the fish to the sauce, and continue to cook for another minute, or until the fish is cooked through. Garnish with the scallions and serve at once.

# Crunchy Fish with Tender Eggplant

*While my non-Chinese schoolmates were at home eating—or resisting—such common vegetables as spinach and broccoli, I was happily consuming what was then an exotic and unfamiliar vegetable: Chinese eggplant.*

*My mother would prepare it as a separate vegetable dish, or she would combine it with meat or fish for a hearty and tasty meal.*

*This dish is one of my favorites. It combines the soft, delicate, tender texture of eggplant with pan-fried fish. The combination of*

*(continues on page 71)*

# Chinese Eggplant

Eggplant is a popular and inexpensive food found throughout China. The white-skinned variety was the first that English-speaking people encountered; hence the name. Nonetheless, this versatile food may be ivory, purple, or even light green in color. It is native to India and Southeast Asia and has been cultivated in China since 600 B.C. The original Chinese name translates as "Malayan purple melon," indicating that Chinese traders brought it from the Malay Peninsula. Although it is botanically a fruit, it is consumed as a vegetable. The size and shape vary from large and plump to small and thin. The most common type, the large purple variety, is easily available in the U.S.; the Chinese prefer the more delicate flavor of the Chinese variety, which is smaller and thinner and sweeter. Fortunately, these are becoming more readily available in supermarkets now.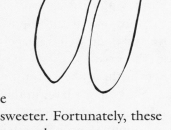

Try to find the long thin light-purple variety known as Chinese or Japanese eggplant. They look like young zucchini and tend to be sweet and tender with fewer seeds. They are also easier to prepare, because they don't need to be salted and rinsed.

Look for eggplants with unwrinkled, firm, smooth, unblemished skin. They should have a hollow sound when tapped.

Chinese normally do not peel eggplants, since the skin preserves texture, taste, and shape. The large eggplants that are most often found in supermarkets should be cut according to the recipe, sprinkled with a little salt, and left to sit for twenty minutes. They should then be rinsed and any liquid blotted dry with paper towels. This process extracts bitter juices and excess moisture from the vegetable before it is cooked, giving a truer taste to a dish. The eggplant also absorbs less moisture as a result. The procedure is unnecessary if you are using Chinese eggplants.

*these two distinct flavors and textures is typically Chinese. It was a most pleasing and very satisfying home-cooked dish.*

Serves 4

1 pound Chinese eggplants or regular eggplant
2 teaspoons salt, if using the regular eggplant
2 cups plus 3 tablespoons peanut oil
1 pound firm white fish fillet, such as sea bass or halibut
1 teaspoon salt
Cornstarch, for dusting
2 tablespoons coarsely chopped garlic
2 tablespoons finely shredded fresh ginger
3 tablespoons finely chopped scallions
2 tablespoons dark soy sauce
3 tablespoons Shaoxing rice wine or dry sherry
3 tablespoons Chinese black rice vinegar
2 tablespoons sugar
1 tablespoon roasted and ground Sichuan peppercorns (see
    page 72)
2 teaspoons chili bean sauce (see page 276)
1/2 teaspoon freshly ground black pepper
1/2 cup homemade chicken stock (page 60) or reduced-salt
    canned broth
2 teaspoons Asian sesame oil

Roll-cut the Chinese eggplant by slicing at a slight diagonal, then rolling the eggplant 180 degrees and slicing again at a slight diagonal. If you are using the regular, large eggplant, trim and cut into 1-inch cubes. You will need to salt the large eggplant. Sprinkle the cubes with the 2 teaspoons of salt and leave them in a sieve to drain for 20 minutes. Then rinse them under cold running water and pat them dry with paper towels.

Heat a wok or large frying pan over high heat until it is hot. Pour in the 2 cups of peanut oil, and when it is very hot and slightly smoking, deep-fry the eggplant pieces for a few minutes until they are tender, in two batches. Drain well in a colander and then on paper towels.

Cut the fish into bite-size pieces and sprinkle evenly with the 1 teaspoon of salt. Now dust them evenly with the cornstarch, shaking off any excess.

Pour off the oil, allow to cool, and store (or reserve) for the next time you are deep-frying eggplant. Wipe the wok clean and reheat, and when it is hot, swirl in 3 tablespoons of fresh oil. Pan-fry the fish until it is crispy and brown. Remove the fish and drain on paper towels. Pour off most of the oil, leaving 1 tablespoon. Reheat the wok; toss in the garlic, ginger, and scallions; and stir-fry for 2 minutes. Now pour in the rest of the ingredients except the fish and the sesame oil. Bring the mixture to the boil, return the eggplant to the wok, and continue to cook over high heat until the eggplant is tender, then return the fish and reheat. Stir in the sesame oil. Serve at once.

# Sichuan Peppercorns

## *(Zanthoxylum simulans)*

Also called fagara, wild pepper, Chinese pepper, and anise pepper, Sichuan peppercorns are an ancient spice known throughout China as "flower peppers" because they look like flower buds opening. Used originally and extensively in Sichuan cooking (hence their popular name), they are enjoyed in other parts of China as well. Their reddish-brown, rusty color and strong, pungent odor distinguish them from the hotter black peppercorns, with which they may be used interchangeably. Not related to peppers at all, they are the dried berries of a shrub that is a member of the prickly-ash family known as fagara. Their smell reminds me of lavender; their taste is sharp and slightly numbing to the tongue, with a clean, lemonlike, woody spiciness and fragrance. It is not the peppercorns that make Sichuan cooking so hot but, rather, the chili pepper. These peppercorns are one of the components of five-spice powder. They can be ground in a conventional peppermill but should be roasted (see below) beforehand to bring out their full flavor.

An inexpensive item, they are sold wrapped in cellophane or plastic bags in Chinese stores. Avoid packets with dark seeds; they should be a vibrant rusty reddish-brown color. They are best when the package is vacuum-packed, for they quickly lose their special aroma if left out too long. They will keep indefinitely if stored in a well-sealed container.

## To roast Sichuan peppercorns:

Heat a wok or heavy frying pan to a medium heat. Add the peppercorns (you can cook up to about ¼ cup at a time) and stir-fry them for about 5 minutes, until they brown slightly and start to smoke. Remove the pan from the heat and let them cool. Grind the peppercorns in a peppermill or clean coffee grinder, or with a mortar and pestle. Sift the ground peppercorns through a fine mesh and discard any of the hard hulls. Seal tightly in a screw-top jar to store. Alternatively, keep the whole roasted peppercorns in a well-sealed container and grind them when required.

# Steamed Trout with Fried Garlic

*Steaming fish is a great southern Chinese tradition and was my mother's favorite method of cooking fish, for it preserves the purest flavors of the fish. However, fresh fish in the 1950s and 1960s was not as abundant in Chicago's Chinatown as it is today. We were fortunate when we were able to get fresh trout, a delicacy that requires quick gentle cooking, in which none of the taste is masked. Steaming allowed the trout to remain moist and tender at the same time. It was a perfect dish for a working mother.*

*The fried garlic at the end added a crunchy aromatic touch.*

*Serves 2*

73

2 small whole trout, cleaned
1/4 teaspoon kosher salt
1 tablespoon finely julienned fresh ginger
2 teaspoons light soy sauce

## Garnish

2 tablespoons finely julienned scallions
2 tablespoons fresh coriander leaves
1 tablespoon peanut oil
2 garlic cloves, peeled and thinly sliced

Pat the trout dry inside and out with paper towels. Rub the trout evenly with the salt.

Next set up a steamer, or put a rack into a wok or deep pan, and fill it with 2 inches of water. Bring the water to a boil over high heat. Put the trout on a heatproof plate and scatter the ginger evenly over the top, then drizzle the soy sauce on. Put the plate of trout into the steamer or onto the rack. Cover the pan tightly and gently steam the trout until it is just cooked, about 5 minutes.

Remove the plate of cooked trout and scatter the scallions and coriander leaves over the top. Heat the oil in a small saucepan, toss in the garlic slices, and brown them. Pour the garlic-oil mixture over the top of the fish. Serve at once.

# Crispy Fried Five=Spice Trout

*This is an elegant trout dish which we often had at home for a quick lunch or dinner. With its clean and delicate taste and texture, all that it needs is the touch of an aromatic seasoning to complement its own unique flavor. At our table, it was served with rice, a fast stir-fried vegetable dish, and usually soup made the night before and simply reheated. An easy four-course meal in about half an hour.*

Serves 2

2 small whole trout, cleaned
$1/2$ teaspoon five-spice powder
$1/2$ teaspoon salt
Freshly ground black pepper to taste
1 tablespoon flour
2 tablespoons peanut oil

### Garnish

1 lemon, quartered
Fresh coriander sprigs

Blot the trout dry inside and out with paper towels.

Mix the five-spice powder with the salt and pepper and sprinkle this evenly over the trout. Dust the outside of the trout thoroughly with the flour.

Heat a wok or large frying pan over high heat until it is hot. Add the oil, and when it is very hot and slightly smoking, turn the heat down to medium and pan-fry the 2 trout for 3 minutes, until they are brown and crispy, then turn them over and pan-fry the other sides. When the fish are cooked, in about 5 minutes total, remove them to a warm platter.

Garnish with lemon wedges and fresh coriander. Serve at once.

# Crispy Fish Roll

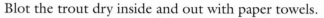

*Among the many banquet dishes I enjoyed as a child, this one, with moist fresh minced fish encased in a crispy crust, was especially memorable. I have never seen it served outside my uncle's restaurant, which makes me wonder if this is a Chinese-American invention or an authentic Chinese dish. My guess is that it is one of my uncle's ad hoc inspirations.*

*But it really doesn't matter, because it is absolutely delicious. Caul fat, the lacy membrane from the abdominal cavity of the pig (which can be obtained from a butcher), encloses a tasty mixture of fish chopped and blended into a well-seasoned paste. The package is fried until very crispy, then sliced and served with lemon wedges and seasoned with salt and pepper. The magic touch, I discovered, was a bit of pork fat, which gives the roll a richness of taste and flavor. The caul fat also serves to keep the roll moist.*

*This fish filling can easily be made in a food processor, and it can be prepared hours in advance of the frying. However, it should be fried and sliced at the last possible moment. It is served with Roasted Salt and Pepper (recipe follows), which can also be prepared ahead.*

Serves 4—6

1 pound firm white fish fillets, such as rockfish,
    sea bass, or halibut
1/4 pound pork fat
1 egg white
2 teaspoons salt
1 1/2 teaspoons freshly ground black pepper
1 teaspoon cornstarch
1 tablespoon cold water
1/2 pound caul fat, for wrapping
Potato starch or cornstarch, for dusting
3 cups peanut oil, for deep-frying

## Garnish

Lemon wedges
Roasted Salt and Pepper (recipe follows)

Mince the fish and blend it with the pork fat, egg white, salt, pepper, cornstarch, and water in a food processor until you have a smooth paste.

Cut the caul fat into 4 pieces 12 by 18 inches. Lay out 1 piece of caul fat, place a quarter of the fish mixture on 1 short end, fold in the sides, and roll up tightly. Dust the fish roll with the starch and set aside. Continue until you have four fish rolls ready.

Heat a wok or large frying pan

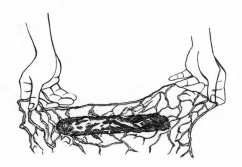

over high heat until it is hot. Pour in the oil, and when it is very hot and slightly smoking, drop in the fish rolls and fry for 6 minutes, or until they are brown and crispy. Remove and drain well on paper towels.

Slice the rolls into bite-size portions and serve at once with the lemon wedges and Roasted Salt and Pepper dip.

## Roasted Salt and Pepper

3 tablespoons Sichuan peppercorns
4 tablespoons kosher salt

Heat a wok or heavy frying pan to medium heat. Toss in the peppercorns and the salt and stir-fry until the mixture begins to smoke slightly and brown a little. Then grind it, using a blender, a clean coffee grinder, or a mortar and pestle. This can be made days before you use it. If you make it ahead, be sure it is well sealed in a jar until you are ready to use it.

# Crispy Butterflied Shrimp

*Butterflying shrimp is a standard in almost every Chinese-American restaurant. An incision is made from head to tail, and the shrimp is flattened into a butterfly outline. It is not hard to do at home once you get the hang of it. Butterflying the shrimp allows for fast cooking—perfect for restaurants that need to get their food out quickly.*

*The shrimp are served fried, which is not the preferred Chinese way of preparing shellfish of any sort. There are many other Chinese versions of this dish, but I am sure that the addition of a breaded coating is an American innovation that has now been introduced into China.*

*Serves 4*

## Spicy Sweet=and=Sour Sauce

*First make this simple sauce and set aside.*

3 tablespoons Chinese white rice vinegar
2 tablespoons sugar
2 teaspoons light soy sauce
2 teaspoons chili bean sauce (see page 276)

Combine all the ingredients in a small bowl, mix well, and let sit for at least 5 minutes before serving.

## Shrimp

1 pound peeled and deveined shrimp (1¼ pounds with
   shells on)
1 teaspoon salt
½ teaspoon freshly ground white pepper
1 teaspoon Asian sesame oil
2 teaspoons light soy sauce
1 teaspoon Shaoxing rice wine or dry sherry
½ cup all-purpose white flour
2 eggs, beaten
¾ cup dried bread crumbs
1½ cups peanut oil

Rinse the deveined shrimp in cold water and blot them dry on paper towels. Then butterfly the shrimp by making a deep cut along the back without cutting through. The shrimp will then open flat like an open book. Now combine the shrimp with salt, pepper, sesame oil, soy sauce, and rice wine and set aside for 20 minutes.

Remove the shrimp from the marinade, dust with flour, dip them in the egg, then roll them in the bread crumbs, shaking off any excess.

Heat a wok or large frying pan over

high heat until it is hot. Pour in the peanut oil; when it is very hot and slightly smoking, turn the heat to medium, and fry the shrimp for 3 minutes, or until they are golden brown. It is best to do this in two batches. Drain them well on paper towels and serve at once with the dipping sauce opposite.

*Chinese fish merchant cleaning fish, late 1800s*

# Tasty Shrimp Toast

*Although this dish is now popular in Hong Kong, I believe it to be a purely Chinese-American invention. Shrimp lends itself to many cooking techniques, including steaming and deep-frying shrimp balls in dim-sum menus, and making shrimp paste stuffing for fish or vegetables. But to combine shrimp with toast is, to me, a uniquely Western idea.*

*That being said, the dish is popular, tasty, and easy to make. The small amount of fatty pork adds richness and enhances the other flavors; the dry bread absorbs the oils and spices. Perhaps the dish was invented by frugal Chinese-American chefs with stale bread on hand—much the way "French toast" evolved.*

Makes about 30 pieces, serving 4—6 as an appetizer

## Shrimp Paste

1 pound shrimp, peeled, deveined, and finely chopped
1/4 pound fatty ground pork
1/2 pound fresh water chestnuts, peeled and chopped, or
   1/4 pound canned, chopped
1 teaspoon salt
1/4 teaspoon freshly ground white pepper
3 tablespoons finely chopped scallions
2 teaspoons finely chopped ginger
2 teaspoons light soy sauce
1 teaspoon sugar
1 teaspoon Asian sesame oil
1 teaspoon cornstarch
1 egg white

10 thin slices dry white bread
Potato flour or cornstarch, for dusting
2 cups peanut oil, for deep-frying

In a food processor, combine all the ingredients for the shrimp paste and process until they are just blended. A bit of texture in the paste is desirable.

Trim any crust from the bread and cut it into 3-by-1-inch rectangles. If the bread is fresh, toast until light brown; this step is not necessary if the bread is dry. Spread the paste about 1/4 inch thick on the bread pieces. Dust the paste side lightly with the potato flour.

Heat a wok or deep pan until it is hot. Pour in the peanut oil, and when the oil is hot, turn the heat to moderate and deep-fry the shrimp toasts, paste side down, for 3 minutes, or until golden brown. Regulate the temperature from time to time so that the oil does not get too hot. Then turn them over and fry on the other side for another minute. Remove with a slotted spoon and drain on paper towels. Serve at once.

# Easy Shrimp with Crispy Snow Peas

*This was a very popular dish at our family restaurant. It could be prepared in minutes in our hot woks, so our customers were able to order and enjoy their dish without much waiting. Snow peas, with their sweet taste and crispy texture, make a nice contrast to the soft and succulent shrimp. A relatively rare vegetable and perceived as an exotic ingredient in the 1960s, snow peas are today a staple in the local supermarket.*

*This altogether delectable dish is as easy to make at home as it was to prepare for our "take-out" customers.*

Serves 4

2 tablespoons salt
1 pound medium shrimp, peeled and deveined
1 egg white
2 teaspoons cornstarch
2 teaspoons Asian sesame oil
1 teaspoon salt

1 cup peanut oil

1 tablespoon finely shredded fresh ginger
2 teaspoons coarsely chopped garlic
1/2 pound snow peas, trimmed
1 teaspoon salt
Freshly ground black pepper to taste
2 tablespoons Shaoxing rice wine or dry sherry
3 tablespoons finely shredded scallions
1/2 cup homemade chicken stock (page 60) or reduced-salt
    canned broth
1 teaspoon sugar
1 teaspoon cornstarch mixed with 2 teaspoons water

2 teaspoons Asian sesame oil

Fill a large bowl with cold water, add 1 tablespoon of salt, and gently wash the shrimp in the salt water. Drain and repeat the process. Then rinse the shrimp under cold running water, drain, and blot them dry with paper towels.

Mix the shrimp with the egg white, cornstarch, sesame oil, and salt in a medium-sized bowl, then refrigerate for about 20 minutes.

Heat a wok until it is very hot and then add the peanut oil. When the oil is very hot, remove the wok from the heat and immediately add the coated shrimp, stirring vigorously to keep them from sticking. When the shrimp turn slightly pink, quickly drain them and all of the oil in a stainless-steel colander set in a bowl. Reserve 1½ tablespoons of the oil and discard the rest.

Reheat the wok over high heat, and when it is hot, add the reserved oil. Immediately toss in the ginger and garlic to stir-fry for 10 seconds. Quickly toss in the snow peas, salt, pepper, rice wine, scallions, chicken stock, and sugar. Continue to stir-fry for another minute, then add the cornstarch mixture and continue to cook for still another minute. Now toss in the shrimp, and when they are reheated thoroughly, stir in the sesame oil. Serve at once with plain rice.

Variation: As a substitute for snow peas, you can use frozen peas, corn, asparagus, sugar snaps, or fresh water chestnuts.

# Classic Shrimp with Lobster Sauce

*This was perhaps the most popular dish in my uncle's restaurant. We used to laugh in the kitchen, because the sauce contains no lobster. In fact, to improve the profits from the dish, we were instructed to cut down on the shrimp and to fill up the dish with less expensive ground pork and egg. It was nevertheless delicious, because it combined aromatic and pungent black beans, garlic, and ginger—an aroma that always evokes memories of good food and eating. There may appear to be a lot of ingredients, but nothing is difficult to prepare; just get everything lined up and you'll find this is a relatively simple dish to do at home.*

Serves 4

1 pound shrimp, peeled and deveined
1 egg white
2 teaspoons cornstarch
1 teaspoon salt
1 teaspoon Asian sesame oil
1/2 teaspoon freshly ground white pepper
1 cup peanut oil or 2 cups water (see variation)

## Sauce

1 1/2 tablespoons peanut oil
1 1/2 tablespoons finely chopped ginger
2 teaspoons finely chopped garlic
1 1/2 tablespoons coarsely chopped black beans
1/2 pound fatty ground pork
1 1/2 tablespoons Shaoxing rice wine or dry sherry
1 tablespoon light soy sauce
2 teaspoons dark soy sauce
2 teaspoons sugar
1/2 teaspoon salt
1/4 teaspoon freshly ground white pepper
2 teaspoons sesame oil
1/2 cup homemade chicken stock (page 60) or reduced-
   salt canned broth
1 tablespoon cornstarch dissolved in 2 tablespoons water

1 egg, beaten

## Garnish

2 tablespoons finely chopped scallions

Rinse the shrimp in cold water and pat them dry with paper towels. Mix the shrimp with the egg white, cornstarch, salt, sesame oil, and pepper. Refrigerate for 20 minutes.

Heat a wok until it is very hot and then drizzle in the peanut oil. When the oil is very hot, remove the wok from the heat, and immediately toss in the shrimp, stirring vigorously to keep them from sticking. As soon as the shrimp turn white, in about 2 minutes, quickly drain them through a stainless-steel colander set in a bowl. Discard the oil.

Reheat the wok or heat a large frying pan over high heat until it is hot. Swirl in the 1½ tablespoons of peanut oil, and when it is very hot and slightly smoking, toss in the ginger, garlic, and black beans and stir-fry for 30 seconds. Then dump in the ground pork, breaking it up, and continue to stir-fry for 2 minutes. Now toss in the rest of the sauce ingredients except the dissolved cornstarch. Bring the sauce to a boil, stir in the cornstarch to thicken, then return the shrimp to the wok and reheat thoroughly. Stir-fry everything for 1 minute. Now pour in the beaten egg in a steady stream, stirring slowly all the while. When the egg has barely set, remove the wok from the heat, pour the contents onto a warm serving platter, garnish with the scallions, and serve at once.

> Variation: If you choose to use water instead of oil, bring it to a boil in a saucepan. Remove the saucepan from the heat and immediately add the shrimp, stirring vigorously to keep them from sticking. When the shrimp turn white, after about 2 minutes, quickly drain them through a stainless-steel colander set in a bowl. Discard the water.

# Curried Shrimp with Vegetables

*This tasty dish is found in many Chinese-American restaurants and is a fine offering when prepared properly. Unfortunately, when overcooked shrimp are served with overthickened curry sauce, the result is an unappealing starchy blob. Curried dishes are not typical of Chinese cookery, so when we do make them, a good cook takes care that they are done correctly.*

*Here is a version that I am sure you will find quite delicious. The secret is to salt the shrimp and then coat them with a protective batter of egg white and cornstarch. This procedure protects the shrimp from the hot oil, keeping it moist and juicy inside. These extra steps will ensure a delectable dish.*

*Serves 4*

1 pound shrimp, peeled and deveined
1 tablespoon salt
1 egg white
2 teaspoons cornstarch
1 teaspoon salt
1 teaspoon Asian sesame oil
½ teaspoon freshly ground white pepper

2 cups peanut oil or water (see variations)

1½ tablespoons peanut oil
1 large onion, thinly sliced
1½ tablespoons finely chopped ginger
2 teaspoons coarsely chopped garlic
1 large green pepper, seeded and sliced
2 tablespoons Shaoxing rice wine or dry sherry
2 teaspoons Madras curry powder or paste
1 teaspoon salt
½ teaspoon freshly ground white pepper
3 tablespoons chicken stock or water
2 teaspoons Asian sesame oil

## Garnish

2 tablespoons finely shredded scallions

Sprinkle the shrimp with the salt and soak in cold water for 5 minutes. Drain well and pat them dry with paper towels.

Mix together thoroughly the shrimp, egg white, cornstarch, salt, sesame oil, and pepper. Let sit, refrigerated, for 20 minutes.

Heat a wok until it is very hot and then pour in the peanut oil. When the oil is very hot, remove the wok from the heat and immediately dump in the shrimp, stirring vigorously to keep them from sticking. When the shrimp turn white, in about 2 minutes, quickly drain them and all of the oil in a stainless-steel colander set in a bowl. Discard the oil.

Reheat the wok or heat a large frying pan over high heat until it is hot. Swirl in the 1½ tablespoons peanut oil, and when it is very hot and slightly smoking, add the onion, ginger, and garlic and stir-fry for 2 minutes. Then toss in the green pepper, along with the rice wine, curry powder, salt, and pepper. Stir-fry the mixture for 1 minute. Return the shrimp to the wok, add the stock, and stir gently for 1 minute to warm the shrimp. Stir in the sesame oil.

Turn onto a platter, garnish with the scallions, and serve at once.

Variations: If you choose to use water instead of oil, bring it to a boil in a saucepan. Remove the saucepan from the heat and immediately add the shrimp, stirring vigorously to keep them from sticking. When the shrimp turn white, in about 2 minutes, quickly drain them and all of the water in a stainless-steel colander set in a bowl. Discard the water.

Other vegetables could be substituted for the green pepper: snow peas, green peas, asparagus, sugar snaps, onions, or scallions.

## Shrimp Paste

(also known as shrimp sauce)

This paste or sauce is made from pulverized salted shrimp that are then allowed to ferment. As shrimp paste, the mixture has been dried in the sun and cut into cakes. The cakes are rarely found outside Asia. However, shrimp *sauce* that has been packed in a thick, moist state directly in jars is available. Once packed, the light-pink shrimp sauce slowly turns grayish, acquiring a pungent flavor as it matures. Popular in South Chinese cooking, this ingredient adds a distinctive flavor and fragrance to dishes. Although the odor of shrimp sauce takes getting used to, remember that the cooking process quickly tones down its aroma and taste. It is similar to anchovy paste in texture, though stronger in taste and odor. It can be found at Chinese grocers or supermarkets.

Kept in the refrigerator, it will last indefinitely.

# Home-Style Stir-Fried Scallops with Fragrant Shrimp Paste

*Chinese love seafood in any form, and the fresher the better. Where I grew up, in Chicago's Chinatown, there was always fresh fish sitting on bins of chipped ice as well as dried seafood gracing the shelves and glass cabinets of the local Chinese market. You could smell the pungent ocean aroma of the dried scallops, shark's fin, dried fish, and squid. It was one of the unique smells of my childhood.*

*At home, my mother would also use other seafood enhancements, such as shrimp paste, to add a dimension to her stir-fried dishes. One of my favorites was this fresh scallop recipe. Just a small amount of shrimp paste transforms ordinary scallops into a special savory treat. It is also a very easy dish to assemble and to prepare, and thus is perfect for today's busy cook.*

*Serves 4*

1 1/2 pounds scallops
1 1/2 tablespoons peanut oil
1 tablespoon finely shredded fresh ginger
1 tablespoon coarsely chopped garlic
1 tablespoon Shaoxing rice wine or dry sherry
2 teaspoons shrimp paste (see box opposite)
1 teaspoon sugar
1/2 teaspoon salt
1/2 teaspoon freshly ground white pepper
3 tablespoons finely chopped scallions
2 teaspoons Asian sesame oil

Pick through the scallops and remove the tough muscles. Drain on paper towels and pat dry.

Heat a wok or large frying pan over high heat until it is hot. Swirl in the peanut oil, and when it is very hot and slightly smoking, toss in the ginger and garlic and stir-fry for 10 seconds. Immediately toss in the scallops and stir-fry them for 2 minutes. Then spoon in the rice wine, shrimp paste, sugar, salt, and pepper. Continue to stir-fry for 3 minutes, until the scallops are firm and cooked through. Now toss in the scallions and sesame oil and continue to stir-fry for another minute. Serve at once with plain rice.

# Savory Black Bean Clams

*As the poorest of the poor, the first Chinese immigrants in America (mainly in California) scratched out a meager living as best they could. Fortunately, they were used to such a challenge, given the dire poverty that had marked their lives in China. One basic need was readily supplied: California was rich in edibles, including many that the Spanish and Anglo residents shunned. (In the old* Kung Fu *TV series, there were many scenes in which the hero satisfied his hunger with the most unlikely edibles found in the midst of the desert.)*

*Clams, for example, were in those days spurned by the non-Chinese. But the Chinese immigrants discovered and adopted such foods and turned them into delicious meals. Combining the clams with fermented black beans and, when possible, with a bit of meat and the traditional spices, they created a tasty dinner that in essential ways took their souls back to the homeland.*

*Serves 4*

6 pounds medium-sized fresh clams, scrubbed
2 tablespoons peanut oil
3 tablespoons coarsely chopped fermented black beans
2 tablespoons coarsely chopped garlic
1 1/2 tablespoons finely chopped ginger
3 tablespoons finely chopped scallions
1/2 pound ground beef or pork
2 tablespoons light soy sauce
2 teaspoons dark soy sauce
2 tablespoons Shaoxing rice wine or dry sherry
1 teaspoon sugar
1/2 cup homemade chicken stock (page 60) or reduced-salt
    canned broth
2 teaspoons Asian sesame oil

## Garnish

1/2 cup fresh coriander sprigs

Soak the clams in several changes of cold water to allow them to expel any sand and grit.

Heat a wok or large frying pan over high heat until it is hot. Drizzle in the peanut oil, and when it is very hot and slightly smoking, toss in the black beans, garlic, ginger, and scallions and stir-fry for 20 seconds. Stir in the meat and stir-fry for 2 minutes. Now throw in the clams and continue to stir-fry for 1 minute. Stir in the soy sauces, rice wine, sugar, and chicken stock, cover, and cook over high heat for 3 minutes, or until the clams start opening. Uncover and continue to cook, removing the clams as they open to a large platter. Discard any clams that remain closed. Finally, stir in the sesame oil. Ladle the mixture over the clams, garnish with the fresh coriander, and serve at once.

# Easy Steamed Fresh Oysters

*Growing up Chinese-American meant enjoying seafood in all forms: fresh, of course, but also dried, salted, smoked, and in sauce form. My Chinese-American friend Lillian Chou remembers that one of her favorite treats as a child was the dried salted squid she would chew on like candy. It remains to this day a real comfort food for her.*

*The diversity of seafood we Chinese-Americans ate contrasted sharply with the food habits of the general American public. Our seafood dishes had intense flavors and myriad forms. When we ate fresh seafood, we mostly preferred it steamed, a technique designed to bring out all the delicate natural essences of the food.*

*In our homes, even oysters were steamed rather than eaten raw, as in this recipe. A bit of ginger and scallion, finished off with a wisp of hot oil, turns ordinary oysters into a marvelous delicacy. It makes a wonderful first course.*

*Serves 4*

16 large fresh oysters
Seaweed or kosher salt
1 tablespoon finely shredded fresh ginger
2 tablespoons light soy sauce
3 tablespoons finely shredded scallions
2 tablespoons peanut oil

### Garnish

Fresh coriander sprigs

Scrub the oysters clean; shuck them open by removing the top shell. Keep the oysters and juices intact in the bottom shell. Lay seaweed or kosher salt on a heatproof platter. Place the open oysters on their bottom shells on top of the seaweed or salt. This will keep them from rocking and spilling their juices. Scatter the ginger and soy sauce over the open oysters.

Next set up a steamer, or put a rack into a wok or deep pan, and fill it with 2 inches of water. Bring the water to the boil over high heat. Gently lower in the platter so that it sits firmly on the rack. Turn the heat to low and cover the wok tightly. Steam gently for 5 minutes.

Remove the oysters from the steamer and scatter the scallions evenly over them. Heat a wok or large frying pan over high heat until it is hot. Swirl in the oil, and when it is very hot and slightly smoking, pour this hot oil all over the oysters. Garnish with coriander sprigs. They are now ready to serve.

# Smoky Dried Oysters with Vegetables

*This unusual dish—oysters wrapped in iceberg lettuce—is a rare treat almost always reserved for family banquets. It is considered a classic, and with good reason, for it is refreshing, savory, and very satisfying.*

*The array of spices and seasonings enliven the robust sea taste of the oysters—even the iceberg lettuce takes on a deeper meaning.*

*I remember as a child using my fingers to dip into this very soft and sensuous platter of food. Fingers before forks, and before chopsticks as well!*

*The preparation requires a lot of chopping, but then there is only a simple stir-fry to do and you have a festive party dish.*

Serves 4

¹/₂ pound dried oysters* or canned smoked oysters
1 head iceberg lettuce, separated into leaves
1¹/₂ tablespoons peanut oil
2 tablespoons coarsely chopped garlic
1 tablespoon finely chopped fresh ginger
3 tablespoons finely chopped scallions
¹/₂ pound ground pork
¹/₄ cup finely chopped bamboo shoots
2 tablespoons finely chopped Smithfield ham
1 cup finely chopped fresh water chestnuts
3 tablespoons finely chopped fresh coriander
¹/₄ cup homemade chicken stock (page 60) or reduced-salt
   canned broth
5 tablespoons oyster sauce
2 teaspoons sugar
¹/₂ teaspoon salt
Freshly ground black pepper to taste

* Can be found at Chinese groceries and supermarkets.

Soak the dried oysters overnight. Remove any hard bits. Drain and finely chop them. If you are using canned smoked oysters, you can skip this step.

Carefully remove the lettuce leaves from the head and trim them all around to make attractive cups.

Heat a wok or large frying pan over high heat until it is hot. Swirl in the oil, and when it is very hot and slightly smoking, toss in the garlic, ginger, and scallions and stir-fry for 20 seconds. Then dump in the ground pork and dried oysters and continue to stir-fry for 3 minutes. Now toss in the bamboo shoots, ham, and water chestnuts and continue to stir-fry for 3 minutes, breaking up the ground pork. Sprinkle in the fresh coriander, pour in the chicken stock, oyster sauce, sugar, salt, and pepper, and continue to stir-fry for 3 minutes more.

Turn the mixture onto a serving platter and surround it with the lettuce cups.

Each guest puts a helping of the smoky dried oysters and vegetables into a lettuce cup and rolls it up like a taco, then eats it with his or her fingers.

# Stir=Fried Fresh Crabs

*Over twenty years ago, when I gave one of my first cooking classes, I prepared a live crab for the wok. My students were rather taken aback as I went through the process of dismembering the crab. But I was only doing as I had been taught.*

*Like my many Chinese-American friends, I grew up knowing that the only crab worth cooking was one that was alive up to the point of cooking. We were taught, correctly, that crab deteriorates as soon as it dies, to the detriment of its flavor and texture. In Chinese cookery, only the freshest of ingredients are to be used, and this applies especially to fish and shellfish.*

*Thus, it made sense only to prepare live crabs, dispatching them quickly and, as my uncles would have said, "with merciful merciless-ness." And once you've tasted fresh crab so prepared, the unique taste, texture, and silkiness of the crabmeat is incomparable. Freshness will have a new meaning—as we Chinese-Americans were taught.*

*This simple dish is easy to make once the crabs have been cut up. A simple stir-fry accented by bracing ginger and sharp scallions, it is a crab lover's gustatorial heaven.*

Serves 4–6

3–4 pounds live or freshly cooked crabs in the shell
2 tablespoons peanut oil
2 tablespoons finely sliced garlic
3 tablespoons finely julienned fresh ginger
4 whole scallions, sliced
2 teaspoons salt
Freshly ground black pepper to taste
2 tablespoons Shaoxing rice wine or dry sherry

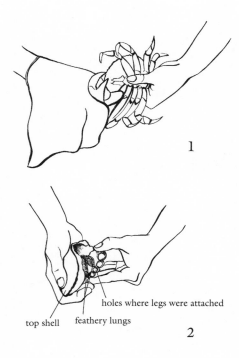

1

If you are using live crabs, hold each crab on its back. (1) With a thick towel, immediately twist off the large claws. Then twist off the small legs. Scrub the shells under cold running water. (2) Now separate the top shell from the crab body. (3) Remove the feathery lungs, the mouth, and the tail. Scrub the shell and the crab body under cold running water.

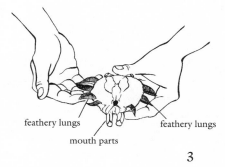

holes where legs were attached

top shell    feathery lungs

2

feathery lungs    feathery lungs

mouth parts

3

(4) Remove the stomach sac.

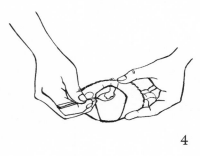

4

(5) Quarter the crab body with a large knife or cleaver. Then crack the claws and legs with the flat of the cleaver.

5

If you are using cooked crabs, simply clean and quarter them and crack as described above.

Heat a wok or large frying pan over high heat until it is hot. Swirl in the oil, and when it is very hot and slightly smoking, toss in the garlic, ginger, and scallions and stir-fry for 20 seconds. Then chuck in the crab pieces, salt, pepper, and rice wine. Stir-fry everything over high heat for about 15 minutes (if using cooked crab, 5 minutes will be enough). Turn it onto a large, warm serving platter and serve at once.

# Steamed Lobster with Duck Eggs

*This was a favorite both at our restaurant and at home, where it was almost always featured at family banquets. We kept the live lobsters in tanks at the restaurant, and my job was to prepare them when the orders came in.*

*The Chinese clientele insisted on the freshest possible seafood—hence the tanks of live lobsters—and they understood that the steaming technique was the best, subtlest, and most delicate way to enjoy this wonderful crustacean. Instead of butter, our version came with a tasty custard of preserved duck eggs. The small bit of pork is added to the custard to make the expensive lobster go further. This recipe makes for a very special meal.*

Serves 2–4

1¹/₂-pound live lobster
¹/₄ pound ground pork
2 beaten eggs
¹/₂ teaspoon salt
¹/₄ teaspoon freshly ground white pepper
¹/₂ teaspoon sugar
2 salted duck eggs*
3 tablespoons finely shredded scallions
1¹/₂ tablespoons finely shredded fresh ginger
2 tablespoons peanut oil
2 teaspoons Asian sesame oil

* Available at Chinese groceries and supermarkets.

Clean and split the lobster in half, then lightly crack the claws and back shell and lobster legs with the side of a cleaver or large knife. (Chinese usually cut up lobsters live, but you can blanch them for 2 minutes first, if you prefer.)

In a bowl, mix together the pork, eggs, salt, pepper, and sugar. Crack open and separate the duck eggs, pouring the duck egg whites into the bowl with the beaten egg and pork. Mix well. Take the salted duck egg yolks, which are firm, cut them in half, and set aside.

Pour the egg-pork mixture into a deep heatproof 8-to-10-inch plate and arrange the lobster halves in an attractive manner on top. Then place the duck egg yolks between the lobster pieces.

Next set up a steamer, or put a rack in a wok or deep pan, and fill it with 2 inches of water. Bring the water to a boil over high heat. Carefully lower the plate with the lobster onto the rack. Turn the heat to low and cover the wok or pan tightly. Steam gently for 10–12 minutes, or until the lobster is cooked and the custard has set.

Scatter the scallions and ginger over the dish. Heat a pan until it is very hot, then swirl in the peanut and sesame oils. When they are smoking, pour the oils over the lobster
and serve at once.

# Mussels in Curry Sauce

*As a child, sitting quietly through our family meals, I listened to innumerable stories, told more than once, about how delightfully different, and better, fresh seafood was in Hong Kong. I heard descriptions of restaurant holding tanks wherein live fish and shellfish were kept until the final moment of cooking them to ensure complete freshness.*

*Cooking techniques and remembrances of past seafood dishes would be topics of discussion as we ate. The Chinese way of cooking seafood was a difficult act to follow in America, but we did our best.*

*My uncle would buy live crabs, lobsters, clams, or mussels— because these were the only live seafoods available. He would stir-fry them in a hot wok and season the dish with a mild curry sauce—curry being an unusual but not unknown southern Chinese flavoring. I well remember this delicious mussel treat as one which we all enjoyed with our chopsticks and fingers.*

Serves 4–6

1½ tablespoons peanut oil
3 tablespoons finely sliced garlic
1 tablespoon finely shredded fresh ginger
3 pounds fresh mussels, well scrubbed
2 tablespoons Madras curry powder
2 tablespoons Shaoxing rice wine or dry sherry
1½ tablespoons light soy sauce
1 teaspoon sugar
¼ cup homemade chicken stock (page 60) or reduced-salt
  canned broth

## Garnish

3 tablespoons finely chopped scallions
3 tablespoons finely chopped fresh coriander

Heat a wok or large frying pan over high heat until it is hot. Swirl in the oil, and when it is very hot and slightly smoking, toss in the garlic and ginger and stir-fry for 20 seconds, then chuck in the mussels and stir-fry for 1 minute. Now sprinkle in the curry powder and pour the rice wine and soy sauce over the mussels. Sprinkle on the sugar and ladle in the stock. Cover and continue to cook for 5 minutes, or until all the mussels have opened. Discard any that have difficulty opening.

Give everything a final stir, scatter the scallions and coriander on top, and serve at once with rice.

# Stir=Fried Crunchy Conch

*As a child of eleven, working in my uncle's restaurant, I disliked a number of things that I never got used to. One of them involved the preparing of conch. Every other Thursday in the summer season, as the youngest member of the kitchen staff, I had to go through an eighty-pound burlap sack of live conch. I would break open the shells with a hammer, clean out the messy parts, and salvage the edible footlike muscle part. This was tedious, wearying work, and I know I broke at least three hammers during my apprenticeship.*

*Conch is a Caribbean seafood, unknown in China. But the Chinese love shellfish, and if they encounter something edible in an alien form their cooks will turn it into a Chinese dish. Conch is related to the more prestigious abalone, and like that delicacy it can be tenderized and eaten raw or cooked in various ways. In our restaurant, the conch was refrigerated right next to other delicacies reserved for Chinese patrons of our "second menu": bird's nest, shark's fin, and sea cucumber. Such exotic offerings drew Chinese from all over Chicago to my uncle's restaurant.*

*Despite the galley-slave labors of my childhood, I love stir-fried conch to this day. It is even more enjoyable now that I don't have to face eighty-pound sacks of the stuff! Fresh conch is the best, but the frozen works nicely.*

*This recipe makes the best of the conch's chewy texture by matching it with delightful seasonings and color. Chinese cooking is ideal for conch, because it needs to be cooked quickly or it will get tough.*

Serves 4

1 pound frozen or fresh conch meat
1 1/2 tablespoons peanut oil
3 cloves garlic, peeled and crushed
2 ginger slices, 3 inches by 1/8 inch
1/2 cup peeled and sliced fresh water chestnuts
1 cup snow peas, trimmed
1 tablespoon light soy sauce
2 teaspoons Shaoxing rice wine or dry sherry
1 teaspoon sugar
1 teaspoon salt
1/2 teaspoon freshly ground black pepper
1/2 cup homemade chicken stock (page 60) or reduced-salt
   canned broth
2 teaspoons cornstarch mixed with 1 tablespoon water
2 teaspoons Asian sesame oil

Slice the conch meat in half horizontally, then crosswise and lengthwise into 1-inch pieces.

Heat a wok or large frying pan over high heat until it is hot. Drizzle in the peanut oil, and when it is very hot and slightly smoking, toss in the garlic and ginger and stir-fry for 20 seconds. Then dump in the conch, water chestnuts, and snow peas. Continue to stir-fry for 1 minute. Now drizzle in the soy sauce, rice wine, sugar, salt, pepper, and chicken stock. When the mixture has come to a boil, slowly stir in the cornstarch mixture, stirring all the while. As soon as the sauce has slightly thickened, stir in the sesame oil and transfer the contents to a platter. Serve at once.

# Aromatic Garlic Squid

*Many of my fellow Chinese-Americans have shared my experience of enjoying squid, long before it was called calamari. We used to keep many of our traditional Chinese foods a secret, for we were afraid our American friends would find them a bit too exotic. At home, however, we loved our "strange" foods, such as this simple garlic squid, which my mother often made. It took her a little time to prepare, but, then, she did all the cleaning of the squid herself; today most markets offer prepared squid. Then it was quickly stir-fried in a hot wok. The aromas always provided proof that we were lucky to be Chinese and to be eating so well. At our table, this squid was accompanied by a soup, a vegetable, and a meat dish— and, of course, rice.*

*Serves 4*

1½ pounds squid, fresh or frozen
1½ tablespoons peanut oil
3 tablespoons finely sliced garlic
1 tablespoon finely shredded ginger
1 teaspoon salt
½ teaspoon freshly ground black pepper
2 teaspoons dried chili flakes
1 teaspoon Asian sesame oil

The edible parts of the squid are the tentacles and the body. If it has not been cleaned by your fishmonger, you can do it yourself. (1) Pull the head and tentacles away from the body.

1

2

(2) Then pull off and discard the skin. Using a small sharp knife, split the body in half.

3

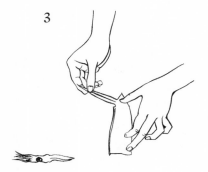

(3) Remove the transparent bony section. Wash the halves thoroughly under cold running water and then pull off and discard the skin.

4

(4) Cut the tentacles from the head, cutting just above the eye.

(5) You may also have to remove the polyp or beak from the base of the ring of tentacles. If you are using frozen squid, make sure it is properly thawed before cooking it.

5

Cut the squid meat into 1½-inch strips. Blanch the strips and the tentacles in a large pot of boiling water for 5 seconds. The squid will firm up slightly and turn an opaque white color. Remove and drain immediately in a colander. Allow the squid to drain for at least 5 minutes in the colander.

Heat a wok or large frying pan over high heat until it is hot. Swirl in the peanut oil, and when it is very hot and slightly smoking, toss in the garlic and ginger and stir-fry for 15 seconds. Then sprinkle in the salt, black pepper, and chili and stir-fry for 30 seconds. Toss in the squid and stir-fry vigorously for 1 minute. Finally, drizzle in the sesame oil and give the mixture a quick stir, mixing well. Serve immediately with other dishes or with rice.

# Amy Tan and the
# Joy of Chinese Food Club

Amy Tan, who has written so evocatively about growing up Chinese-American, is a good friend, and we often share childhood reminiscences. Food is as central a part of family life for her as it has always been for me.

She was born in Oakland, California, but lived for a while in Fresno, in the Central Valley, where her father was the minister of the First Chinese Baptist Church. Christian though she was, her world was Chinese through and through.

Like my mother, Amy's mother had grown up in a family with cooks and servants to attend to the kitchen work. Both her mother and her grandmother were expert cooks and extremely knowledgeable about Chinese cuisine. Her grandmother maintained she had so sensitive a palate that she could tell the precise area a certain type of noodle came from. Certainly both her grandmother and her mother, Amy says, drew upon their experiences and memories of China to guide their cooking in America.

Amy's mother never took a cooking lesson. She knew what had to be done because she had learned by osmosis and cooking was part of the essential experience of living. She used only the freshest ingredients, and she knew instinctively how to balance tastes and colors carefully, never making the mistake of using too many or too few seasonings and spices. Whenever the family ate out in Chinese restaurants, she would invariably complain that the food was too salty or too spicy, too sweet or too sour, that the fish was overcooked, too much soy sauce had been used, and the soup was not hot enough. Clear, distinct tastes are the hallmarks of good Chinese cooking, especially of the South China–Hong Kong style. But as I have mentioned before, restaurateurs here had quickly caught on to the fact that the heavy, sweet mixed sauces of the Chinese restaurants in those days were what the American palate preferred—and in the restaurant business, as elsewhere, the customer is always right.

Amy recalls that the typical family meal at her house consisted of five separate dishes, the way they ate in China. The family would enjoy at least one vegetable dish, fresh fish or prawns, one or two meat dishes, and, of course, rice. Usually a soup—something like a simple egg drop soup with tomato—would accompany the meal.

In retrospect, she often wonders how her mother managed the shopping, all the preparation, and the actual cooking of these meals. Her mother worked nights as a nurse, and she must have had to rush about every day to find the various fresh ingredients she insisted on. Although Amy's father loved to cook, too, his pastoral duties kept him busy seven days a week, and he didn't have much spare time.

Each meal would begin with a prayer of thanks to God and a remembrance of both the living and the dead. Once these formalities were over, the good food was fully enjoyed, along with family news and gossip.

One special dish that Amy recalls her mother making for a festival or anniversary was dried shredded pork, prepared by cooking down over two days a large chunk of fresh ham and then seasoning, drying, and shredding it—the whole process taking days. Her mother would make her own pickled spicy cabbage—called "la-la" by the children—and radishes pickled with vinegar and chili.

Birthdays, naturally, were special occasions, but the meals were a trial: her mother would always prepare live fresh crabs, and Amy as a child could not bear to see those crabs being slowly cooked to death. She felt the same way when live fresh fish were brought home and she would watch them flopping about on the kitchen table before being dispatched. In this regard, Amy and I agree that she was acting much more American than Chinese: in China there is no empathy for any living thing designated as food—an understandable attitude in a society that has known devastating famines and chronic food shortages throughout its history.

Amy's mother had always wanted to open a restaurant, a specialty place that offered only pot stickers or *jiao zi* (poached dumplings). And, indeed, her dumplings were famous among family and friends. She would make the dough from scratch, roll it out into a long roll, then cut off pieces and roll them out into doughy circles. These she would fill with pork, shredded squash, ginger, and other ingredients. She had no recipes. She simply tasted, looked, smelled, felt, and hefted the dough to decide whether it was right. And it always was, even if it was a little different each time.

Although Amy claims she is not a good cook, eating good Chinese food three times a day every day as a child taught her nose and palate unforgettable lessons. Until she entered high school, Amy ate every meal at home, including lunch. So her memories of food are almost totally Chinese. She even recalls the smell of wet newspaper as an essential element: the newspaper would be spread out on the kitchen table, around which Mother, the girls, Auntie, and family friends would gather to prepare the foods, snapping off the ends of yellowy soybean sprouts (out of three to four pounds of whole sprouts, only one pound of edible sprouts), cleaning fish and seafood (deveining the shrimp, cracking the crabs), splashing seasonings and pickled vegetables over many kinds of foods—making for an unforgettable wet-newspaper smell.

In 1956, an aunt and uncle were permitted to leave China with their four children and came to stay with Amy's parents for two years. Amy remembers it as a time of total immersion for her in Chinese customs and in the Shanghai dialect. Auntie and Mother would decide (not always easily or without rancor) on the meals of the day, and the preparations were carried out with all the children participating. Amy remembers vividly the loud talk, the delightful snacks and sweets, "shee fan" or "jook" (rice porridge) at midnight, the hustle and bustle of the kitchen, the delicious family meals, the warm, loving relationships, the extended celebrations of the Chinese New Year—in short, a happy childhood.

Amy remembers how uneasy she was as a teenager, by which time the family's circle of friends had expanded to include a few non-Chinese, when American friends would come to dinner. Most Americans, she found, were rather timid about unusual food; they still had a steak-and-potatoes mentality then and knew nothing about tofu or bean curd, cooked squid or jellyfish, whole fish on a platter with eyes glaring out in what seemed a reproach. "It was as if we had served a whole cow."

Naturally, for those used to a diet of hamburgers or Mrs. Paul's fishsticks, what Mrs. Tan served inevitably raised a few eyebrows. Recently, at a book signing, Amy recognized one of her high-school friends, who said, "I am so glad you remember me. I remember the frog heads and other weird things your mother used to make." Hardly a dish that Mrs. Tan ever made, but this kind of remark brings back the acute embarrassment that Amy felt as a youngster.

Like many Chinese-American children, Amy Tan found that, try as she might to adapt to other cuisines, her Chinese roots were too strong. When she lived in Europe in the late 1960s and it was difficult to get the proper Chinese ingredients for home cooking, the Chinese restaurants she ate in were mostly Indonesian or Vietnamese and lacked the authentic flavors of her mother's cooking.

Today her favorite foods remain Chinese. She loves the comfort foods of home: dumplings, wontons, oysters in ginger, scallions, and garlic; salt plums, salted watermelon, salted anything; clean tastes, no heavy gravies; fresh vegetables, the black Chinese mushrooms. In short, the stuff of her childhood.

These tastes and predilections were enhanced when she and her mother visited her sisters in Shanghai in the 1980s. Like Mother Tan in the good old days, the sisters shopped every morning for such delicacies as live eels and fresh fish and seafood. Amy loved the early-morning breakfasts they enjoyed together at the market: rich and tasty broth with brown bread and dim-sum treats. Then the family would go home, spread newspapers on the kitchen table, and prepare the day's meals. Once again, that smell of wet newspaper, the peeling of fruits and vegetables and the slicing of meats and fish, the talk, the ordered chaos, the good food, the warmth, love, affection, and close family ties. I like to call it Amy Tan's Joy of Chinese Food Club.

# POULTRY

Nostalgic Chicken Subgum

Delectable Black Bean Chicken Wings

Lemon Chicken

Almond Chicken

Stir-Fried Chicken with Glazed Walnuts

Chinese-Style Roast Chicken

Sweet-and-Sour Chicken

Black Bean Chicken with Bitter Melon

Spicy Curried Chicken

Stir-Fried Chicken with Asparagus and Mushrooms

Stir-Fried Chicken with Vegetables

Silky Steeped Chicken

Crispy Chinese-Style Fried Chicken

Tomato-Curry Chicken

Braised Red Bean Curd Chicken

Classic Kung Pao Chicken

Home-Style Steamed Chicken with Mushrooms

Classic Moo Goo Gai Pan

Pineapple Duck

King Wah's Pressed Almond Duck

A Chinese-American Thanksgiving Turkey

Banquet-Style Crispy Squabs

Minced Squab in Lettuce Leaves

# Nostalgic Chicken Subgum

*This is probably one of the best-known Chinese-American dishes,*
*appearing on countless menus in many Chinese restaurants.*
*Curiously enough, the Chinese name implies "ten gold treasures"*
*stir-fried with chicken—in America, mostly chicken breast. It uses*
*a simple method of combining chicken with whatever vegetables*
*are in season and inexpensive. You can easily make this recipe*
*your own by improvising with your choice of vegetables. Cooked*
*properly, it makes a delightful, easy chicken dish that is tasty*
*with plain rice.*

Serves 4

3/4 pound boneless, skinless chicken breasts
1 egg white
2 teaspoons cornstarch
1 teaspoon salt
1/4 teaspoon freshly ground white pepper
1 teaspoon Asian sesame oil
1/2 cup peanut oil or 1 cup water (see variations) and 2
   tablespoons peanut oil
3 cloves garlic, peeled and lightly crushed
1 small onion, peeled and sliced
4 ounces celery heart, sliced crosswise
1 small zucchini, cut into 1/2-inch-thick slices
1 red pepper, seeded and cut into 1-inch squares
1 green pepper, seeded and cut into 1-inch squares
4 ounces fresh water chestnuts, peeled and sliced, or canned
5 scallions, cut into 2-inch slices
1 tomato, cut into 8 wedges
1/4 pound Napa cabbage, coarsely shredded
1/4 pound bok choy, washed and cut into 2-inch slices

## Sauce

1 1/2 tablespoons oyster sauce
2 tablespoons Shaoxing rice wine or dry sherry

4 tablespoons homemade chicken stock (page 60) or
    reduced-salt canned broth
1 teaspoon cornstarch mixed with 2 teaspoons water
1 teaspoon salt
1/4 teaspoon freshly ground black pepper
2 teaspoons Asian sesame oil

Cut the chicken into 1-inch cubes and combine it with the egg white, cornstarch, salt, pepper, and sesame oil. Chill in the refrigerator for at least 20 minutes.

Heat a wok until it is very hot and then add the peanut oil. When the oil is very hot, remove the wok from the heat and immediately add the chicken pieces, stirring vigorously to keep them from sticking. As soon as the chicken pieces turn white, in about 2 minutes, quickly drain the chicken in a stainless-steel colander set in a bowl to catch the oil. Reserve 2 tablespoons of the drained oil and discard the rest.

Heat a wok or large frying pan over high heat until it is hot. Swirl in the reserved 2 tablespoons of oil (or 2 fresh tablespoons of peanut oil if you used water), and when it is very hot and slightly smoking, toss in the garlic and onion and stir-fry for 10 seconds. Then scatter in the celery hearts, zucchini, peppers, and water chestnuts and continue to stir-fry for 2 minutes. Finally, toss in the scallions, tomato, Napa cabbage, and bok choy and continue to stir-fry for another 2 minutes, until the vegetables are just tender. Mix together the sauce ingredients, pour into the wok, and bring to a simmer. Return the chicken to the sauce and give the mixture a few turns to mix well. Serve at once.

Variations: If you choose to use water instead of oil, bring it to a boil in a saucepan. Remove the saucepan from the heat and immediately add the chicken pieces, stirring vigorously to keep them from sticking. When the chicken pieces turn white, in about 2 minutes, quickly drain the chicken and all of the water in a stainless-steel colander set in a bowl. Discard the water.

Feel free to substitute other types of vegetables, such as snow peas, sugar snaps, carrots, or leeks. One of the beauties of this recipe is that you can so easily improvise according to what's in season: a spring version with asparagus, peas, and snow peas; an autumn version with carrots, leeks, celeriac, and turnips.

# Delectable Black Bean Chicken Wings

*I could never understand my American classmates when they turned their noses up at chicken wings. For me, they were the choicest and tastiest morsels of the chicken. We used to feast on them at home because they were cheap, although I didn't know that at the time. In our household, my mother would cook them in the morning and I would bring them to school with me. I loved the curiosity my lunch would arouse as I unwrapped my lunch of chicken wings with their pungent black bean odor. I felt superior and contented in the knowledge that my lunch was better.*

Serves 4

1¹/₂ pounds chicken wings
1 tablespoon light soy sauce
1¹/₂ tablespoons Shaoxing rice wine or dry sherry
¹/₂ teaspoon salt
1 teaspoon sugar
1 teaspoon Asian sesame oil
2 teaspoons cornstarch

1¹/₂ tablespoons peanut oil
1¹/₂ tablespoons finely chopped fresh ginger
1¹/₂ tablespoons finely chopped garlic
2 tablespoons finely chopped shallots
2 tablespoons finely chopped scallions
3 tablespoons coarsely chopped fermented black beans
1 tablespoon light soy sauce
1 tablespoon Shaoxing rice wine or dry sherry
¹/₂ teaspoon salt
¹/₂ teaspoon freshly ground black pepper
¹/₂ cup homemade chicken stock (page 60), reduced-salt canned broth, or water

## Garnish

2 tablespoons finely chopped scallions

Mix the chicken wings with the soy sauce, Shaoxing rice wine or dry sherry, salt, sugar, sesame oil, and cornstarch. Let the chicken marinate for about 1 hour, then drain any excess marinade from the chicken and discard.

Heat a wok or large frying pan over high heat until it is hot. Swirl in the peanut oil, and when it is very hot and slightly smoking, dump in the chicken wings. Stir-fry for 5 minutes, or until the chicken begins to brown. Then toss in the ginger, garlic, shallots, scallions, and black beans and stir-fry for 2 minutes. Now pour in the soy sauce, rice wine, salt, pepper, and stock. Bring the mixture to a boil and then reduce the heat. Cover the wok or pan and simmer for 15 minutes, or until the chicken is cooked. Uncover, bring the heat up to high, and continue to cook until most of the liquid has evaporated. Transfer to a large platter and serve at once. This dish can be made ahead of time and reheated, and it is also delicious served cold. Garnish with scallions.

# Lemon Chicken

*Lemons were introduced into China hundreds of years ago, probably from Persia. Like all citrus fruits, the lemon was deemed to possess magical and spiritual qualities in addition to its most pleasant sweet-sour tang. Lemon works well as a flavoring with many foods.*

*I do not recall my mother's ever making this popular dish, but I know it was an occasional item in my school cafeteria. It was frequently ordered in our restaurant, almost always by non-Chinese.*

*Here I offer two versions of the recipe. The first is more authentically Chinese, the chicken being velveted (that is, coated with egg white and delicately cooked in warm oil); the second is the more familiar American "take-home" version, with the pieces of chicken coated in a batter, then tossed in a lemon sauce.*

*Serves 4*

# The Authentic Version

*This version uses oil to cook the chicken briefly, until the flesh is succulent and velvety; hence the term "velveted." You can use water instead of oil.*

1 pound boneless, skinless chicken breasts
1 egg white
1 teaspoon salt
2 teaspoons cornstarch
1 cup peanut oil or 2 cups water (see variation)

## Sauce

1/2 cup homemade chicken stock (page 60) or
    reduced-salt canned broth
2 tablespoons fresh lemon juice
1 tablespoon sugar
1 tablespoon light soy sauce
2 teaspoons Shaoxing rice wine or dry sherry
1 tablespoon finely sliced garlic
2 dried and crushed red chilies
1 tablespoon grated lemon zest
1 teaspoon cornstarch blended with
    1 teaspoon water

Cut the chicken breasts into 1½-inch cubes. Mix the chicken with the egg white, salt, and cornstarch in a bowl and refrigerate for about 20 minutes.

Heat a wok until it is very hot and swirl in the oil. When the oil is very hot, remove the wok from the heat and immediately add the chicken pieces, stirring vigorously to keep them from sticking. As soon as the chicken pieces turn white, in about 2 minutes, quickly drain the chicken and all of the oil in a stainless-steel colander set in a bowl. Discard the oil.

Mix together in a saucepan all the ingredients for the sauce except the cornstarch mixture, and bring it to a simmer. Slowly drizzle in the cornstarch mixture, stirring all the while. When the sauce has slightly thickened, toss in the chicken, coating well with the sauce. Turn onto a platter and serve at once.

Variation: If you choose to use water instead of oil, bring it to a boil in a saucepan. Remove the saucepan from the heat and immediately add the chicken pieces, stirring vigorously to keep them from sticking. When the chicken pieces turn white, in about 2 minutes, quickly drain the chicken and all of the water in a stainless-steel colander set in a bowl. Discard the water.

## The Chinese=American Version

*Chicken breasts in batter tend to be dried out and uninteresting. I have altered this classic Chinese-American version by using thighs instead of breast meat, for a tastier dish. Many Chinese chefs use potato starch to enhance crispiness.*

1 pound boneless, skinless chicken thighs
1 teaspoon salt
1/2 teaspoon freshly ground white pepper
1 teaspoon Asian sesame oil
1 teaspoon light soy sauce
1 teaspoon Shaoxing rice wine or dry sherry
1 teaspoon cornstarch

### Batter

1/2 cup potato starch or cornstarch
1/4 cup all-purpose unbleached white flour
1 teaspoon baking powder
1 teaspoon baking soda
Salt and freshly ground black pepper to taste
2 teaspoons peanut oil
1/2 cup water

2 cups peanut oil, for deep-frying

### Sauce

¹/₂ cup homemade chicken stock (page 60) or reduced-salt
   canned broth
2 tablespoons fresh lemon juice
1 tablespoon crushed fermented black beans
1 tablespoon sugar
1 tablespoon light soy sauce
2 teaspoons Shaoxing rice wine or dry sherry
1 tablespoon finely sliced garlic
2 dried red chilies, crushed
1¹/₂ tablespoons lemon zest
2 teaspoons Asian sesame oil
2 teaspoons cornstarch blended with 1 teaspoon water

Cut the chicken into 1-inch pieces and evenly coat them with the salt, pepper, sesame oil, soy sauce, Shaoxing rice wine, and cornstarch.

Mix the batter ingredients in a medium-sized bowl with a whisk and beat mixture until it is smooth.

Heat a wok or deep pan until it is hot and swirl in the oil. When the oil is slightly smoking, turn the heat down. Remove the chicken pieces from the marinade and stir them into the batter. Lift the chicken from the batter with a slotted spoon and deep-fry the chicken pieces for 3 minutes in several batches. Place the deep-fried chicken pieces on a tray lined with paper towels to drain.

Mix all the sauce ingredients except the cornstarch mixture in a saucepan and bring it to a simmer. Then, in a slow drizzle, add the cornstarch mixture, stirring all the while.

Place the deep-fried chicken on a platter, drizzle the sauce over, and serve at once.

# Almond Chicken

*This is almost as popular a Chinese-American dish as the more familiar cashew chicken. In China nuts are often paired with poultry, but I believe this dish is an American innovation: in China almonds are rare. Nuts add a crunch and special tastes to any dish. In Chinese-American restaurants only breast meat was served to Americans. Chinese patrons prefer the more robust flavor and chewy texture of thighs and wings. In our restaurant, we saved the legs and thighs for our Chinese customers. However, almond chicken was always made with white breast meat.*

*Many of the traditional Chinese-American restaurants prepare a dark-brown sauce, a sort of ready-made gravy that is artificially colored to make our American customers more comfortable with Chinese dishes, and that is what is usually served with almond chicken. But here I offer a lighter and, I believe, more delicious version without the heavy gravy.*

*Serves 4*

1 pound boneless, skinless chicken breasts
1 egg white
1 teaspoon salt
2 teaspoons cornstarch
1 cup peanut oil, or 2 cups water (see variations) and
   1 tablespoon peanut oil
1 tablespoon light soy sauce
1 tablespoon Shaoxing rice wine or dry sherry
2 tablespoons finely chopped scallions
2 ounces roasted whole almonds

Cut the chicken into 1-inch cubes. In a medium-sized bowl, mix the chicken with the egg white, salt, and cornstarch. Refrigerate for at least 20 minutes.

Heat a wok until it is very hot and then swirl in the oil. When the oil is very hot, remove the wok from the heat and immediately add the chicken pieces, stirring vigorously to keep them from sticking. As soon as the chicken pieces turn white, in about 2 minutes, quickly drain the chicken and all of the oil in a stainless-steel colander set in a bowl. Discard all but 1 tablespoon of the oil.

Reheat the wok (or heat it and swirl in 1 tablespoon of oil if you used water instead of oil) and pour in the soy sauce, rice wine, and drained chicken. Continue to stir-fry for 2 minutes, then toss in the scallions and roasted almonds and give the mixture 2 stirs. Transfer the contents of the wok to a platter and serve at once.

Variations: If you choose to use water instead of oil, bring it to a boil in a saucepan. Remove the saucepan from the heat and immediately add the chicken pieces, stirring vigorously to keep them from sticking. When the chicken pieces turn white, in about 2 minutes, quickly drain the chicken and all of the water in a stainless-steel colander set in a bowl. Discard the water.

You can substitute cashews, peanuts, or walnuts for the almonds.

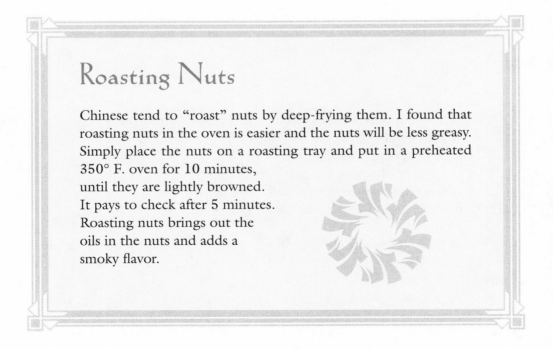

# Roasting Nuts

Chinese tend to "roast" nuts by deep-frying them. I found that roasting nuts in the oven is easier and the nuts will be less greasy. Simply place the nuts on a roasting tray and put in a preheated 350° F. oven for 10 minutes, until they are lightly browned. It pays to check after 5 minutes. Roasting nuts brings out the oils in the nuts and adds a smoky flavor.

# Stir=Fried Chicken with Glazed Walnuts

*This Hong Kong–inspired recipe has become very popular in recent years in Chinese restaurants from New York to Chicago to San Francisco. Although it requires two steps, the results are well worth making for a special dinner party. The walnuts can be prepared well ahead, and once made the dish can be assembled rather quickly. You can make a variation using pecans instead of walnuts, changing it immediately to a contemporary Chinese-American dish.*

*Serves 4*

1/2 cup (1/2 recipe) Glazed Walnuts (page 118)
1 pound boneless, skinless chicken breasts
1 egg white
1 teaspoon salt
1 teaspoon Asian sesame oil
2 teaspoons cornstarch
1 cup peanut oil or water (see variation)
1 tablespoon peanut oil
2 teaspoons coarsely chopped garlic
1 teaspoon finely chopped fresh ginger
2 tablespoons finely chopped scallions
2 tablespoons Shaoxing rice wine or dry sherry
1 1/2 tablespoons light soy sauce
Salt and freshly ground black pepper to taste

Make the Glazed Walnuts the day or night before.

Cut the chicken breasts into 1-inch cubes. Mix the chicken with the egg white, salt, sesame oil, and cornstarch in a small bowl, and refrigerate for about 20 minutes.

Heat a wok until it is very hot and then pour in 1 cup of peanut oil. When the oil is very hot, remove the wok from the heat and immediately toss in the chicken pieces, stirring vigorously to keep them from sticking. As soon as the chicken pieces turn white, in about 2 minutes, quickly drain the chicken and all of the oil in a stainless-steel colander set in a bowl. Discard the oil.

Wipe the wok clean and reheat it until it is very hot, then swirl in 1 tablespoon of peanut oil. Toss in the garlic, ginger, and scallions and stir-fry for a few seconds. Now toss the drained chicken, the rice wine, and the soy sauce in the wok and stir-fry the mixture for another 2 minutes. Sprinkle on salt and freshly ground black pepper to taste. Toss in the Glazed Walnuts, give the mixture several stirs, and serve at once.

Variation: If you choose to use water instead of oil, bring it to a boil in a saucepan. Remove the saucepan from the heat and immediately add the chicken pieces, stirring vigorously to keep them from sticking. When the chicken pieces turn white, in about 2 minutes, quickly drain the chicken and all of the water in a stainless-steel colander set in a bowl. Discard the water.

## Glazed Walnuts
Serves 4

1/2 pound shelled walnuts
1/4 cup granulated sugar
1 1/2 cups peanut oil

Bring a medium-sized pot of water to a boil. Toss in the walnuts and cook for about 10 minutes to blanch them. Drain the nuts in a colander or sieve, and then pat dry with paper towels and spread them to dry on a baking tray. Sprinkle the sugar over the walnuts and roll them around in it to cover them completely. Place the tray of sugared walnuts in a cool, drafty place to dry. Leave them for at least 2 hours, preferably overnight. (The recipe can be done ahead to this point.)

Heat the oil in a wok to moderate heat. Fry a batch of the walnuts for about 2 minutes, or until the sugar melts and the walnuts turn golden. (Watch the heat to prevent burning.) Remove the walnuts from the oil with a slotted spoon or strainer. Lay them on a nonstick tray or rack to cool. (Do not drain them on paper towels: the sugar will stick when it dries.) Deep-fry and drain the rest of the walnuts in the same way. Once cooled, the Glazed Walnuts can be kept in a sealed glass jar for about 2 weeks. Serve them with cocktails as appetizers or stir-fried with chicken or shrimp.

# Chinese=Style Roast Chicken

*In China, roasting foods is a technique that has traditionally been reserved for commercial bakers and grocers. Large ovens are expensive to build and to use, and are thus a rarity in the average private home, where space is in any case quite limited.*

*However, in America it is a different story. Even fifty years ago, an urban home or apartment with a range almost always had an oven. So, with their legendary flexibility and adaptability, Chinese-Americans quickly invented recipes that took advantage of the roasting capabilities of the oven.*

*Here is a recipe my uncle put together for a favorite dish he would enjoy on his day off. We used to gather at his home for Monday-night dinner, and this is one of the centerpieces of the meal he would serve. It is quite delectable and easy to make—an unusual roast chicken that is extremely aromatic and very tasty.*

Serves 4–6

1 tablespoon bean sauce (see page 276)
2 tablespoons light soy sauce
1 tablespoon Shaoxing rice wine or dry sherry
1 tablespoon crushed rock sugar or granulated sugar
3 star anise
1 whole piece cinnamon bark or cinnamon stick
2 teaspoons whole roasted Sichuan peppercorns
   (see page 72)
1/4 cup homemade chicken stock (page 60) or reduced-salt
   canned broth
1 tablespoon peanut oil
3 slices fresh ginger, 2 inches by 1/8 inch
3 whole garlic cloves, crushed
3 whole scallions
8 sprigs fresh coriander
4–5-pound whole chicken
4 tablespoons honey

In a bowl, whisk together the bean sauce, soy sauce, rice wine, sugar, star anise, cinnamon bark, peppercorns, and chicken stock.

Heat a wok or large frying pan over high heat until it is hot. Swirl in the oil, and when it is very hot and slightly smoking, toss in the ginger, garlic, and scallions and stir-fry for 1 minute. Pour the mixture from the bowl into the wok and simmer for 2 minutes. Remove the wok from the heat, toss in the fresh coriander, and allow the mixture to cool thoroughly.

Dry the chicken thoroughly inside and out with paper towels. Pin down the neck flap with a skewer. Pour the mixture from the bowl into the cavity and truss the end of the chicken so that it is tightly secured.

Bring a large pot of water to a boil, then add the honey. With a large strainer, dip the chicken in and out of this water several times. Hang the chicken in a dry cool place or in front of a fan and allow it to dry thoroughly. Place a tray under the chicken to catch any liquid that may drip. This should take about 45 minutes.

Preheat the oven to 450° F. Place the chicken on a rack in a roasting pan. Roast for 15 minutes, then turn the temperature down to 350° F. and continue to roast for 1 hour, or until the juices run clear. Drain any liquid from the chicken, keep warm, and serve alongside the chicken. Allow the chicken to rest for 25 minutes before carving.

# Sweet=and=Sour Chicken

*I am convinced that this dish is a concoction of some Chinese-American restaurant. In China, chicken is considered to have such a delicate flavor that it would be a travesty to flavor it with a sweet-sour sauce: beef, yes; pork, yes; chicken, and especially chicken breast, no. Again, I envision a proprietor thinking, "The Americans love sweet-and-sour pork; why not chicken, of which we have many leftovers?"*

*Here I offer a more balanced, more authentically Chinese approach: the sweet-sour sauce is muted so as not to overwhelm the chicken; and I use chicken thigh meat, which can better stand up to an assertive sauce.*

*Serves 4*

1 pound boneless, skinless chicken thighs or 1¹/₂ pounds
   with skin and bones
1 teaspoon salt
¹/₂ teaspoon freshly ground black pepper
1 teaspoon Asian sesame oil
2 teaspoons light soy sauce
1 teaspoon Shaoxing rice wine or dry sherry
1 teaspoon cornstarch

## Batter

¹/₂ cup potato starch or cornstarch
¹/₄ cup all-purpose unbleached white flour
1 teaspoon baking powder
1 teaspoon baking soda
1 teaspoon salt
¹/₂ teaspoon freshly ground black pepper
2 teaspoons Asian sesame oil
¹/₂ cup water

2 cups peanut oil, for deep-frying

## Sauce

3 tablespoons Chinese black rice vinegar
2 tablespoons sugar
1¹/₂ tablespoons light soy sauce
1 teaspoon dark soy sauce
2 teaspoons Shaoxing rice wine or dry sherry
2 teaspoons Asian sesame oil

3 tablespoons slant-cut scallions

Cut the chicken into 1-inch pieces and mix it with the salt, pepper, sesame oil, light soy sauce, Shaoxing rice wine, and cornstarch.

Mix the batter ingredients in a medium-sized bowl with a whisk and beat until smooth.

Heat a wok or deep pan until it is hot, then swirl in the oil. When it is slightly smoking, turn the heat down. With chopsticks or whisk, blend the chicken batter. Put the chicken in the batter and mix well. Remove the chicken from the batter with a slotted spoon and deep-fry the pieces for 3 minutes in several batches. Place the deep-fried chicken pieces on a tray lined with paper towels to drain.

Blend all the sauce ingredients in a small pan and warm through until the sugar dissolves.

Place the deep-fried chicken on a platter, drizzle the sauce over it, garnish with the scallions, and serve at once.

# Black Bean Chicken with Bitter Melon

*In the summer months, our next-door neighbors in Chicago used to bring us bitter melon plucked fresh from their tiny garden. They knew it was one of our favorite vegetables. Bitter melon is, quite frankly, for most people an acquired taste, although I certainly don't recall anything but the enjoyment of eating this unusual vegetable in the various ways my mother prepared it. However, it was to my advantage that, as I was told, I inherited my taste buds from my grandmother, a wonderful cook who loved bitter melon.*

*When it is combined with black beans, it at once enlivens prosaic chicken and creates a pungent and savory dish that will always remind me of the height of summer.*

*Bitter melon adds a unique dimension to many dishes. It is well worth trying, and is readily available in season at Chinese groceries.*

*Serves 4*

1 pound bitter melon
1 pound boneless, skinless chicken thighs or 1½ pounds
   with skin and bones
1 tablespoon light soy sauce
1½ tablespoons Shaoxing rice wine or dry sherry
½ teaspoon salt
1 teaspoon sugar
1 teaspoon Asian sesame oil

2 teaspoons cornstarch

1 tablespoon peanut oil

1 tablespoon finely chopped fresh ginger

1¹/₂ tablespoons coarsely chopped garlic

1 tablespoon finely chopped shallots

1¹/₂ tablespoons finely chopped scallions

2¹/₂ tablespoons coarsely chopped fermented black beans

¹/₄ cup homemade chicken stock (page 60) or reduced-salt
canned broth

## Garnish

2 tablespoons finely chopped scallion tops

Wash the bitter melon, cut it in half lengthwise, and remove the seeds.
Cut the melon into thin (¹/₄-inch) slices and blanch in a pot of boiling water
for 2 minutes. Remove with a slotted spoon and drain well on paper towels.

Cut the chicken into bite-size pieces. Mix the soy sauce, Shaoxing rice
wine or dry sherry, salt, sugar, sesame oil, and cornstarch together and pour
it over the chicken, blending well. Let the chicken marinate for about 1 hour,
then drain it and discard the marinade.

Heat a wok or large frying pan over high heat until it is hot. Swirl in the
peanut oil, and when it is very hot and slightly smoking, dump in the chicken.
Stir-fry it for 5 minutes, or until the chicken begins to brown. Toss in the ginger, garlic, shallots, scallions, and black beans and stir-fry for 2 minutes. Pour
in the stock and bring everything to a boil, then reduce the heat. Cover the
wok or pan and simmer for 12 minutes, or until the chicken is cooked; stir in
the bitter melon and cook for another 3 minutes. This dish can be cooked
ahead of time and reheated, and it is also delicious served cold.

# Stir=Fried Chicken with Asparagus and Mushrooms

*One key characteristic of Chinese-American cooking is its adaptability. Here is a popular dish found only in Chinese restaurants in this country. Shredded chicken is quickly velveted and then stir-fried with American vegetables—asparagus and brown mushrooms. The unique American produce is paired with ancient tradition, and the result is a dish unlike any found anywhere in China. A quick and easy recipe that is healthy and tasty at the same time, it is delicious accompanied by plain white rice.*

Serves 4

1 pound boneless, skinless chicken breasts
1 egg white
1 teaspoon salt
1 teaspoon Asian sesame oil
2 teaspoons cornstarch

$1/2$ pound fresh bean sprouts
$1/2$ pound asparagus
$1/2$ pound fresh mushrooms
$1^1/2$ cups peanut oil or water (see variation)
1 tablespoon peanut oil
1 tablespoon light soy sauce
2 teaspoons Shaoxing rice wine or dry sherry
$1^1/2$ teaspoons salt
1 teaspoon sugar
2 teaspoons Asian sesame oil
3 tablespoons finely shredded scallions

Julienne the chicken into very thin shreds and combine these with the egg white, salt, sesame oil, and cornstarch in a bowl. Mix well, and refrigerate for about 20 minutes.

Trim the bean sprouts, slant-cut the asparagus thinly, and slice the mushrooms finely.

Heat a wok until it is very hot and then add the 1½ cups peanut oil. When the oil is hot, remove the wok from the heat and immediately toss in the chicken shreds, stirring vigorously to keep them from sticking. As soon as the chicken shreds turn white, in about 2 minutes, quickly drain the chicken and all of the oil in a stainless-steel colander set in a bowl. Discard the oil.

Wipe the wok clean and reheat it over high heat. When it is hot, swirl in the 1 tablespoon of peanut oil, then add the asparagus and mushrooms and stir-fry for 3 minutes. Now swirl in the soy sauce, rice wine, salt, and sugar and continue to stir-fry for 2 minutes. Put the drained chicken and bean sprouts in the wok, stir to mix well, and swirl in the sesame oil. Toss in the shredded scallions, give the mixture a few more stirs, and then turn it onto a warm serving platter. Serve at once.

Variation: If you choose to use water instead of oil, bring it to a boil in a saucepan. Remove the saucepan from the heat and immediately add the chicken shreds, stirring vigorously to keep them from sticking. When the chicken shreds turn white, in about 2 minutes, quickly drain the chicken and all of the water in a stainless-steel colander set in a bowl. Discard the water.

# Spicy Curried Chicken

*Curry is not an indigenous Chinese spice. The term "curry" stands for no single spice or flavor. Different curries have different taste characteristics. The idea of crushing and combining various whole spices entered China by way of Chinese merchants who had traveled to India. Curry became popular in South China because of the commercial connections that area enjoyed with Southeast Asia.*

*In the process of assimilation, curry was modified and adapted to the Cantonese taste, resulting in a milder version than in India. This is the "curry" taste found in Chinese-American homes and restaurants.*

*I remember the distinct aroma of mild curry wafting through our house when my mother so spiced up a chicken dish. It was an easy way to add an exotic touch to our dinner. Even as a child, I knew somehow that curry was not really Chinese.*

Serves 4

1 pound boneless, skinless chicken thighs or
   1¹/₂ pounds with skin and bones
1 tablespoon light soy sauce
2 teaspoons Shaoxing rice wine or dry sherry
1 teaspoon Asian sesame oil
2 teaspoons cornstarch

1 tablespoon peanut oil
2 tablespoons finely sliced garlic
1 large onion, finely sliced
1 pound (2 large) red or green peppers,
   seeded and sliced
¹/₂ cup canned coconut milk
¹/₂ cup homemade chicken stock (page 60) or
   reduced-salt canned broth
2 tablespoons Madras curry powder or paste
2 teaspoons sugar
1 teaspoon salt
1¹/₂ tablespoons Shaoxing rice wine or
   dry sherry
2 tablespoons light soy sauce
1 teaspoon cornstarch blended with 1 tablespoon water

Cut the chicken into bite-size pieces. Mix them with the soy sauce, rice wine, sesame oil, and cornstarch to coat.

Heat a wok or large frying pan over high heat until it is hot. Swirl in the peanut oil, and when it is very hot and slightly smoking, dump in the chicken and stir-fry for 5 minutes, until the pieces are lightly browned. Remove them from the wok with a slotted spoon and pour off most of the fat and oil, leaving about 2 tablespoons.

Reheat the wok until it is very hot. Toss in the garlic and onion and stir-fry for 3 minutes, or until the onion is soft and brown. Then toss in the peppers and continue to stir-fry another 2 minutes. Now pour in the rest of the ingredients, except the cornstarch mixture. Continue to cook the vegetables over high heat for another 2 minutes. Return the drained chicken to the wok and stir-fry for another 2 minutes, pour in the cornstarch mixture, and cook for 30 seconds. Coat the chicken thoroughly with the sauce and serve at once.

# Stir=Fried Chicken with Vegetables

*Chicken with vegetables is both a classic dish and a standard family meal, a familiar item in every Chinese-American restaurant and home. In restaurants, all too frequently the chicken is overcooked; or it has not been velveted (an extra step). In either case, the results are not as satisfactory as when the ingredients are cooked properly.*

*Here is that classic dish prepared the right way. The different ingredients are all treated with respect and added appropriately in separate steps. This makes for a most pleasing meal.*

Serves 4

1 pound boneless, skinless chicken breasts
1 egg white
1 teaspoon salt
2 teaspoons cornstarch
1 1/2 cups peanut oil, or 1 1/2 cups water (see variations) and 1
    tablespoon of peanut oil
2 teaspoons salt
1/2 pound peeled and sliced fresh water chestnuts, or canned
1/2 pound trimmed snow peas
1/2 pound bean sprouts
1 tablespoon Shaoxing rice wine or dry sherry
2 tablespoons light soy sauce
1 teaspoon sugar
1/4 teaspoon freshly ground white pepper

Garnish

2 tablespoons finely sliced scallions

Cut the chicken breasts into slices or strips. Mix them with the egg white, salt, and cornstarch in a small bowl, and refrigerate for about 20 minutes.

Heat a wok or large frying pan over high heat until it is hot. Pour in the oil, and when it is very hot and slightly smoking, remove the wok from the heat and immediately add the chicken slices, stirring vigorously to separate them and keep them from sticking. When the chicken pieces turn white, in about 2 minutes, quickly drain the chicken and all of the oil in a stainless-steel colander set in a bowl. Reserve 1 tablespoon of the oil and discard the rest.

Wipe the wok clean. Reheat (or heat) the wok until it is very hot, then add the 1 tablespoon of drained oil that you have saved (or 1 tablespoon of fresh peanut oil if you used water). Toss in the salt, water chestnuts, and snow peas and stir-fry them for 1 minute. Add the rest of the ingredients. Return the chicken to the wok and stir-fry the mixture for another 2 minutes. Garnish the dish with the scallions and serve at once.

> Variations: If you choose to use water instead of oil, bring it to a boil in a saucepan. Remove the saucepan from the heat and immediately add the chicken pieces, stirring vigorously to keep them from sticking. When the chicken pieces turn white, in about 2 minutes, quickly drain the chicken and all of the water in a stainless-steel colander set in a bowl. Discard the water.
>
> Other vegetables can be substituted, such as asparagus, broccoli, zucchini, and mushrooms.

# Silky Steeped Chicken

*Lillian Chou is a superb Chinese-American chef who has worked at the famous Le Cirque restaurant in New York as a pastry chef. She told me of a very common experience among Chinese-Americans. On the occasion of Ching Ming, a Chinese festival honoring the dead, Lillian would prepare various foods for the feast and picnic with her family. However, she was always very reluctant to tell any of her American friends what was on the menu for the occasion, for fear they would think her a bit unusual ("weird," in her word), if not quite eccentric. The dishes included foods and ingredients that are literally foreign to the American palate.*

*Many of my Chinese-American friends and I have had the same experience. We were Chinese at the same time as we were American. But the culinary cultures of the twain are so oddly dissimilar that at certain points we were all living in two worlds.*

*I was taught that even the dead must have good food. The custom was, then, to offer tasty morsels to our ancestors and the dearly departed. But we, the living, were pragmatic enough not to waste good material on spiritual sustenance. After a sufficient but very brief time, we would proceed to consume the delectable offerings.*

*As far as I can remember, there was always a chicken dish, this being a most propitious offering. It was invariably made by slowly steeping the chicken so that the result was a moist and subtle delicacy. Here the gentlest possible heat is used, to keep the flesh of*

*Lillian Chou with friends at a Chinese banquet*

*the chicken extremely moist and flavorful with a satiny, almost velvetlike texture.*

*This chicken dish is not difficult to make. The chicken simmers in liquid for a few minutes; then the heat is turned off, the pot tightly covered, and the chicken left to steep until done. I still think it is one of the best ways to cook chicken. Of course, the luscious dipping sauce may have something to do with my appreciation of this honorable treat. Scallions and ginger root, jolted to the full fragrance by a quick dousing of hot peanut oil, offer the perfect flavor combination.*

*Made ahead of time, this dish is usually served at room temperature. Your ancestors and your family will be happy if you offer it to them.*

*Save the steeping liquid for cooking rice or as a base for chicken stock.*

Serves 4

3¹/₂–4-pound free-range chicken
1 tablespoon salt
6 slices fresh ginger, 2 inches by ¹/₈ inch
6 whole scallions

## Cantonese=Style Dipping Sauce

4 tablespoons finely chopped scallions, white part only
2 teaspoons finely chopped fresh ginger
2 teaspoons salt
2 tablespoons peanut oil

Rub the chicken evenly with the salt. Put the chicken in a pot large enough to hold it, cover with water, and bring to a boil. Toss in the ginger and scallions. Cover tightly, reduce the heat, and simmer for 20 minutes. Turn off the heat and leave covered tightly for 1 hour.

To make the sauce, put the scallions, ginger, and salt in a stainless-steel bowl and mix well. Heat a wok until it is hot, then add the oil. When the oil is very hot and smoking, pour it on the scallions, ginger, and salt and mix well. The sauce is now ready.

Remove the chicken to a chopping board. Strain and save the liquid, which can be used as a base for making stock or for cooking rice. Cut the chicken into bite-size pieces and arrange them on a platter. Serve the sauce on the side.

# Crispy Chinese-Style Fried Chicken

*Chinese-Americans always celebrated with banquets such impor-tant events as a marriage, a seventieth birthday (in Chinese tradition, too, "three score and ten" is an auspicious occasion), or a funeral. These were noisy family affairs held in restaurants, with children running around and adults singing and talking loudly, the men's voices especially fortified by rounds of drinking—usually whiskey or cognac mixed with soft drinks. I remember these occasions fondly. The highlight was always the food, and each dish would be examined critically and judged by the highest standard: the taste test. Comparisons with how, and how much better, the dish would have been cooked in China were inevitable. It must have been hard to cook for such an informed and critical audience.*

*As a child, I always enjoyed this fried chicken dish, regularly served at so many banquets. It was greeted with much antici-pation by the family members at the table. The skin had to be crackling crispy and the flesh perfectly moist. As my mother rightly pointed out, our fried chicken was vastly superior to the American version. I naturally agreed as I ate it with gusto. And any leftovers (a rarity, it is true) were carefully divided among the guests at each table to take with them when they left, with no pretense whatsoever that the treats were meant for the dog at home. Sandwiches made with this chicken were delicious.*

*Serves 4–6*

131

## Simmering Sauce

2 quarts water
2 whole pieces Chinese cinnamon bark or cinnamon sticks
$1/2$ cup dark soy sauce
3 tablespoons light soy sauce
$1/4$ cup Shaoxing rice wine or dry sherry
3 whole star anise
2 tablespoons finely shredded fresh orange peel
3 slices fresh ginger, 2 inches by $1/8$ inch
2 scallions
5 tablespoons crushed rock sugar or granulated sugar

$31/2$–4-pound chicken

## Glaze

3 tablespoons honey
1 cup water
2 tablespoons dark soy sauce
2 tablespoons Chinese black rice vinegar

4 cups peanut oil, for deep-frying

## Garnish

1 whole lemon, cut in wedges
Roasted Salt and Pepper (page 77)

Mix all the ingredients for the simmering sauce in a large casserole or pot and bring the mixture to the boil. Then turn the heat down to a simmer. Lower in the chicken and simmer slowly for 30–40 minutes, covered, turning the chicken from time to time so that it is cooked evenly. Remove the chicken and let it cool on a rack for at least 3 hours. The skin of the chicken should be completely dried and feel like parchment paper.

In a pan or wok, heat the glaze ingredients to boiling point. Baste the chicken several times with this glaze. Let the chicken dry again, for another 2 hours, keeping it in a very cool and airy place but not in the refrigerator.

Heat the oil in a large wok and carefully lower in the chicken. Deep-fry it on one side until it is a rich, dark brown color and very crisp. Then carefully turn it over and let it brown on all sides. Remove it with a strainer and drain well on paper towels. Allow the chicken to cool so that you can handle it. Cut the chicken into bite-size pieces and arrange them on a warm platter. Serve with lemon wedges and Roasted Salt and Pepper.

# Braised Red Bean Curd Chicken

*This home-style dish could easily have come straight out of South China, and it probably did. It has been a standard item on the family tables of countless Chinese-American homes.*

*And it is typical of the hearty cooking my mother would prepare on an autumn or winter evening in Chicago. That is to say, this is a cold-weather dish.*

*One virtue of this treat is that my mother could make it the night before, or before she set off for work in the morning. Then, in the evening, she would reheat some soup, stir-fry some seasonal vegetables, and reheat this casserole, bringing it all together for a satisfying warm meal.*

*Fermented red bean curd works its magic by infusing the dish with robust flavors and zest. The use of potatoes is definitely an American touch: Chinese-American home cooking at its best.*

*Serves 4*

1¹/2 pounds boneless, skinless chicken thighs
1 tablespoon Shaoxing rice wine or dry sherry
1 tablespoon light soy sauce
2 teaspoons Asian sesame oil
2 teaspoons cornstarch

1 pound russet potatoes
1¹/2 tablespoons peanut oil
2 tablespoons finely shredded fresh ginger
3 tablespoons fermented red bean curd*
1 teaspoon salt
¹/2 teaspoon freshly ground black pepper
1 teaspoon five-spice powder
2 cups homemade chicken stock (page 60) or reduced-salt
   canned broth
1 tablespoon Shaoxing rice wine or dry sherry
2 tablespoons dark soy sauce
2 teaspoons Asian sesame oil
1 teaspoon sugar

* Can be found in Chinese supermarkets and groceries.

Cut the chicken into 2-inch pieces and mix them with the rice wine, soy sauce, sesame oil, and cornstarch. Set aside.

Peel the potatoes and cut into 1-inch chunks.

Heat a wok or large frying pan over high heat until it is hot. Swirl in the peanut oil, and when it is very hot and slightly smoking, toss in the chicken pieces and stir-fry for 5 minutes, until they are lightly browned. Drain off all the excess fat and oil. Now toss in the ginger and bean curd, mix well, and stir-fry for 2 minutes. Throw in the potatoes and stir-fry for another 2 minutes. Sprinkle on the salt, pepper, and five-spice powder. Pour in the chicken stock, rice wine, soy sauce, and sesame oil and sprinkle in the sugar. Mix well and bring the mixture to a simmer. Reduce the heat to low, cover, and cook for 20 minutes. Serve at once, or let it cool and then refrigerate; it reheats beautifully.

# Tomato = Curry Chicken

*Tomatoes are a popular item on modern Chinese-American menus. They are a relatively recent addition to the Chinese cuisine, having been introduced only about one hundred years ago. Chinese-American cooks, finding tomatoes in abundance in their adopted land, quickly recognized their versatility and immediately discovered how their virtues could best be exploited.*

*For Chinese restaurants, it was an ideal ingredient, because tomatoes need little cooking and their color brightens up any dish. Another virtue was that in Chinese culture the color red means happiness.*

*Of the many tomato combinations found on Chinese-American menus, one of my favorites is the following, which mixes chicken with tomatoes and a touch of curry, just enough of the spice to enliven the dish but not so much as to detract from the fresh tomato flavor.*

Serves 4

1 pound boneless, skinless chicken thighs or 1¹/₂ pounds
   with skin and bones
2 tablespoons light soy sauce
2 teaspoons plus 1 tablespoon Shaoxing rice wine or dry
   sherry
1 teaspoon Asian sesame oil
2 teaspoons cornstarch
1 tablespoon peanut oil
1 tablespoon coarsely chopped garlic
1 cup sliced onions
1¹/₂ tablespoons Madras curry powder or paste
2 teaspoons sugar
2 tablespoons oyster sauce
1 pound fresh tomatoes, quartered

Cut the chicken into 1¹/₂-inch pieces and combine it with 1 tablespoon of soy sauce, 2 teaspoons of rice wine, the sesame oil, and the cornstarch. Let the mixture marinate for at least 20 minutes.

Heat a wok or large frying pan over high heat until it is hot. Swirl in the peanut oil, and when it is very hot and slightly smoking, throw in the chicken pieces and stir-fry for 10 minutes, or until the pieces are browned.

Toss in the garlic and onions and stir-fry them for 2 minutes. Sprinkle in the curry powder and sugar. Then pour in 1 tablespoon of rice wine, 1 tablespoon of soy sauce, and the oyster sauce. Finally, toss in the tomatoes and stir-fry for 5 minutes. Serve at once.

# Classic Kung Pao Chicken

*This became one of the most popular dishes in Chinese-American restaurants in the 1970s, when menus began to expand to include many more authentic and traditional examples of Chinese cuisine. It continues to be a great favorite.*

*It is a classic Sichuan dish that has gone through many mutations. From my research, its first appearance in the U.S. was in New York, and subsequently it spread to menus throughout the country. There is hardly a Chinese restaurant in America that does not offer the dish today. Unfortunately, many restaurants began to Americanize the dish into something I don't think anyone from Sichuan, China, would recognize. Try this version, the closest recipe to the original.*

*Serves 4*

1 pound boneless, skinless chicken breasts
1 egg white
1 teaspoon salt
1 teaspoon Asian sesame oil
2 teaspoons cornstarch

2 cups peanut oil, or 2 cups water (see variation) and
   1¹/₂ tablespoons peanut oil
2 dried red chilies, split lengthwise
¹/₄ cup shelled raw peanuts
1 tablespoon finely sliced garlic
1 tablespoon finely chopped scallions
2 teaspoons finely chopped fresh ginger
2 tablespoons homemade chicken stock (page 60) or
   reduced-salt canned broth
2 tablespoons Shaoxing rice wine or dry sherry
1¹/₂ tablespoons dark soy sauce
2 teaspoons sugar
2 teaspoons Chinese black rice vinegar
1 teaspoon salt
2 teaspoons Asian sesame oil
1 teaspoon cornstarch mixed with 2 tablespoons
   water

Cut the chicken into 1-inch cubes. Mix the chicken thoroughly with the egg white, salt, sesame oil, and cornstarch.

Heat a wok until it is hot and then add the oil. When the oil is very hot, remove the wok from the heat and immediately add the chicken pieces, stirring vigorously to keep them from sticking. As soon as the chicken pieces turn white, in about 2 minutes, quickly drain them and all of the oil through a stainless-steel colander set in a bowl. Discard all but 1¹/₂ table-spoons of oil.

Reheat the wok with the 1¹/₂ tablespoons of reserved oil. (If you used the water method, swirl 1¹/₂ tablespoons of fresh oil.) When the wok is very hot, toss in the chilies and stir-fry for a few seconds, until they blacken slightly. Toss in the peanuts, garlic, scallions, and ginger and stir-fry for 1 minute, until they are lightly browned. Add the cooked chicken pieces, the stock, rice wine, soy sauce, sugar, vinegar, salt, and sesame oil, then stir in the cornstarch mixture. Continue to stir-fry for 2 minutes. Serve at once with rice.

Variation: If you choose to use water instead of oil, bring it to a boil in a saucepan. Remove the saucepan from the heat and immediately add the chicken pieces, stirring vigorously to keep them from sticking. When the chicken pieces turn white, in about 2 minutes, quickly drain the chicken and all of the water in a stainless-steel colander set in a bowl.

# Home=Style Steamed Chicken with Mushrooms

*Steamed chicken appeared often on our Chinese-American tables. In China roasting was limited to professional roasting houses or restaurants—big ovens were very expensive and thus quite rare. To steam chicken was relatively simple and inexpensive (the steaming water would be used for other cooking purposes). Every-one had a steaming setup at home. Chinese-Americans continued to use the technique even after they could well afford ovens and grills.*

*Moreover, a gently steamed chicken was preferred over the roasted version, which was often dry. The chicken was succulent and tender, and its delicate flavor remained intact. Sometimes, as a special treat, the chicken was paired with smoky Chinese mushrooms, which gave the dish an added dimension of flavor.*

*At home we would always drizzle the juices from the steam-*
*ing chicken over rice.*

1 cup Chinese dried black mushrooms
3–3½-pound cut-up whole chicken or unboned chicken
   breasts and thighs
2 tablespoons Shaoxing rice wine or dry sherry
1½ tablespoons light soy sauce
2 tablespoons oyster sauce
2 teaspoons Asian sesame oil
1 teaspoon sugar
1 teaspoon salt
½ teaspoon freshly ground black pepper

## Garnish

3 tablespoons finely chopped scallions

Soak the mushrooms in warm water for 20 minutes. Then drain them
and squeeze out the excess liquid. Remove and discard the stems and set aside
the caps.

Cut the chicken into bite-size pieces, chopping through the bones with
a decisive whack, and put it in a bowl with the rice wine, soy sauce, oyster
sauce, sesame oil, sugar, salt, and pepper. Mix well.

On a heatproof platter, arrange the chicken with the marinating ingredients and mushrooms, interspersing the caps with the pieces of chicken.

Set up a steamer or put a rack into a wok or deep pan. Fill the steamer
with about 2 inches of hot water. Bring the water to a simmer. Put the plate
with the chicken into the steamer or onto the rack. Cover the steamer tightly
and gently steam over medium heat for 40 minutes, or until the chicken is
cooked. Replenish the water in the steamer from time to time as needed.

Remove from the steamer, garnish with the scallions, and serve at once
with plain rice.

# Classic Moo Goo Gai Pan

*This classic dish appeared on almost every Chinese restaurant menu when I was growing up. In Cantonese, it simply means "mushrooms with chicken slices." And perhaps it became popular because mushrooms were a food with which most Americans would be familiar.*

*Whatever the reasons for its popularity, Chinese restaurants loved serving it, because it was easy to make and allowed a great profit margin. Unfortunately, but predictably, many of the restaurateurs cut corners and used canned button mushrooms instead of the traditional and more flavorful, but expensive, dried black mushrooms. Here is a more authentic and elaborate version of that classic dish.*

*Serves 4*

1 pound boneless, skinless chicken breasts
1 egg white
1 teaspoon salt
Freshly ground white pepper to taste
2 teaspoons cornstarch
1/2 cup Chinese dried black mushrooms
1 cup fresh bean sprouts
1/2 pound trimmed snow peas
1/2 cup fresh water chestnuts, or canned
1 1/2 cups peanut oil or water (see variation)
1 1/2 tablespoons peanut oil
2 tablespoons finely sliced garlic
4 finely shredded scallions
1 tablespoon light soy sauce
2 tablespoons oyster sauce
2 teaspoons Shaoxing rice wine or dry sherry
Salt and freshly ground black pepper to taste
1 teaspoon sugar
2 teaspoons Asian sesame oil

Cut the chicken into thin slices and combine these with the egg white, 1 teaspoon of salt, the white pepper, and the cornstarch in a bowl. Mix well, and refrigerate for about 20 minutes.

Soak the mushrooms in warm water for 20 minutes. Then drain them and squeeze out the excess liquid. Remove and discard the stems, and finely shred the caps into thin strips.

Meanwhile, trim off the bean sprouts' ends, finely shred the snow peas lengthwise, and slice the water chestnuts.

Heat a wok or large frying pan over high heat until it is hot. Swirl in the 1½ cups of peanut oil, and when it is very hot and slightly smoking, remove the wok from the heat, and immediately add the chicken pieces, stirring vigorously to keep them from sticking. When the chicken pieces turn white, about 2 minutes, quickly drain the chicken and all of the oil in a stainless-steel colander set in a bowl.

Reheat the wok or large frying pan over high heat until it is hot. Swirl in the 1½ tablespoons of oil, and when it is very hot and slightly smoking, toss in the garlic and stir-fry for 20 seconds. Then toss in the mushrooms, bean sprouts, snow peas, water chestnuts, and scallions and stir-fry for 2 minutes. Finally, drizzle in the soy sauce, oyster sauce, and rice wine. Sprinkle in the salt and pepper to taste and the sugar and continue to stir-fry for 2 minutes. Return the drained chicken to the wok, heat through, stir to mix well, and drizzle in the sesame oil. Give the mixture a few stirs and then turn it onto a warm serving platter. Serve at once with plain rice.

Variation: If you choose to use water instead of oil, bring it to a boil in a saucepan. Remove the saucepan from the heat and immediately add the chicken pieces, stirring vigorously to keep them from sticking. When the chicken pieces turn white, in about 2 minutes, quickly drain the chicken and all of the water in a stainless-steel colander set in a bowl. Discard the water.

# Pineapple Duck

*I used to find quite amusing the attitudes of some of my fellow Americans toward Chinese food. Their knowledge of Chinese cuisine had come mainly by way of dining at Trader Vic's, in San Francisco. This popular restaurant features what I call "pseudo-Asian-Pacific food," served with cute Chinese-style paper umbrellas sticking out of potent mixed drinks, all in a pleasant tropical environment. It was a clever concept to get Americans to accept and enjoy "foreign" food in an exotic atmosphere made reassuringly familiar by Hollywood.*

*My uncles in the restaurant trade had many Chinese friends who worked at Trader Vic's, and they tell me this interesting combination—Chinese roast duck served with pineapple slices—was a very popular dish. Although the recipe is not quite authentic except for the duck, it does make sense to serve the sweetly acidic pineapple as a counterbalance to the robust richness of the duck. I am sure that, had pineapples been available to them, Chinese chefs would long ago have added them to the canon of classical Chinese cookery.*

*American Long Island ducks are a variety of the Chinese Peking duck. The cooking process here will rid the duck of most of the fat.*

Serves 4–6

San Francisco Chinatown
delicatessen

2 tablespoons bean sauce (see page 276)

2 tablespoons light soy sauce

1¹/₂ tablespoons Shaoxing rice wine or dry sherry

1¹/₂ tablespoons rock sugar or granulated sugar

3 star anise

1 large piece or whole piece cinnamon bark or stick

2 teaspoons roasted whole Sichuan peppercorns
   (see page 72)

¹/₂ cup homemade chicken stock (page 60) or reduced-salt
   canned broth

1 tablespoon peanut oil

3 slices fresh ginger, 2 inches by ¹/₈ inch

6 whole garlic cloves, crushed

5 whole scallions

12 sprigs fresh coriander

5–5¹/₂-pound whole duck, excess fat from cavity removed

2 cups water

2 tablespoons dark soy sauce

4 tablespoons honey

## Garnish

1 pineapple, peeled, cored, and cut into slices, or sprigs of
   fresh coriander

In a bowl, whisk together the bean sauce, light soy sauce, rice wine, sugar, star anise, cinnamon bark, peppercorns, and chicken stock.

Heat a wok or large frying pan over high heat until it is hot. Swirl in the oil, and when it is very hot and slightly smoking, toss in the ginger, garlic, and scallions and stir-fry for 1 minute. Pour the mixture from the bowl into the wok and simmer for 2 minutes. Remove the wok from the heat and toss in the fresh coriander. Allow the contents to cool thoroughly.

Dry the duck thoroughly inside and out with paper towels. Secure the neck flap with a skewer. Pour the mixture from the bowl into the cavity, and then skewer to close up the end of the duck so that it is tightly secured. The liquid is now inside the duck cavity. Tie a long string around the duck's neck or around its body.

Bring 1 cup of water to the boil, then add the dark soy sauce and honey.

With a large ladle, baste the duck with this liquid several times. Now hang the duck in a dry cool place or in front of a fan and allow it to dry thoroughly. This should take about 2 hours. The duck skin should be dry to the touch, like parchment paper.

Preheat the oven to 450° F. Place the duck on a rack in a roasting pan. Add 1 cup of water to the roasting pan. Roast for 10 minutes, turn the temperature down to 350° F., and continue to roast for 1 hour and 10 minutes, until the duck is thoroughly cooked and most of the fat is drained out. Allow the duck to rest for 20 minutes before cutting it up: First cut away the wings. Then remove the thighs and legs and chop into two pieces. Separate the breast into halves. Finally, cut all the meat into bite-size pieces and arrange them. Garnish with pineapple slices or fresh coriander and serve at once.

# King Wah's Pressed Almond Duck

*This imaginative American-style adaptation of the Cantonese classic pressed duck dish was one of the most popular offerings in my uncle's restaurant. The Chinese themselves prefer either a roast duck or Peking duck. Our American patrons loved this version, because it is delicious, and also perhaps because, after preparation, although it is clearly duck, it does not require any skill in carving: convenience food, not fast food. And I am sure that an added appeal was that it was fried and had a crispy texture. The almonds and Chinese seasonings, of course, add a pleasing touch of the exotic.*

*Once the duck has been braised, it is boned, floured, and then fried. It is quite aromatic and delicious in this version.*

*Serves 4—6*

3¹/₂–4-pound duck, fresh or frozen

Sauce

4 cups homemade chicken stock (page 60) or reduced-salt
   canned broth
4 cups dark soy sauce

1½ cups light soy sauce
1½ cups Shaoxing rice wine or dry sherry
¼ pound rock sugar
5 whole star anise
3 whole Chinese cinnamon barks or cinnamon sticks

6 tablespoons chopped roasted almonds
2 tablespoons finely chopped scallions
2 tablespoons finely chopped ham
2 beaten eggs
Potato starch or cornstarch, for dusting
4 cups peanut oil

Cut the duck in half lengthwise. Dry the halves thoroughly with paper towels. Combine all the sauce ingredients in a large pot and bring the mixture to a boil. Add the duck halves and turn the heat down to a simmer. Cover the pot and slowly braise the duck for 1 hour, or until it is tender.

Skim from the surface of the liquid the large amount of fat that will be left when the duck is cooked. Allow the duck to cool, and once the sauce has cooled, remove any lingering surface fat and reserve.

When the duck is quite cool, carefully remove all the bones, keeping the meat and skin intact. Place the duck halves between 2 pieces of plastic wrap and press the meat and skin together with your hands. Remove the wrap and distribute the almonds, scallions, and ham evenly over the duck. Now baste the duck halves with the beaten egg and dust with cornstarch.

Next set up a steamer, or put a rack into a wok or deep pan, and fill it with 2 inches of water. Bring the water to a boil over high heat. Put the duck on a heatproof plate and then carefully lower it into the steamer or onto the rack. Turn the heat to low and cover the wok or pan tightly. Steam gently for 20 minutes. Allow the duck to cool thoroughly. The dish can be completed to this stage a day in advance.

When you are ready to serve the duck, heat a wok or large frying pan over high heat until it is hot. Pour in the oil, and when it is very hot and slightly smoking, carefully lower the duck halves, skin side down, and deep-fry until they are crispy. Remove, and drain well on paper towels. Heat some of the reserved braising liquid and serve sauce with the duck.

Save remaining liquid in freezer for future braised dishes.

# A Chinese=American Thanksgiving Turkey

*Most Americans sit down to a Thanksgiving dinner of roast turkey and bread stuffing with all the trimmings. In my house we had a Chinese-American version of this very American treat. I have since learned that many of my fellow Chinese-Americans enjoyed versions similar to my mother's turkey. Ours was usually stuffed with a glutinous-rice mixture, which Chinese cooks usually used for chicken. Most often the turkey was steamed first, then roasted briefly to make the skin crisp and to give the turkey a nice color. This very Chinese method ensured that the large bird stayed moist, unlike the usual American-style product.*

*My mother used a large enamel turkey roaster to steam the bird. In China, because only restaurants had ovens, we would have fried the turkey after the steaming to give the skin color and crispiness. In America, we made the most of our oven. My mother always got the smallest turkey possible. I wonder if it was because of our small oven or the tiny refrigerator that we had. Or perhaps she couldn't stand to have turkey leftovers for weeks on end.*

*The turkey bones can be deliciously recycled in a Turkey "Shee Fan" (page 250). I was always impressed by my mother's ways of using leftover turkey: for example, in stir-fried dishes, or as a stuffing in bean curd, or shredded into soups.*

*Much of the work involved in this recipe can be done ahead of time: the rice stuffing can be made even days ahead and kept refrigerated. Once steamed, the turkey is really cooked. A quick roast serves only to give it the desired golden-brown skin. It is truly a Chinese-American creation.*

Serves 10–12

12–14-pound fresh or frozen turkey
2 tablespoons Asian sesame oil
3 tablespoons kosher salt
1 tablespoon freshly ground black pepper

## Rice and Sausage Stuffing

3 cups glutinous rice (also known as sweet rice)
1 cup dried black mushrooms

1¹/2 pounds ground pork
3 tablespoons light soy sauce
4 tablespoons Shaoxing rice wine or dry sherry
2 teaspoons Asian sesame oil
1 teaspoon salt
¹/2 teaspoon freshly ground black pepper, plus more to taste
2 tablespoons peanut oil
¹/2 cup finely chopped scallions
2 tablespoons finely chopped fresh ginger
1 pound Chinese pork sausage, chopped (see page 168)
¹/2 pound fresh water chestnuts, peeled and coarsely
   chopped, or canned
3 cups homemade chicken stock (page 60) or reduced-salt
   canned broth

3 cups homemade chicken stock or reduced-salt canned
   broth, for the sauce

Dry the turkey inside and out with paper towels, reserving the giblets. Rub skin with sesame oil. Mix the salt and pepper and rub this evenly over the turkey and set aside. You may do this a day in advance; cover the turkey in plastic wrap and refrigerate. Coarsely chop the turkey giblets and set aside.

Put the glutinous rice in a large bowl, cover it with cold water, and soak for at least 2 hours or overnight. Drain thoroughly.

Soak the mushrooms in warm water for 20 minutes. Then drain them and squeeze out the excess liquid. Remove and discard the stems and coarsely chop the caps.

Combine the ground pork with 1 tablespoon of soy sauce, 1 tablespoon of rice wine, the sesame oil, salt, and pepper and set aside for 20 minutes.

Heat a wok or large frying pan over high heat until it is hot. Swirl in the peanut oil, and when it is very hot and slightly smoking, toss in the scallions and ginger and stir-fry for 3 minutes. Then dump in the pork and the reserved turkey giblets and stir-fry for 3 minutes, breaking up the pork. Now toss in the mushrooms, Chinese sausage, glutinous rice, and water chestnuts and continue to stir-fry for 3 minutes, or until everything is thoroughly mixed. Pour in the chicken stock and the remaining soy sauce and rice wine and mix well. Taste for salt and add several good grindings of freshly ground black pepper. Reduce the heat to low, cover, and cook for 20 minutes, stirring from time to time.

Remove from the heat and allow it cool thoroughly.

## Cooking the Turkey

Using your hands, carefully separate the skin of the turkey breast from the meat. Then insert a thin layer of stuffing between the turkey breast and skin. Next, loosely fill the cavity of the turkey with the stuffing and close with a skewer. Any remaining stuffing can be spooned into a heatproof baking dish, steamed for 40 minutes, and served separately.

Place the turkey on a deep heatproof platter on a rack in a large roasting pan or turkey roaster. Add enough hot water to the pan or roaster to come to 1 1/2 inches beneath the rack. Cover the pan or roaster tightly with a lid or aluminum foil. Bring the water to a simmer, turn the heat to low, and gently steam for 3 1/2 hours, or until the thigh juices run clean when pricked. Be sure to replenish the steaming water from time to time, as necessary. Remove the turkey from the platter, reserving any juices that may have collected. Discard the steaming water.

Preheat the oven to 350° F. Place the cooked turkey on a rack in a roasting pan and cook for 25 minutes, then increase the temperature to 450° F. and roast for another 15 minutes, until the turkey is golden brown.

Make the sauce. While the turkey is roasting, combine the chicken stock and the reserved turkey juices in a saucepan. Bring the mixture to a boil and reduce it by half. Taste and adjust for seasoning by adding salt and pepper.

Remove the turkey from the oven and allow it to rest for 20 minutes before carving. Serve the carved turkey and stuffing with the sauce.

*Kent Wong's family at Thanksgiving dinner*

# Banquet=Style Crispy Squabs

*This dish stands out vividly in my memory of attending Chinese banquets in Chicago's Chinatown as a child. Even in those days, squab was a rather expensive food and eaten only in restaurants and on special occasions. Murmurs of delight always greeted this dish when it came to the banquet table.*

*The squab was briefly braised, dried, and then deep-fried just before serving. And the result was fit for an emperor—who, indeed, was among the very few who could afford the dish in the good old days.*

*The skin would be crisp and crackling, while the rich dark meat of the squab retained its rich flavor but was also nicely moist. It was traditionally served with a squeeze of lemon and Roasted Salt and Pepper.*

*Serves 4*

2 squabs, about ³/₄ pound each
4 slices fresh ginger, 2 inches by ¹/₃ inch
6 whole scallions
6 cups water
¹/₂ cup dark soy sauce
3 tablespoons light soy sauce
¹/₂ cup Shaoxing rice wine or dry sherry
8 tablespoons crushed rock sugar
1 teaspoon salt
3 whole Chinese cinnamon barks or cinnamon sticks
3 whole star anise
1 piece Chinese dried citrus peel or fresh orange peel
3 cups peanut oil, for deep-frying

## Garnish

Lemon wedges
Roasted Salt and Pepper (page 77)

Bring a large pot of water to a boil. Blanch the squabs in the boiling water for about 2 minutes. This helps to rid them of impurities and tightens the skin. Remove the squabs from the pot and discard the water.

149

Put the ginger, scallions, water, soy sauces, rice wine, sugar, salt, cinnamon, star anise, and citrus peel together in a large pot and bring to a boil. Lower the blanched squabs into the pot. Reduce the heat to a simmer and cover the pot tightly. Simmer for about 30 minutes, or until the squabs are just tender. Remove them with a slotted spoon and let them dry on a plate, or hang them up in a cool, dry, airy place for at least 2 hours. The braising liquid, once cooled, can be stored in a plastic container and frozen for future use.

After 2 hours, the skin of the squabs should feel like parchment paper. Just before you are ready to serve them, heat the oil in a large wok. When it is hot, lower the squabs in and deep-fry them until they are crisp and deep brown in color. Turn them over frequently with a slotted spoon so that all sides are crisp and browned. This should take 5–8 minutes. Drain the cooked squabs on paper towels and let them cool for a few minutes. Using a heavy cleaver or knife, chop each one into 4–6 pieces and arrange on a warm serving platter. Serve at once with lemon wedges and Roasted Salt and Pepper.

# Minced Squab in Lettuce Leaves

*For many of us who grew up in Chinatown, the big social events were banquets celebrating or commemorating weddings, birthdays, funerals, and Chinese New Year. Even the funeral banquets were full of socializing, among young and old, and much gaiety, rather like the traditional Irish wake.*

*Banquets were normally huge affairs, with at least 150 people attending. The highlight was always the meal. There would be a procession of dishes (ten was the customary number) featuring expensive ones such as lobster, whole fish, duck, and of course squab.*

*I recall that the most anticipated dish was this one, consisting of minced squab, stir-fried with an assortment of other ingredients, enclosed in an iceberg lettuce leaf (a definite American influence), with dashes of hoisin sauce. This delicacy was eaten like a taco, which made it ideal for children. It was delicious and certainly the most fun dish of the evening.*

*Serves 4–6*

2 whole squabs, about ³/₄ pound each
¹/₂ pound ground pork
2 tablespoons Shaoxing rice wine or dry sherry
1 tablespoon light soy sauce
4 teaspoons Asian sesame oil
2 teaspoons cornstarch
1 head iceberg lettuce
2 tablespoons peanut oil
2 tablespoons coarsely chopped garlic
3 tablespoons finely chopped scallions
1 cup chopped celery
¹/₂ cup chopped canned bamboo shoots
1 tablespoon dark soy sauce
3 tablespoons oyster sauce
¹/₂ teaspoon salt
1 teaspoon sugar
¹/₄ teaspoon freshly ground black pepper
Hoisin sauce, for dipping

Strip all the meat from the squabs and chop it coarsely. Combine the chopped squab meat with the pork, 1 tablespoon of rice wine, the light soy sauce, 2 teaspoons of sesame oil, and the cornstarch. Mix well and let it marinate for about 20 minutes.

Separate and wash the lettuce leaves, wiping off any excess water, and set them aside.

Heat a wok or large frying pan over high heat until it is hot. Swirl in the peanut oil, and when it is very hot and slightly smoking, toss in the garlic, scallions, and squab mixture and stir-fry for 5 minutes. Then toss in the celery and bamboo shoots and continue to stir-fry for 2 minutes. Now pour in the remaining rice wine, the dark soy sauce, oyster sauce, and remaining sesame oil. Continue to stir-fry 1 minute. Finally, sprinkle on the salt, sugar, and pepper and continue to stir-fry 2 minutes.

Place the mixture on a platter. Arrange the lettuce leaves on a separate platter, put the hoisin sauce in a small bowl, and serve at once.

# Chinese Restaurant Menus:

## Selecting from Column A/Column B

Despite the new culinary opportunities available to them, most Americans remain stuck in the old "Chinese-American" menu. It will take them some time to move easily from the open to the "secret" menu, from the "A" column to the "B" column. Every Chinese restaurant, even today, has such a divided menu. Patrons may be seated at adjoining tables, yet they may be experiencing entirely different foods, if one group is Chinese and the other American. Because restaurateurs want to please their customers, they give them what they already like and are used to. However, if Americans ask for guidance and are willing to try something completely new and different, then the proprietors will oblige.

In my uncle's restaurant, we had two menus. In those days, we knew that Americans would not savor braised sea cucumber, bird's nest soup with egg white, or braised shark's fin. These were delicacies enjoyed by our knowledgeable Chinese patrons but would most certainly have driven our American customers away. So we had a menu for them, with the usual suspects listed: chow mein, etc., etc.

The menu was printed in English as well as Chinese characters but not always completely translated. We knew that "Whole Fresh Pike with Ginger and Scallions" did not have to be translated, because our American customers did not like a whole fish on the table, eyes, fins, bones, tail, and all. In fact, they generally ordered only shrimp and lobster among our fish and seafood offerings. They preferred pork and beef, and deep-fried foods. A steamed dish was really too subtle for most of them.

The same division applied to vegetables. Even today, Americans do not like them, especially if they are unusual. They stuck to celery, cabbage, and snow peas (a real exotic!) while our Chinese customers enjoyed mustard greens, fresh water chestnuts, Chinese cabbage and spinach, bitter melon (this being, I will grant you, an acquired taste even for Chinese), and bok choy. It is true that some of our basic one-dish lunches—a stir-fry of meat and vegetables served with rice, for example—might be ordered by Americans, but we knew we had to watch the flavorings and be very careful with the fermented black beans, ginger, and garlic.

Today, we can see the changes that have occurred. Americans are getting bolder; their palates are becoming receptive to new tastes and combinations of foods. The day will come when the words of a New York Chinatown restaurateur, written on his menu in 1916, will be confidently accepted by all patrons: "Our Chinese chef is the originator of many delectable dishes with queer-sounding names, but good to look at and even better to eat." When that day comes, the double menu, the American and the "secret" menus, will disappear—and good riddance!

---

### Bill of Fare

ALL DISHES COOKED TO ORDER
The discriminating public will appreciate the
fact that in the Oriental Restaurant
all dishes are cooked to order

炒穿花面 32 CHOW TUNE FAR MEIN (Fried Noodles with Boneless Chicken, Bamboo Shoots, Water Chestnuts and Ham).............$1.50

炒奇花面 33 CHOW SUE JU KAY FAR MEIN (Fried Noodles, with Boneless Chicken, Lobster, Mushrooms, Water Chestnuts and Bamboo Shoots) .........................$2.00

#### OMELETS

鷄芙荣旦 34 GUY FOO YONG DUN (Chicken Omelet).. 75c

火腿旦 35 FOO HOY DUN (Omelet with Ham)........ 50c

芙蓉旦 36 PLAIN OMELET ......................... 35c

芙蓉虾 37 FOO YONG HA (Omelet with Lobster)..... 75c

炒生虾 38 CHOW SANG HA (Fried Live Lobster, with Vegetables) ........................... 75c

八寶芙蓉 39 BAT BOW FOO YONG (Omelet with Chicken, Lobster, Mushrooms, Bamboo Shoots and Water Chestnuts)............$2.00

三生芙蓉 40 SAM SANG FOO YONG (Omelet with

---

# EGGS

# Egg Foo Young

*My American friends used to be surprised when I told them that Egg Foo Young is the name of an authentic classical Chinese dish but that what they were served in Chinese-American restaurants bore no relation to the original. The American version represents the worst aspect of the tendencies of Cantonese cooks to give the foreign customers what they wanted—in this case dry, crispy omelets drenched in a brown sauce, served with plenty of soy sauce on the table. From the proprietor's point of view, this dish was cost-effective, because the omelet could be prepared ahead of time—as if such a thing were really acceptable!—and its deficiencies buried under a sloppy brown sauce next to mounds of rice. All that the customers knew was that it wasn't what they got at home, nor was it huevos rancheros, so it had to be Chinese.*

*The original Cantonese version is a work of culinary art. The "Foo Young" in the name of the dish is really "furong" and literally means "egg white," which is also used to describe hibiscus, commonly known as the "white Chinese rose."*

*Eggs are remarkably nutritious and versatile foods. They are good boiled or poached, fried or scrambled, by themselves or mixed with other foods; they are used to thicken liquids into solids, to lighten the texture of a foam, and to stabilize oil-and-water sauces. But they require delicate treatment if they are not to harden into a tasteless gummy mass.*

*Thus, in the Chinese version of Egg Foo Young, the eggs can never be prepared ahead of time. The omelet will fail if proper care is lacking. But the true version is a beautiful as well as a delicious dish, as pretty as a hibiscus, its delicate flavors dancing lightly on the palate. In today's Chinese restaurants, you can now experience the delightful original.*

*Though there are many versions of Egg Foo Young, which may include mushrooms, almonds, shrimp, crab, etc., this Chinese-American version, which consists of chicken and vegetables, was the most popular in the restaurant I worked in.*

Serves 4

# The American Version

¹/2 pound boneless, skinless chicken breasts, cut into
    1-inch cubes
1 egg white
¹/2 teaspoon salt
1 teaspoon cornstarch

1 cup peanut oil, or 2 cups water (see variation) and
    2 tablespoons peanut oil

¹/4 cup diced onion
1 tablespoon coarsely chopped garlic
¹/4 pound fresh water chestnuts, peeled and diced, or
    4 pieces canned water chestnuts, diced
¹/2 cup diced celery
¹/2 cup bean sprouts
¹/4 cup seeded and diced green pepper
¹/4 cup diced fresh tomato
1 teaspoon salt
¹/2 teaspoon freshly ground black pepper

4 eggs
1 teaspoon salt
¹/2 teaspoon freshly ground white pepper
1¹/2 teaspoons Asian sesame oil

## Sauce

1 cup homemade chicken stock (page 60) or
    reduced-salt canned broth
2 teaspoons light soy sauce
1¹/2 tablespoons dark soy sauce
¹/2 teaspoon salt
¹/2 teaspoon freshly ground black pepper
1 tablespoon cornstarch mixed with 2 tablespoons
    water
2 teaspoons Asian sesame oil

Combine the chicken with the egg white, salt, and cornstarch, mix well, and refrigerate for 20 minutes.

Heat a wok until it is very hot and then add the peanut oil. When the oil is very hot, remove the wok from the heat and immediately add the chicken pieces, stirring vigorously to keep them from sticking. When the chicken pieces turn white, in about 2 minutes, quickly drain the chicken and all of the oil in a stainless-steel colander set in a bowl. Reserve 6 tablespoons of the oil.

Reheat the wok and add 2 tablespoons of the reserved oil (you need fresh peanut oil at this point if you used water). When the wok and oil are hot, toss in the onion and garlic and stir-fry for 2 minutes. Then chuck in the water chestnuts, celery, bean sprouts, green pepper, tomato, salt, and pepper and stir-fry the mixture for 1 minute. Remove from the heat and allow to cool.

Whisk the eggs lightly with the salt, pepper, and sesame oil. Toss in the chicken and the cooked vegetables, drained from the wok, and mix well.

Heat the wok and when it is hot, add the remaining 1/4 cup of reserved oil (you need to add fresh peanut oil if you used water for cooking the chicken). When it is hot, ladle about one-fifth of the egg mixture into the oil and fry until it is crispy and brown. Turn over and fry the other side. Remove and drain well on paper towels. Repeat four or five times, until you have used up the mixture. Put the Egg Foo Young on a heatproof platter and keep warm in the oven.

In a saucepan, heat the chicken stock, soy sauces, salt, and pepper, and once it is hot, turn the heat down and slowly drizzle in the cornstarch mixture, stirring all the while. When the sauce has thickened, stir in the sesame oil. Ladle this gravy on the Egg Foo Young and serve.

> Variation: If you choose to use water instead of oil, bring it
> to a boil in a saucepan. Remove the saucepan from the heat and
> immediately add the chicken pieces, stirring vigorously to keep
> them from sticking. When the chicken pieces turn white, in
> about 2 minutes, quickly drain the chicken and all of the water
> in a stainless-steel colander set in a bowl. Discard the water.

## An Authentic Chinese Version

*I came across this version of a typical egg stir-fried dish in a
remote village on one of my many trips to China. It is simple
and easy and makes the most of fresh ingredients.*

2 teaspoons Asian sesame oil
1¹/₂ teaspoons salt
¹/₂ teaspoon freshly ground black pepper
6 eggs
2 tablespoons peanut oil
1 small onion, peeled and sliced
2 garlic cloves, peeled and crushed
2 medium-sized ripe tomatoes, cut into 8 wedges each
¹/₄ pound bean sprouts

Stir the sesame oil, 1 teaspoon of salt, and the pepper into the eggs and
beat the mixture thoroughly.

Heat a wok or large frying pan over high heat until it is hot. Drizzle in
the peanut oil, and when it is very hot and slightly smoking, toss in the onion
and garlic and stir-fry for 20 seconds. Then chuck in the tomatoes, bean
sprouts, ¹/₂ teaspoon of salt, and the eggs. Continue to cook, stirring constantly, until the eggs are set, about 5 minutes. Quickly slide on a platter and
serve at once.


# Home=Style Fried Eggs
# with Oyster Sauce


*While my classmates were enjoying their eggs with bacon or ham,
I was savoring this classic dish. My mother would fry the eggs in
a wok very quickly at high heat. She would use peanut oil, which
does not burn easily and imparts a slight nutlike flavor to the
delicate eggs. The result was an egg dish with a crispy exterior and
a soft interior, and a subtle contrast of flavors. The eggs were
served on a platter, sprinkled with a good-quality oyster sauce,
with plain white rice on the side. It makes a delectable breakfast
or lunch, and the eggs alone are often served as a side dish in a
multicourse Chinese dinner.*

*Two important points to remember: cook the eggs quickly,
over high heat, so the white is crispy, but do not overcook them; use*

*a good-quality oyster sauce—the best you can find, because here price is usually a good indication of quality.*

*Serves 4*

2 tablespoons peanut oil
4 eggs
Salt and freshly ground black pepper to taste
3 tablespoons oyster sauce

Heat a wok or large frying pan over high heat until it is hot. Add the oil; when it is very hot and slightly smoking, turn the heat down to low and crack each egg into the wok, keeping the yolks intact.

Continue to pan-fry the eggs over low heat until they are crispy and set. Salt and pepper to taste. Carefully remove the eggs from the wok with a spatula and let them drain on paper towels. Place them on a platter, drizzle with oyster sauce, and serve at once.

# Quick and Easy Corn and Egg

*Along with tomatoes and white and sweet potatoes, corn was brought into China from the New World within the last few centuries. That is only recently, as China measures things. All of these foods quickly became staples in the Chinese diet. Until the 1950s, corn kernels in China were rather tough and not very sweet. Consequently, corn was usually boiled, and its sweet potential was discovered only when Chinese came to America. It became one of the favorite foods of Chinese-Americans, and is certainly one of mine: I love it in all ways, canned, frozen, and, best of all, fresh.*

*On Sundays when corn was in season, my mother would make this quick, easy, and inexpensive treat, adding a few of her Chinese flavorings to make a wonderful dish. Try it as an alternative to your usual eggs and you will see why I have such fond memories.*

*Serves 4*

1 pound (about 3 ears) fresh corn on the cob, or 1 cup
    frozen or canned corn
4 eggs, lightly beaten
1 teaspoon Asian sesame oil
Pinch of salt

1 tablespoon butter
2 teaspoons peanut oil
1 teaspoon finely chopped garlic
1 teaspoon finely chopped ginger
3 tablespoons finely chopped scallions
1 teaspoon salt
$1/2$ teaspoon freshly ground black pepper

If you are using fresh corn on the cob, clean it and remove the kernels
with a sharp knife or cleaver; you should end up with about 1 cup. Set aside.
If you are using frozen corn, place it in a small bowl and let it thaw at room
temperature.

Combine the eggs with the sesame oil and salt and set aside.

Heat a wok or skillet until it is hot, and heat the butter and peanut oil
until the butter has melted. Then toss in the garlic and ginger and stir-fry for
10 seconds. Stir in the corn and continue to stir-fry for 2 minutes. Toss in the
scallions, salt, and pepper. Finally, reduce the heat to medium, add the eggs,
and stir to scramble the eggs, continuing to cook for another 2 minutes, or
until the eggs have set. Serve at once.

# The Ubiquitous Egg Roll

*The ubiquitous egg rolls Americans know as Chinese-American food have nothing to do with eggs and even less with the original Chinese dish. Instead of the leaden Chinese-American versions, the spring rolls of China are light, delicate, and delectable crispy morsels of small treats. In China, very little meat is used in the filling, which consists mostly of savory stir-fried fresh seasonal vegetables evoking the theme of spring—hence their name. The most famous ones are from Shanghai, but equally good are the ones from South China. In America, unskilled cooks made a parody of this popular delicacy. Here I offer the two versions: the first, based on the Chinese-American version but drastically updated; the other, the genuine version from China.*

## Sweet-and-Sour Dipping Sauce
Serves 4

1/2 cup canned tomatoes, pureed
2 tablespoons sugar
3 tablespoons Chinese white rice vinegar
2 teaspoons light soy sauce

Heat all the ingredients in a small saucepan and simmer for 5 minutes over very low heat. Transfer the sauce to a small bowl to cool. Make this sauce ahead of time and cool until ready to use.

## Chinese-American Egg Rolls

Makes about 15 to 20, serving 4

### Filling

1/2 cup Chinese dried black mushrooms
1 1/2 tablespoons peanut oil
2 tablespoons finely chopped garlic
2 teaspoons finely chopped ginger
3 tablespoons finely chopped scallions
1/2 pound ground pork

2 cups shredded cabbage
$^1/_2$ cup canned bamboo shoots, drained, rinsed, and shredded
1 cup bean sprouts
1 teaspoon salt
$^1/_4$ teaspoon freshly ground black pepper
1 tablespoon light soy sauce
2 teaspoons Shaoxing rice wine or dry sherry
2 teaspoons Asian sesame oil

## Sealing Paste

2 tablespoons flour
2 tablespoons water

1 package egg roll wrappers (leftover wrappers can be saved
   and frozen for future use)
2 cups peanut oil

Soak the mushrooms in warm water for 20 minutes. Then drain them and squeeze out the excess liquid. Remove and discard the stems, and finely shred the caps into thin strips.

Heat a wok or large frying pan over high heat until it is hot. Drizzle in the peanut oil, and when it is very hot and slightly smoking, add the garlic, ginger, and scallions and stir-fry for 10 seconds. Chuck in the pork and cabbage and continue to stir-fry for 3 minutes. Add the bamboo shoots, bean sprouts, salt, pepper, soy sauce, and rice wine and stir-fry the mixture for 2 minutes, stirring continuously to mix well. Finally, stir in the sesame oil and remove from the heat. Put the mixture into a colander set in a bowl to drain and allow it to cool thoroughly.

Mix the flour and water until you have a smooth paste.

Place about 4 tablespoons of filling on one end of each egg roll skin, fold in both sides, and roll up tightly. Use the flour mixture to seal the edge.

Heat a wok or large frying pan until it is hot and swirl in the peanut oil. When the oil is quite hot, gently drop in as many egg rolls as will fit easily in one layer. Fry them carefully, turning until the egg rolls are golden brown on the outside and cooked inside, about 4 minutes. Adjust the heat as necessary. Take the egg rolls out with a slotted spoon and drain on paper towels. You will have to do this in several batches. Serve them at once, hot and crispy, with the Sweet-and-Sour Dipping Sauce.

# Chinese Spring Rolls

*Here the spring rolls are wrapped in a light flour pancake, known as "Shanghai spring roll wrappers." They are lighter because the dough does not contain egg.*

Makes about 15 to 20, serving 4

## Filling

1/2 cup Chinese dried black mushrooms
1 1/2 tablespoons peanut oil
1 tablespoon finely chopped garlic
2 teaspoons finely chopped ginger
3 tablespoons finely chopped scallions
1/2 pound shrimp, peeled and deveined
2 cups shredded Napa cabbage
1/2 cup canned bamboo shoots, drained, rinsed, and
    shredded
1 cup bean sprouts
1 teaspoon salt
1/2 teaspoon freshly ground black pepper
1 tablespoon light soy sauce
2 teaspoons dark soy sauce
2 teaspoons Shaoxing rice wine or dry sherry
2 teaspoons Asian sesame oil

## Sealing Paste

2 tablespoons flour
2 tablespoons water

1 package Shanghai spring roll wrappers (leftover wrappers
    can be saved and frozen for future use)*
2 cups peanut oil

* Available at Chinese groceries or supermarkets.

Soak the mushrooms in warm water for 20 minutes. Then drain them and squeeze out the excess liquid. Remove and discard the stems, and finely shred the caps into thin strips.

Heat a wok or large frying pan over high heat until it is hot. Swirl in the peanut oil, and when it is very hot and slightly smoking, toss in the garlic, ginger, and scallions and stir-fry for 10 seconds. Add the shrimp, mushrooms, and Napa cabbage and continue to stir-fry for 3 minutes. Toss in the bamboo shoots, bean sprouts, salt, and pepper; add the soy sauces and rice wine, and stir-fry for 5 minutes, stirring to mix well. Finally, stir in the sesame oil and remove from the heat. Put the mixture into a colander set in a bowl to drain, pressing out any excess moisture, and allow it to cool thoroughly.

Mix the flour and water until you have a smooth paste.

(1) Place about 4 tablespoons of filling on one end of each spring roll skin, (2) fold in each side, and (3) roll up tightly. Use the flour mixture to seal the edge.

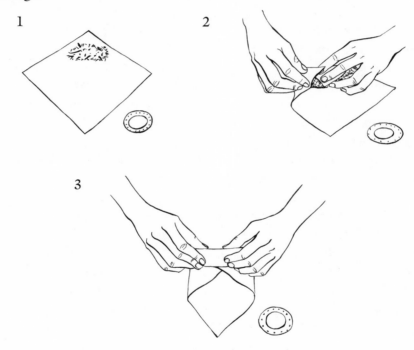

Heat a wok or large frying pan until it is hot and pour in the peanut oil. When the oil is quite hot, gently drop in as many spring rolls as will fit easily in one layer. Carefully fry them, turning from time to time, until the spring rolls are golden brown on the outside and cooked inside, about 4 minutes. Adjust the heat as necessary. Take the spring rolls out with a slotted spoon and drain on paper towels. You will have to do this in several batches. Serve them at once, hot and crispy, with the Sweet-and-Sour Dipping Sauce (page 162).

# Stir=Fried Eggs with Barbecued Pork

*Here is yet another delightful variation on the egg theme: conge-
nial eggs and Chinese barbecued pork.*

*This recipe brings back memories of my Chicago childhood.
My mother's cousin, whom I knew as Third Uncle, was the Chinatown roaster. He had the professional ovens, and he would prepare
all of the roast duck, whole roast pig, and barbecued pork for the
entire Chinese community, as well as for festivals and banquets.
Whenever he visited our home, he would bring with him some
samples of the delights he had prepared that day.*

*I remember his place of business. It always smelled so good to
me. He had special ovens in which marinated pork strips were
suspended and slowly roasted until they were suffused with the
aromas and flavors of different spices. I particularly remember
the slightly charred, caramelized crust of the pork and my enjoyment of all the crispy bits.*

*Any leftover barbecued pork was sliced the next day and stir-
fried with eggs and Chinese chives, usually from the neighbor's
garden. Chinese chives are mild, small versions of the onion. They
have no bulb; only the green shoots are eaten. In China, which has
relatively few food herbs (medicinal herbs are abundant), garlic
chives are very popular as a flavoring herb. Chinese green chives
have a distinctive pungency that adds richness to stir-fried dishes.
You can buy them fresh at Chinese markets or groceries. Garlic
and Chinese green chives should be deep green and fresh-looking,
not wilted and tired. Substitute regular chives from your local
supermarket if you can't find the Chinese ones.*

*This recipe really represents memories of home cooking at its
simple best.*

*Serves 2—4*

6 beaten eggs
2 teaspoons Asian sesame oil
1 teaspoon salt
1 1/2 tablespoons peanut oil

½ pound sliced Chinese barbecued pork* or cooked ham
2 bunches Chinese chives* or regular chives, diagonally cut
    into 1-inch segments
6 sliced scallions

* Available from Chinese groceries or supermarkets.

In a medium-sized bowl, mix the eggs with the sesame oil and salt and reserve.

Heat a wok or large frying pan over high heat until it is hot. Swirl in the peanut oil, and when it is very hot and slightly smoking, throw in the pork slices and stir-fry for 2 minutes. Now pour in the beaten eggs and stir-fry, stirring constantly, until the eggs begin to set, in about 2 minutes.

Toss in chives and scallions and continue to stir-fry for 3 minutes. Quickly place on a platter and serve at once.

# Stir-Fried Eggs with Chinese Sausage

*As hard and as long as my mother worked every day, she insisted that we have a complete Chinese meal with at least three or four different dishes every night. Like most working mothers, she tried to make quick and easy meals that were nevertheless good and wholesome. This recipe was one that met her very high standards of savory taste. It takes literally but a few minutes to assemble and to cook.*

*She sometimes varied the recipe according to what was in the market—for example, tossing in Chinese chives or green garlic shoots that a neighbor would give us in the spring.*

*These eggs and sausages also make a simple but delightful luncheon dish.*

*Serves 2—4*

6 beaten eggs
1 teaspoon salt
2 teaspoons Asian sesame oil
1½ tablespoons peanut oil
3 Chinese pork sausages, sliced (see box)
6 scallions, sliced

In a medium-sized bowl, whisk the eggs lightly with the salt and sesame oil and reserve.

Heat a wok or large frying pan over high heat until it is hot. Swirl in the peanut oil, and when it is very hot and slightly smoking, throw in the sausages and stir-fry for 2 minutes. Now pour in the beaten eggs and stir-fry, stirring constantly, until the eggs begin to set, in about 2–3 minutes. Toss in the scallions and continue to stir-fry another minute. Quickly place on a platter and serve at once.

## Chinese Sausages

Chinese sausages look exactly like thin, dry salami and are about six inches long. They are made from duck liver, pork liver, or pork meat and are hung on strings and dried. They are deep burgundy red in color, with white flecks of fat. Their tasty flavor varies according to type, but they are sweet rather than spicy, with a rich aroma. They must be steamed before eating or used with other foods, such as eggs or in stuffing. Chinese sausages can be found at Chinese groceries or supermarkets. They freeze well. You can also buy them through specialty-food mail-order companies. Look for firm sausages. Most of the Chinese sausages called for in this book are the most common variety, made with pork meat.

# Shark's Fin with Eggs

*As a practical matter, the Chinese character for "shark's fin"*
*should also stand for "special occasion." Any recipe involving*
*shark's fin means a formal banquet in a restaurant or at home,*
*celebrating something special.*

*In my childhood, we rarely had shark's fin—it was much too*
*expensive for our limited household budget. But I had an uncle*
*who loved to gamble, and he especially loved the "sport of kings."*
*Whenever one of his long shots came in, we all celebrated with one*
*or another recipe calling for shark's fin. Most often, we would*
*enjoy the delicacy in a soup, double-steamed for many hours with*
*a fresh whole chicken. My mother would soak the fins for hours and*
*then braise them for another few hours with scallions and ginger*
before *cooking them with the soup.*

*However, my favorite was and remains shark's fin simply*
*stir-fried with eggs, as in this version. The rich soft egg contrasts*
*nicely with the* al dente *texture of the shark's fin. Fortunately, the*
*hours of soaking and braising are no longer necessary: it is possible*
*now to buy already prepared shark's fins. They may be found in*
*the frozen-food section of most Chinese groceries or supermarkets.*

Serves 2–4

6 beaten eggs
2 teaspoons Asian sesame oil
1 teaspoon salt
1¹/₂ tablespoons peanut oil
6 tablespoons finely shredded Smithfield ham
¹/₂ pound prepared frozen shark's fin,* thawed
6 sliced scallions

* Available at Chinese groceries or supermarkets.

In a medium-sized bowl, whisk the eggs lightly with the sesame oil and
salt and reserve.

Heat a wok or large frying pan over high heat until it is hot. Swirl in the
peanut oil, and when it is very hot and slightly smoking, toss in the ham and

shark's fin and stir-fry for 3 minutes. Now pour in the beaten eggs and stir-fry, stirring constantly, until the eggs begin to set, in about 2–3 minutes. Toss in the scallions and continue to stir-fry another minute. Quickly place on a platter and serve at once.

# Steamed Savory Custard

*Comfort food* par excellence. *In this most satisfying dish, eggs are beaten with stock or water, and the result is a savory delicacy. The custard is smooth as silk, with just the right body and texture. A more substantial dish can be made with the addition of ground pork to the custard.*

*Such quickly made home-cooked dishes were ideal for busy Chinese-American mothers like mine, who had to work and then come home to prepare meals for hungry family members. This one is literally whipped together in minutes.*

Serves 4

2 teaspoons light soy sauce
1 teaspoon Shaoxing rice wine or dry sherry
1 teaspoon Asian sesame oil
1/4 teaspoon salt
4 eggs, beaten
1 1/2 cups homemade chicken stock (page 60) or reduced-salt
   canned broth
Peanut or vegetable oil, to coat bowl
2 tablespoons oyster sauce

## Garnish

3 tablespoons finely chopped scallions

Mix together thoroughly the soy sauce, rice wine, sesame oil, salt, eggs, and chicken stock.

Rub a heatproof shallow bowl with peanut oil or vegetable oil, then pour in the beaten egg mixture.

Next, set up a steamer, or put a rack into a wok or deep pan, and fill it with 2 inches of water. Bring the water to a boil over high heat. Carefully lower the bowl into the steamer or onto the rack. Turn the heat to low and cover the wok or pan tightly. Steam gently for 15 minutes, or until the custard has set.

Remove the custard and drizzle oyster sauce over the top. Scatter the scallions over all and serve at once with rice.

# MEAT

Home-Style Pork and Egg Custard Loaf

Chop Suey

Mrs. Tsai's Pork Dumplings

Sweet-and-Sour Pork My Way

Succulent Barbecued Spareribs

Mrs. Wong's Braised Pig Snout

Meaty Stir-Fried Pork Liver

The Tsai Family's Red Roast Pork

Lao Zhou's Lionhead Meatballs

Savory Pork with Pickled Vegetables

Steamed Pork Loaf with Salted Duck Eggs

Steamed Pork Loaf with Salted Fish

Steamed Pork Loaf with Chinese Sausages

Sweet-and-Sour Pig's Feet

Roast Pork Belly

Easy Stir-Fried Pork with Scallions

Simple Stir-Fried Ground Pork

Stir-Fried Beef with Broccoli

Traditional Pepper Beef

Rich Braised Beef

My Mother's Savory Oxtail Stew

Pickled Mustard Greens with Beef

Stir-Fried Beef with Tomato and Egg

Classic Stir-Fried Beef with Oyster Sauce

The Tsai Family's Mongolian Beef

Northern-Style Lamb with Garlic

# Home-Style Pork and Egg Custard Loaf

*Pork and egg custard was true comfort food in my family. My mother would make it often, because it was cheap, easy, and frankly delicious. Just a small amount of meat, which she could easily stretch with the eggs. The result was a silky, tender, savory custard, which I still love today. I am not sure most non-Chinese would appreciate the soft texture of the eggs, which are barely set. Perhaps the mushiness of the dish is what makes it comfort food. The trick is to steam the custard gently, so the eggs do not toughen. My mother used an old aluminum pot, because our wok was not big enough. A small rack transformed it into an efficient steamer. Unlike the Steamed Savory Custard (page 170), this recipe includes pork.*

Serves 4

1/4 pound ground pork
2 teaspoons light soy sauce
1 teaspoon Shaoxing rice wine or dry sherry
1/2 teaspoon salt
1/4 teaspoon freshly ground black pepper
1 teaspoon Asian sesame oil
1 teaspoon cornstarch
1 tablespoon peanut oil, plus more to coat bowl

## Custard

3 eggs, beaten
1 1/2 cups homemade chicken stock (page 60) or reduced-salt
   canned broth
1 tablespoon Shaoxing rice wine or dry sherry
1/2 teaspoon freshly ground white pepper
1 teaspoon salt

## Garnish

3 tablespoons finely chopped scallions, white part only
1 tablespoon peanut oil
2 tablespoons oyster sauce

Mix the pork with the soy sauce, rice wine, salt, pepper, sesame oil, and cornstarch. Heat a wok or large frying pan over high heat until it is hot. Swirl in the peanut oil, and when it is very hot and slightly smoking, dump in the pork and stir-fry it for 2 minutes, breaking up the meat until it loses its raw look. Drain the meat in a colander set in a bowl, and discard the excess fat and oil. Mix the custard ingredients in another bowl and stir in cooked pork. Lightly oil a heatproof shallow bowl and pour in the custard mixture.

Next set up a steamer, or put a rack into a wok or deep pan, and fill it with 2 inches of water. Bring the water to a boil over high heat. Carefully lower the bowl with the custard into the steamer or onto the rack. Turn the heat to low and cover the wok or pan tightly. Steam gently for 10 minutes, or until the custard has barely set. Remove the custard and sprinkle with the scallions. Meanwhile, heat the peanut oil in a small pan until it begins to smoke, then pour this over the custard. Drizzle on the oyster sauce and serve at once.

# Chop Suey

*This is the quintessential "Chinese-American" dish, and there are many stories, legends, and myths about how it came to be the most popular item on the menu (see box on page 179). We do know that the generic style of this dish is a traditional one in the rural areas of South China (around Canton), the birthplace of most of the early Chinese immigrants to America. That style, however, had little to do with the Chinese-American version. Here I offer both the Chinese original and the Chinese-American recipes. You will discern the differences between them.*

*Serves 4*

## The Classic Chinese=American Version

1 pound pork butt or shoulder, cut into 1-inch cubes

### Marinade

1 tablespoon light soy sauce
2 teaspoons Shaoxing rice wine or dry sherry
1 teaspoon salt
1/2 teaspoon freshly ground black pepper
1 teaspoon Asian sesame oil
2 teaspoons cornstarch

2 tablespoons peanut oil
3 garlic cloves, peeled and crushed
2 cups finely sliced onions
2 cups finely sliced bok choy
2 cups bean sprouts, cleaned
1/2 cup finely sliced celery
1 teaspoon salt
1/2 teaspoon freshly ground black pepper

### Sauce

1/2 cup homemade chicken stock (page 60) or reduced-salt
canned broth

1 tablespoon dark soy sauce
2 teaspoons light soy sauce
1 tablespoon oyster sauce
1 tablespoon Shaoxing rice wine or dry sherry
2 teaspoons cornstarch mixed with 1 tablespoon water

In a medium-sized bowl, mix the pork with the marinade ingredients. Let it marinate for 20 minutes at room temperature.

Heat a wok or large frying pan over high heat until it is hot. Swirl in the peanut oil, and when it is very hot and slightly smoking, toss in the garlic and onions and stir-fry for 1 minute. Dump in the pork and continue to stir-fry for 4 minutes. Then toss in the bok choy, bean sprouts, celery, salt, and pepper, mixing well. Pour in the chicken stock, soy sauces, oyster sauce, and rice wine and continue to cook for another 3 minutes. Slowly drizzle in the cornstarch mixture, stirring all the while, and bring the contents of the wok to a simmer.

Remove from the heat, transfer to a platter, and serve at once.

## The Chinese Version

1 pound lean boneless pork chops
1 tablespoon light soy sauce
2 teaspoons Shaoxing rice wine or dry sherry
1 teaspoon salt
1/2 teaspoon freshly ground black pepper
2 teaspoons Asian sesame oil
1 egg white
1 tablespoon cornstarch

2 cups peanut oil

3 garlic cloves, peeled and crushed
2 tablespoons finely shredded ginger
2 cups snow peas, trimmed
1/2 cup finely shredded scallions
1/4 cup homemade chicken stock (page 60) or reduced-salt
   canned broth
1 tablespoon light soy sauce
2 teaspoons Shaoxing rice wine or dry sherry

2 teaspoons chili bean paste or sauce (see page 276)
1 teaspoon salt
1 teaspoon sugar
¼ teaspoon freshly ground black pepper
1 teaspoon cornstarch mixed with 2 teaspoons water
2 teaspoons Asian sesame oil

Cut the pork into fine shreds about 2 inches long by ⅛ inch wide. In a medium-sized bowl, mix the pork with the soy sauce, rice wine, salt, pepper, and sesame oil. Mix in the egg white and cornstarch and toss until the pork is well coated. Refrigerate for at least 20 minutes.

Heat a wok until it is very hot, and then swirl in the peanut oil. When the oil is very hot, remove the wok from the heat and immediately add the pork shreds, stirring vigorously to keep them from sticking. As soon as the pork begins to lose its raw look, in about 2 minutes, quickly drain the pork in a stainless-steel colander set in a bowl. Discard all but 2 tablespoons of the oil.

Reheat the wok and the oil. When it is hot, toss in the garlic and ginger and stir-fry for 30 seconds. Scatter in the snow peas and scallions and continue to stir-fry for 1 minute. Pour in the stock, soy sauce, and rice wine. Spoon in the chili paste, salt, sugar, and pepper. Stir to mix well, return the pork, and let cook for 2 minutes. Slowly drizzle in the cornstarch mixture. Stir in the sesame oil, transfer to a platter, and serve.

# Mrs. Tsai's Pork Dumplings

*I was fortunate to grow up enjoying not only my mother's well-prepared, delicious food but that of her friends who cooked as well as she did. Mrs. Tsai, for example, our neighbor and my mother's best friend, was renowned in Chinatown as a wonderful home cook and housewife; her fame spread by word of mouth through Chicago's Chinatown. I remember going to her home and enjoying exceptional meals, especially her savory homemade dim-sum snacks. Her pork dumplings were so good that people ordered them for their own "home-cooked" Sunday family dinners and dim-sum*

*(continues on page 181 )*

# Chop Suey

Chinese cuisine depends more upon a certain philosophy and upon certain techniques of preparation and cooking than it does on any particular foods or exotic ingredients such as bok choy or Sichuan peppercorns. Garlic, ginger, and soy sauce, the essential seasonings of authentic Chinese cuisine, are commonly available everywhere in the world. This versatility that does not depend solely on what is produced by the ancestral farm is what makes Chinese cooking so adaptable and so popular throughout the world. Because the philosophy and techniques remain the same, the Chinese style lends itself to the use of new, local, and different ingredients while preserving the authenticity of the classic recipes.

The basic principles of Chinese cooking techniques are universal in their applicability. The various slicing, chopping, dicing, mincing, and other cutting techniques; the steaming, steeping, and braising; the deep-frying, shallow-frying, stir-frying—all these techniques are readily learned and applied. Woks and cleavers are the preferred implements, but skillets and chefs' knives will serve well enough. The Chinese cook in a foreign land takes whatever is at hand and creates a distinctly "Chinese" menu.

This trait provides the basis in legend for the origins of American "chop suey." According to the story, some rough and tough and very hungry miners entered a Chinese restaurant that had been set up among the gold mines and demanded to be fed. The hapless proprietor was short of many supplies, but he quickly steamed some rice, diced, sliced, and roll-cut whatever could pass as a vegetable, stir-fried it with some leftover bits of spiced chicken, and, *voilà*, technique and the pressure of necessity gave rise to an apparently authentic Chinese dish, or at least a reasonable facsimile thereof.

The legend continues that, when the miners asked what this

satisfying dish was called, the proprietor said it was *tsap seui* or, as it was understood, "chop suey." The kernel of truth in this legend is that *tsap seui* in Cantonese means "sundry scraps."

An interesting legend, but a story nonetheless. The great American authority on Chinese food and culture, E. N. Anderson, draws upon Chinese scholarship to show that *tsap seui* (in Mandarin, *tsa sui*) is a traditional dish in the Toisan area, south of Canton, a poor rural section where one would expect every scrap of food to be used, albeit prepared as well and imaginatively as possible. One can understand why restaurateurs would offer such a dish. Better sell it to hungry, nondiscriminating customers than to throw the leftovers out: that, after all, is what hash is, even with a fried egg on top.

By an irony of history and the use of smart marketing, the American version of this dish is now being offered by cosmopolitan restaurants in China itself: "Genuine American Chop Suey Served Here," they proclaim. Yet another global triumph for American pop culture. And, perhaps even more ironic, chop suey is enjoying a revival among third-generation Chinese-Americans who wish to affirm their Americanism without denying their Chinese origins. To them, chop suey is Chinese "soul food" as well as a universal comfort food.

The only unfortunate aspect to the "chop suey story" is that the dish became synonymous with Chinese food. Cantonese cookery especially has had to struggle against this rather deplorable stereotype. Still, chop suey does and can taste good, and it is both economical and nutritious. Every negative stereotype should have such virtues.

*Ming Tsai with his father and uncle enjoying a meal*

luncheons. *In those days, dim sum was not readily available, as it
is today. It was always a rather complicated affair and required
time. However, Mrs. Tsai had so mastered the techniques of making dim sum that she soon had a thriving Sunday sideline—dim
sum to go. If Mrs. Tsai was exceptionally busy, my mother would
go next door to her house and assist her in making her famous
dumplings.*

*I remember very well the bamboo leaves soaking in the bath-
tub of her apartment and, in the cluttered kitchen, tubs of minced
meat and of sweet bean paste filling, and mounds of cooked rice.
Although Mrs. Tsai brought already made wonton wrappers, she
did make her own rice flour dough.*

*My mother and Mrs. Tsai would take turns at the mortar
and pestle, grinding rice flour and almonds into a paste. Things
could get quite hectic. I thought it all a big treat, because my task,
as I saw it, was to stay out of the way and to nibble on any tidbits
I was offered.*

*My favorite was Mrs. Tsai's steamed pork dumplings, filled
with sweet, crisp water chestnuts. It was not difficult to see why her
dumplings were in such demand.*

Serves 4

## Filling

¹/₂ cup Chinese dried black mushrooms
1 pound fatty ground pork butt
¹/₂ cup peeled and chopped fresh or canned
    water chestnuts
2 tablespoons finely chopped canned Sichuan preserved
    vegetables, rinsed*·
¹/₄ pound shrimp, peeled, deveined, and coarsely chopped
1 tablespoon light soy sauce
2 teaspoons dark soy sauce
1 tablespoon Shaoxing rice wine or dry sherry
3 tablespoons finely chopped scallions
1 tablespoon finely chopped fresh ginger
2 teaspoons Asian sesame oil
1 beaten egg white
1 teaspoon salt
¹/₂ teaspoon freshly ground black pepper
2 teaspoons sugar
1 package thin wonton skins (about 40 skins)

\* Available in Chinese groceries or supermarkets.

Soak the mushrooms in warm water for 20 minutes. Drain them and squeeze out the excess liquid. Remove and discard the stems, and finely chop the mushroom caps.

Put the chopped mushrooms and rest of the filling ingredients into a large bowl and mix them well.

(1) Place a portion of filling on each wonton skin. (2) Bring up the sides and press them around the filling mixture.

1

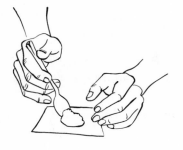

2

3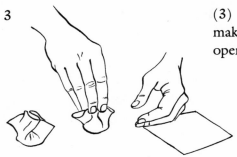

(3) Tap the dumpling on the bottom to make a flat base. The top should be wide open, exposing the meat filling.

Set up a steamer, or put a rack inside a wok or large deep pot. Pour in about 2 inches of water and bring it to a boil. Put the dumplings on a lightly oiled heatproof plate and place this in the steamer or on the rack.

Cover the pot tightly, turn the heat to low, and steam gently for about 20 minutes. You may have to do this in several batches. Serve the dumplings hot. Keep the first batch warm by covering them with foil and placing them in a warm but switched-off oven until all the dumplings are ready to serve at once.

## The Need for Fat

My mother always insisted on using fatty ground pork in her fillings. She wanted at least 30 to 40 percent fat in her meat. This was important, for the pork fat would gently melt, keeping the filling moist and flavorful. Lean fillings meant a dry and tasteless dish—a grave error in my mother's eye. An often heard criticism was that a dish did not have enough pork fat—the equivalent of an Italian's saying there is not enough olive oil, or a Frenchman's saying there is not enough butter or goose fat. Fatty pork can easily be ground from pork butt, which can be ordered from your butcher. This cut is often available as a pork butt roast.

# Sweet=and=Sour Pork My Way

*One Chinese food authority refers to "the sweet-sour glop of over-seas restaurants." He means the sweet-and-sour pork dish served in Chinese-American restaurants. Working in my uncle's restaurant, I could never understand why Americans would order, and seem really to enjoy, the sticky, gluey, much too sweet concoction, topped with bright-red bits of maraschino cherries, and plenty of soy sauce on the rice to boot. It was a mystery to me, except that I knew Americans liked lots of (salt and) sugar, an ingredient that is used but sparingly in China. Not until many years later, during my first visit to Hong Kong, did I discover the authentic sweet-and-sour pork. To my surprise and gratification, instead of a thick, heavy batter and a correspondingly thick, heavy, sweet sauce, I enjoyed the delicate flavor of succulent pork wrapped in a light crispy coating, with a perfectly balanced sweet-and-sour sauce: when it is properly done, one should never be quite sure whether the dish is sweet or sour.*

*Here I offer my modern version, melding the traditional recipe and some Chinese-American touches—but no extra soy sauce or cherries!*

*Serves 4*

1 pound pork butt
1 teaspoon salt
1/2 teaspoon freshly ground black pepper
2 teaspoons light soy sauce
1 teaspoon Shaoxing rice wine or dry sherry
1 teaspoon Asian sesame oil
1 teaspoon cornstarch

## Batter

1/2 cup potato starch or cornstarch
1/4 cup all-purpose unbleached white flour
1 teaspoon baking powder
1 teaspoon baking soda
1/4 teaspoon salt

¼ teaspoon freshly ground black pepper
2 teaspoons Asian sesame oil
½ cup water

2 cups peanut oil, for deep-frying

## Sauce

1 cup homemade chicken stock (page 60) or reduced-salt
   canned broth
3 tablespoons Chinese red rice vinegar or cider vinegar
3 tablespoons sugar
1 tablespoon lemon juice
1 tablespoon light soy sauce
2 teaspoons Shaoxing rice wine or dry sherry
2 tablespoons tomato puree
1 tablespoon lemon zest
2 teaspoons Asian sesame oil
1 tablespoon cornstarch blended with 2 tablespoons water

2 cups peeled, cored 1-inch cubes of fresh pineapple

Cut the pork into 1-inch cubes. Mix it with the salt, pepper, soy sauce, Shaoxing rice wine, sesame oil, and cornstarch, and let it marinate at room temperature for 20 minutes.

Mix the batter ingredients with a whisk in a medium-sized bowl and beat until smooth.

Heat a wok or deep pan until it is hot. Swirl in the peanut oil, and when it is slightly smoking, turn the heat down to medium. Mix the pork with the batter. Remove the pork with a slotted spoon and deep-fry in several batches, for a few minutes each. Place the pork on a tray lined with paper towels to drain.

Mix all the sauce ingredients except the cornstarch mixture in a saucepan and bring it to a simmer. Pour in the cornstarch mixture in a slow drizzle, stirring all the while. Add the pineapple and warm it for 2 minutes. Remove from the heat.

Place the pork on a platter, ladle the sauce over, and serve at once.

# Succulent Barbecued Spareribs

*I grew up with the smug conviction that our barbecued spareribs were always different. I didn't know why they were better; perhaps it was their glistening, lacquered look or their juiciness or their aroma. When I ate barbecued spareribs outside of my Chinese home, they were bland, insipid, and tasteless. Later I learned why: the Chinese marinate their spareribs overnight and cook them slowly at a low temperature, so that the flavors permeate the meat and make it mouth-watering.*

Serves 4

3½ pounds pork spareribs

## Marinade

1 tablespoon finely chopped garlic
1 tablespoon finely chopped ginger
2 tablespoons light soy sauce
2 tablespoons dark soy sauce
2 tablespoons Shaoxing rice wine or dry sherry
1 tablespoon five-spice powder
1½ tablespoons chili bean sauce or paste (see page 276)
1 tablespoon Asian sesame oil
2 teaspoons salt
2 tablespoons sugar
3 tablespoons hoisin sauce

3 tablespoons honey, for roasting

Lay the spareribs on a baking sheet.

Mix the marinade ingredients together and spread this evenly on both sides of the spareribs. Wrap with plastic wrap and refrigerate overnight.

Preheat the oven to 250° F.

Place the spareribs with the marinade in a large roasting pan in one layer, coat with the honey, and cook slowly in the oven, for 2 hours and 15 minutes, or until tender. Pour off any excess fat.

Turn the temperature to 450° F. and continue to cook for 10 minutes, or until the ribs are browned.

Serve at once.

# Mrs. Wong's Braised Pig Snout

*A large majority of first- and second-generation Chinese-Americans were relatively poor. Nevertheless, they ate well. Like African-Americans, they made do with inexpensive and less desirable meats and other foods. Steaks, for example, never appeared on our table. Instead, we usually ate pork and vegetables. And most parts of the pig were very much cheaper than beef.*

*In Chinatowns, Chinese butchers enjoyed a busy trade with all parts of the pig. For example, my friend Steve Wong's mother made this tender braised pig snout with a robust mixture of star anise, soy sauce, and broth. The long simmering turns this seemingly unattractive part of the pork into a tender, luscious treat. The bonus is that the dish reheats extremely well. You can find pig snout at Chinese and other ethnic meat markets.*

Serves 4

1 pound pig snout (see above)
2 slices fresh ginger, peeled, 2 inches by 1/8 inch
4 scallions, cut into 2-inch segments
4 garlic cloves, peeled, crushed slightly, and left whole
3 tablespoons Shaoxing rice wine or dry sherry
1 tablespoon dark soy sauce
2 teaspoons light soy sauce
3 tablespoons hoisin sauce
2 tablespoons chili bean sauce (see page 276)
2 tablespoons crushed Chinese rock sugar or ordinary sugar
3 whole star anise
1 cinnamon stick or bark
1/2 teaspoon freshly ground black pepper
1 teaspoon salt
3 cups homemade chicken stock (page 60) or reduced-salt
   canned broth

## Garnish

3 tablespoons coarsely chopped scallions

Bring a large pot of salted water to a boil. Drop in the pig snout together with the ginger, scallions, and garlic. When the liquid comes to a boil, reduce the heat and simmer for 1 hour, skimming the surface frequently to remove any scum and impurities. Drain the pig snout and remove and discard the garlic, scallions, and ginger, as well as the water.

In a medium-sized casserole, mix the rice wine, soy sauces, hoisin sauce, chili bean sauce, sugar, star anise, cinnamon, pepper, salt, and stock. Bring to a simmer and add the cooked pig snout. Cover, reduce the heat to low, and simmer for 1½ hours, or until the meat is quite tender.

Skim off any surface fat, transfer to a deep dish with the sauce, garnish with the chopped scallions, and serve immediately with plain rice.

# Meaty Stir=Fried Pork Liver

*For those of us who grew up in or near a Chinatown, pork liver was more common than calves' liver, which is what the wider American community ate. Pork liver was inexpensive, and my mother used to pick it up for dinner on her way home. She would blanch the liver before stir-frying it, usually with whatever vegetable was fresh and in season at the same local corner Chinese grocery. I especially love the recipe in which she paired the liver with silk squash, a unique Chinese vegetable (which can be found in Chinese markets) that tasted like a cross between a cucumber and a zucchini. It was tender and sweet and provided a wonderful contrast to the liver in taste and texture.*

Serves 4

1 pound pork liver
2 tablespoons light soy sauce
2 teaspoons Shaoxing rice wine or dry sherry
1 teaspoon sugar
½ teaspoon salt
¼ teaspoon freshly ground black pepper
2 teaspoons potato starch or cornstarch

4 tablespoons peanut oil

2 tablespoons coarsely chopped garlic

1 tablespoon finely chopped ginger

1/2 cup chopped red onion

1 pound silk squash (see recipe introduction), zucchini, or
   cucumber, peeled and roll-cut

3 tablespoons finely chopped scallions

1 tablespoon light soy sauce

1 tablespoon dark soy sauce

1 tablespoon oyster sauce

1 tablespoon Shaoxing rice wine or dry sherry

1 teaspoon sugar

1/4 cup homemade chicken stock (page 60) or reduced-salt
   canned broth

2 teaspoons Asian sesame oil

Cut the liver into 2-inch strips lengthwise and then into thin slices about 1/8 inch thick. Blanch the liver in a pot of boiling water for 1 minute, remove to a colander, and refresh with cold water to stop it from cooking. Blot the liver pieces dry. Mix the light soy sauce, rice wine, sugar, salt, pepper, and potato starch, and stir in the liver.

Heat a wok or large frying pan over high heat until it is hot. Add the peanut oil, and when it is very hot and slightly smoking, toss in the garlic, ginger, and onion and stir-fry for 2 minutes. Then dump in the silk squash and scallions and stir-fry for 2 minutes. Pour in the soy sauces, oyster sauce, rice wine, and sugar and cook for 1 minute. Drizzle in the stock and continue to cook for another 2 minutes. Add the liver and continue to cook for 2 minutes. Finally, stir in the sesame oil and give the mixture several good stirs. Transfer the contents of the wok to a platter and serve at once.

# The Tsai Family's Red Roast Pork

*This is a favorite dish on the family table of my Chinese-American friend Ming Tsai. Unlike a majority of Chinese-Americans, who are of South Chinese ancestry, Ming's family roots are in North China. Shanghai, like Canton, is a coastal city, but it is much farther north. Along with many other North Chinese, the family migrated to Taiwan during the troubled times following World War II.*

*Red Roast Pork is a typical Shanghai dish that became quite popular in Taiwan. It is not usually found in Cantonese house-holds, or in restaurants whose fare characterizes the kind of Chinese-American cooking we know in this country. The fleshy and robust pork shoulder is braised for hours, until it is meltingly tender. Ask your butcher for a piece with both the bone and rind on the meat. In Ming's family kitchen, a large piece was custom-arily cooked for six to eight hours. The resulting sauce is sweet rather than salty. Just before serving, they would cook either bok choy or Napa cabbage in the liquid and then serve the dish with plain white rice, making a nutritionally balanced and delicious family meal.*

*Ming Tsai enjoying hot pot with his brother*

*It is interesting that their original recipe called for white wine, a cooking ingredient that is unusual in Chinese cuisine. The traditional Shaoxing rice wine was until recently quite expensive and hard to obtain. However, here I have followed the Chinese method and used Shaoxing rice wine, which is indeed a wonderful ingredient.*

Serves 6–8

1 pork shoulder with rind and bone, about 6–8 pounds
5 whole star anise
5 whole Chinese cinnamon barks or cinnamon sticks
3 tablespoons cumin seeds
3 dried red chilies
4 pieces (approximately 1¹/₂ by 1¹/₂ inches) dried tangerine peel

## Sauce

4 cups Shaoxing rice wine or dry sherry
6 cups homemade chicken stock (page 60) or reduced-salt canned broth
2 cups dark soy sauce
¹/₂ cup light soy sauce
1 cup crushed Chinese rock sugar or ¹/₂ cup granulated sugar
10 slices fresh ginger, 2 inches by ¹/₈ inch
8 garlic cloves, peeled and crushed
6 whole scallions
1¹/₂ tablespoons salt
1 teaspoon freshly ground black pepper

## Garnish

2 pounds Napa cabbage

Bring a large pot of water to a boil, add the pork shoulder, and when it comes to a boil again, skim, reduce the heat, and simmer gently, partially covered, for 30 minutes. Drain thoroughly.

Place the star anise, cinnamon, cumin seeds, dried chilies, and tangerine peel in a piece of cheesecloth and tie together tightly. Then make the sauce, by combining all the sauce ingredients in a very large pot and bringing the liquid to a simmer. Add the spices tied in the cheesecloth.

Add the blanched pork shoulder and bring it back to a simmer, partially covered, skimming all the while. Now cover the pot tightly and continue to simmer gently for 3 hours, until the pork fat and rind are very soft and tender.

Cut the Napa cabbage into 2-inch chunks. When the pork is done, remove it to a warm platter. Add the cabbage to the pot and cook over high heat for 10 minutes, or until it is very tender. Remove the cabbage to a serving platter. Place the pork on top of the cabbage.

Skim off all the fat and reduce the liquid in the pot to a syrup. Serve with the pork.

# Lao Zhou's Lionhead Meatballs

*Ming Tsai's grandmother Lao Zhou made a delicious classic Chinese dish in which meatballs are braised with Napa cabbage. The result of long patient cooking, it is something that only a loving grandmother seems to have time to make.*

*But these classic Shanghai meatballs are easy to make. The little patience it requires is well rewarded. And the dish reheats nicely.*

Serves 4—6

1 pound Napa cabbage, stalks separated and cut into 2-inch strips
1/2 pound fresh or 6 ounces canned water chestnuts, peeled if fresh, coarsely chopped
1 pound fatty ground pork
1 egg white
4 tablespoons cold water
2 tablespoons light soy sauce
1 tablespoon dark soy sauce
2 tablespoons Shaoxing rice wine or dry sherry
1 1/2 tablespoons sugar

2 teaspoons salt

1/2 teaspoon freshly ground black pepper

Cornstarch, for dusting

3–4 tablespoons plus 2 teaspoons peanut oil

2 garlic cloves, peeled and crushed

2 cups homemade chicken stock (page 60) or reduced-salt
   canned broth

Prepare the Napa cabbage and water chestnuts. Put the pork in a food
processor and pulse with the egg white and cold water for 1 minute. The mixture should be light and fluffy. Do not use a blender, which would make it
too dense. Now add the water chestnuts, soy sauces, rice wine, sugar, salt, and
pepper and process for another 30 seconds, until just coarsely mixed.

Divide the mixture into 6 equal parts and roll each part into a large
meatball. Dust each meatball with cornstarch. Heat a wok until it is hot, then
swirl in the 3–4 tablespoons of oil. When the oil is hot and slightly smoking,
gently lay in the meatballs, turn the heat down, and slowly brown the meatballs all over. Remove the meatballs and set aside.

Clean the wok and reheat. When the wok is hot, swirl in the 2 teaspoons
of oil, then toss in the garlic cloves and stir-fry for 10 seconds. Add the Napa
cabbage and stir-fry for several minutes. Pour in the chicken stock and continue to cook for 2 minutes, until the cabbage leaves are soft. Transfer the
mixture to a heavy casserole and lay the meatballs on top. Bring the contents
of the casserole to a boil, then turn the heat to very low, cover, and simmer
for 1 1/2 hours.

Arrange the cabbage on a platter, lay the meatballs on top, spoon the
sauce over the dish, and serve at once.

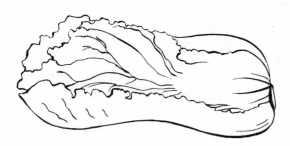

# Savory Pork with Pickled Vegetables

*Every other Saturday at our family restaurant in Chicago, one of the chefs would go down to the basement to fetch a fresh batch of pickled mustard greens, which were stored in large ceramic crocks until ready to use. A favorite recipe and a very popular dish among our patrons called for pickled mustard greens simply stir-fried with slices of pork.*

*Although the taste of raw pickled greens is intensely strong, they mellow with cooking and retain a nice crunchiness. They add a piquant touch to robust meat dishes.*

*One secret is to add a pinch of sugar to balance the tart flavors of the greens—your taste buds and experience will dictate just how much a "pinch" is. Pickled greens are now readily available at Chinese groceries.*

Serves 4

1 pound lean boneless pork chops

## Marinade

2 teaspoons light soy sauce
1 teaspoon Shaoxing rice wine or dry sherry
1 teaspoon sugar
2 teaspoons cornstarch
1 teaspoon Asian sesame oil

2½ tablespoons peanut oil
2 tablespoons finely sliced garlic
¾ cup sliced pickled mustard greens, rinsed (see recipe
    introduction)
2 tablespoons homemade chicken stock (page 60) or
    reduced-salt canned broth
1 tablespoon Shaoxing rice wine or dry sherry
1 tablespoon light soy sauce
2 teaspoons sugar
2 teaspoons Asian sesame oil

Cut the pork into slices 1 inch wide by ¼ inch thick. In a large bowl, mix the sliced meat with the marinade ingredients, let it sit at room temperature for 20 minutes, and drain.

Heat a wok or large frying pan over high heat until it is hot. Swirl in 1½ tablespoons peanut oil, and when it is very hot and slightly smoking, toss in the meat and stir-fry for 1 minute. Immediately remove with a slotted spoon and drain in a colander set in a bowl. Wipe the wok clean and reheat over high heat. Swirl in the remaining peanut oil, toss in the garlic, and stir-fry for 20 seconds. Toss in the pickled mustard greens and stir-fry for 1 minute. Pour in the chicken stock, rice wine, soy sauce, and sugar and continue to stir-fry for 30 seconds. Return the meat to the wok, and continue to stir-fry for 2 minutes. Finally, swirl in the sesame oil and stir twice. Ladle the meat and greens onto a platter and serve at once.

# Steamed Pork Loaf with Salted Duck Eggs

*This dish is well known to many of my fellow Chinese-Americans. It should become a favorite of all Americans, hyphenated or not. I am sure the recipe was first put together a long time ago in the kitchen of a South China peasant family and was the centerpiece of a celebratory feast. Meat loaf may be common on American tables, but in China both pork and duck eggs are rather expensive special treats, hardly the ordinary fare of even wealthy peasants.*

*Unlike our familiar meat loaf, this pork loaf is not baked but steamed with an array of exciting seasonings. In this recipe I follow my mother's customary use of salted duck eggs, which can be found at Chinese groceries. Preserved in brine, the egg yolks harden, and tempting flavors suffuse the whole egg. The eggs thus add much to the already zestful blend of robust pork and spices. The result is a pleasantly rich and aromatic dish that is a true centerpiece for any special meal. One needs only plain rice and a vegetable to make a complete, balanced, nutritious dinner.*

*Serves 2—4*

1 pound fatty ground pork
1 pound fresh water chestnuts, peeled and coarsely chopped
3 tablespoons finely chopped scallions
1 tablespoon light soy sauce
2 teaspoons Shaoxing rice wine or dry sherry
2 teaspoons salt
1 teaspoon sugar
2 teaspoons cornstarch
2 teaspoons Asian sesame oil
1/2 teaspoon freshly ground black pepper
2 salted duck eggs (see recipe introduction)

In a food processor, mix the pork with the water chestnuts until they are finely chopped. Scrape this mixture into a large stainless-steel bowl and toss in the scallions, then pour in the soy sauce and rice wine. Toss in the salt, sugar, cornstarch, sesame oil, and pepper. With your hands, mix well, then turn the meat onto a deep heatproof plate and shape it into a flat loaf. Crack open the duck eggs, discard the whites, and cut the yolks in half. Distribute the yolks over the top of the meat, pressing them into the loaf.

Set up a steamer by putting a rack inside a wok or deep pan. Fill it with about 2 inches of water. Bring the water to a boil, then reduce the heat to a low simmer. Gently set the platter with the loaf in the steamer, cover, and steam vigorously for 20 minutes, or until the pork is done.

Serve immediately.

# Steamed Pork Loaf with Salted Fish

*What goes around comes around. When I was growing up in Chicago many years ago, my mother used to serve salted fish regularly. It was nutritious and cheap. She often served it in this variation of steamed pork loaf. The inexpensive fish extended the pork loaf, as it were, while its briny spiciness added depth to the robust flavor of pork.*

*Because of the salted fish, the mixture stood up well even with our primitive refrigeration. To me, it tasted better served two days later.*

*The salted fish is available at Chinese groceries in dried form and in jars of oil. If you are using the dried salted fish, be sure to soak it in warm water for 20 minutes before chopping; the salted fish in oil does not need soaking—simply drain it.*

Serves 2–4

1 pound fatty ground pork
1 pound fresh water chestnuts, peeled, or 12 ounces canned, coarsely chopped
3 tablespoons finely chopped scallions
6 tablespoons finely chopped drained salted fish in oil or soaked dried fish (see recipe introduction)
1 tablespoon finely chopped fresh ginger
1 tablespoon light soy sauce
2 teaspoons Shaoxing rice wine or dry sherry
1 teaspoon salt
1 teaspoon sugar
2 teaspoons cornstarch
2 teaspoons Asian sesame oil
1/2 teaspoon freshly ground black pepper

In a food processor, mix the pork with the water chestnuts until they are finely chopped. Scrape this mixture into a large stainless-steel bowl and toss in the scallions, chopped fish, and ginger, then pour in the soy sauce and rice wine. Toss in salt, sugar, cornstarch, sesame oil, and pepper. Mix well with your hands. Turn the loaf onto a heatproof deep plate and form into a flat loaf shape. Set up a steamer by putting a rack inside a wok or deep pan. Fill it with about 2 inches of water. Bring the water to a boil, then reduce the heat to a low simmer. Gently set the platter with the loaf in the steamer, cover, and steam vigorously for 25 minutes, or until the pork is done.

Serve immediately.

# Steamed Pork Loaf with Chinese Sausages

*When my uncle made his Chinese sausages for home consumption,
he would always share them with us. My mother would stir-fry
them with vegetables, or mix the sausage meat with ground pork.
One result was this recipe, yet another variation of the popular
steamed pork loaf.*

*Chinese sausages are sweet and savory and are available at
Chinese groceries. This particular recipe was much loved by my
uncle, who was himself a very sweet man.*

Serves 2–4

1 pound fatty ground pork
6 Chinese pork sausages, chopped
1 pound peeled fresh water chestnuts or 12 ounces canned,
  coarsely chopped
3 tablespoons finely chopped scallions
1 tablespoon light soy sauce
2 teaspoons Shaoxing rice wine or dry sherry
2 teaspoons salt
1 teaspoon sugar
2 teaspoons cornstarch
2 teaspoons Asian sesame oil
1/2 teaspoon freshly ground black pepper

In a food processor, mix the pork with the sausages until they are finely
chopped, then add the water chestnuts and mix well. Throw this mixture into
a large stainless-steel bowl and toss in the scallions, then pour in the soy sauce
and rice wine. Toss in the salt, sugar, cornstarch, sesame oil, and pepper. Mix
well with your hands. Turn this onto a heatproof deep plate and form a flat
loaf shape.

Set up a steamer by putting a rack inside a wok or deep pan. Fill it with
about 2 inches of water. Bring the water to a boil, then reduce the heat to a
low simmer. Gently set the platter with the loaf in the steamer, cover, and
steam vigorously for 20 minutes, or until the pork is done.

Serve immediately.

# Sweet=and=Sour Pig's Feet

*The edge of Chicago's Chinatown, on the South Side, was heavily populated by African-Americans. Ethnically segregated as Chicago was, there was nonetheless a great deal of cross-cultural exchange. African-Americans shared the Chinese-American taste for pig's feet. They would often come to Chinatown to buy the treat fresh at Chinese groceries. "Soul food" knows no geographic or ethnic boundaries.*

*I remember the pungent aromas that used to emanate from my mother's kitchen when she made this absolutely delicious version of Sweet-and-Sour Pig's Feet. The unique texture of the skin would melt in my mouth, and I would spend minutes chewing on the delicate little bones, savoring every last bit of flavor.*

*This easy-to-make recipe reheats well and is an unusual way to enjoy an often neglected food.*

Serves 4

2 pounds large, meaty pig's feet, about 4 pieces
1 tablespoon peanut oil
1 tablespoon coarsely chopped fermented black beans
2 garlic cloves, coarsely chopped
1 cup black rice vinegar
2 cups water
1 cup Shaoxing rice wine or dry sherry
2 teaspoons light soy sauce
1 cup crushed rock sugar or ³/4 cup granulated sugar

Have your butcher trim the pig's feet and cut them in half. Blanch the pig's feet for 20 minutes in a large pot of boiling water. Drain well.

Heat a wok or large frying pan over high heat until it is hot. Swirl in the oil, and when it is very hot and slightly smoking, gently lower in the pig's feet, skin side down, and brown for a few minutes. Then toss in the black beans and garlic and continue to brown for another 2 minutes. Now pour in the rest of the ingredients and bring to a boil. Lower the heat, cover, and let simmer for 30 minutes, or until the meat is very tender. Serve at once, or allow it to cool and reheat when desired.

# Roast Pork Belly

*Pork is the "red meat" of Chinese cuisine, and is served to cele-
brate very special occasions. For example, before we would set off
to visit our ancestors' shrines close by the Buddhist temple—in
Chicago—my mother would send me to the local Chinese grocery
to pick up a piece of roast pig that would be part of our offering to
our ancestors. If I arrived early enough in the morning, I could
smell the still-warm pork's toastlike fragrance, which filled the
store. Occasionally, returning home with the prized pork, I would
succumb to temptation and break off a sliver of the crackling skin.
I still remember it as the most satisfying pork I have ever eaten.*

*Now, living far from Chinatown, I have duplicated this
childhood delicacy by roasting a piece of pork belly. It works quite
well and is easy to do. Your ancestors will be as pleased as I am
sure mine were. This delectable crispy treat is perfect with rice.*

Serves 4–6

3 pounds boneless pork belly, with rind (may be ordered
   from your butcher)
4 tablespoons kosher salt
2 tablespoons ground roasted Sichuan peppercorns
   (see page 72)
1½ tablespoons five-spice powder
2 teaspoons freshly ground black pepper
1 tablespoon sugar

Pierce the rind side of the pork with a sharp fork or knife tip until the
skin is covered with fine holes.

Insert a meat hook into the pork to secure it. Bring a pot of water to a
boil and, using a large ladle, pour the hot water over the rind side of the pork
several times. Set the pork belly aside.

Heat a wok until it is hot, then toss in the salt, peppercorns, five-spice
powder, black pepper, and sugar and stir-fry the mixture for 3 minutes, until
it is hot and well mixed. Allow the mixture to cool slightly. When it is cool
enough to handle, rub it on the flesh side of the pork.

Hang the meat to dry for 8 hours or overnight in a cool place or in front of a fan.

Preheat the oven to 450° F.

Place the pork on a rack, rind side up, in a roasting pan. Pour about 1 cup of water into the roasting pan. Roast for 15 minutes. Then reduce the heat to 250° F. and continue to roast for 1 hour. Turn the heat to 350° F. and cook for another hour. Finally, turn back up to 450° F. for 15 minutes. Remove the pork and allow it to cool. Then carve it into bite-size pieces, arrange on a platter, and serve.

# Easy Stir-Fried Pork with Scallions

*This is a basic stir-fried dish in the South Chinese tradition which my mother made when she felt lazy or was pressed for time. It literally took minutes to assemble and cook. Variations were endless: in the spring, she would add asparagus; in the summer, bitter melon, sometimes even cucumber. However, the one I remember best is this version, with just plain scallions. The key to success in this recipe is not to overcook the pork.*

*Serves 4*

1 pound boneless pork loin chops
1 tablespoon Shaoxing rice wine or dry sherry
1 tablespoon light soy sauce
2 teaspoons Asian sesame oil
1 teaspoon cornstarch
8 whole scallions
1 tablespoon peanut oil, plus 1 teaspoon if needed
1 teaspoon salt
1/2 teaspoon freshly ground black pepper
1 teaspoon sugar

Cut the pork into slices about 1/4 inch thick by 2 inches long. Put the sliced pork into a bowl and mix in the Shaoxing rice wine or dry sherry, soy sauce, sesame oil, and cornstarch. Let the mixture sit for 10 minutes so that the pork absorbs the flavors of the marinade. Cut the scallions on the diagonal into 2-inch lengths.

Heat a wok or frying pan to a very high heat. Swirl in the peanut oil, and when it is very hot and slightly smoking, add the pork slices and stir-fry them until they are lightly brown, about 1 minute. Remove the pork and quickly toss in the scallions, salt, pepper, and sugar. If it seems too dry, swirl in 1 more teaspoon of peanut oil. Continue to stir-fry the scallions for 30 seconds, then toss in the pork and stir-fry until the pork is cooked and slightly firm. This should take about 3 minutes. Remove the pork and arrange it on a warm serving platter. Pour any juices remaining in the wok over the pork and serve at once.

# Simple Stir=Fried Ground Pork

*This delicious, easy-to-prepare, and inexpensive dish uses ground pork. The preparation literally takes minutes. In this Chinese-American creation, iceberg lettuce is used as a vegetable, but you can easily substitute spinach, watercress, or Swiss chard. Any leafy vegetable in season will do.*

Serves 4

1½ tablespoons peanut oil
1 pound lean ground pork
½ pound (1 cup) shredded iceberg lettuce
2 tablespoons dark soy sauce
1 tablespoon Shaoxing rice wine or dry sherry
2 teaspoons Asian sesame oil
2 teaspoons sugar
3 tablespoons finely chopped scallions

Heat a wok or large frying pan until it is hot. Swirl in the peanut oil, and when it is very hot and slightly smoking, add the pork and stir-fry it for 2 minutes. Stir constantly to break up any lumps. Toss in the lettuce; pour in the soy sauce, rice wine, and sesame oil. Sprinkle in the sugar and continue to stir-fry for another 3 minutes, or until the pork is cooked. Toss in the scallions and give the mixture several good stirs. Serve at once.

# Jews and Chinese Food

It is well known that, in America, Jews prefer Chinese food above all other ethnic cuisines. As the comedian Jackie Mason put it: "Jewish civilization is six thousand years old; Chinese civilization is four thousand years old. So, where did Jews eat on Sunday night for two thousand years?"

The phenomenon is variously explained. My own view is that Jews are drawn to the cuisine because dairy products are rare. Thus, in a Chinese restaurant the observant Jew doesn't have to worry about the Jewish dietary prohibition against mixing meat and dairy products in the same meal. I know this is but a partial explanation, given how much shellfish and pork are used in Chinese cookery—both of which are also forbidden under Jewish law.

Mimi Sheraton, the food writer, facetiously speculates that the Chinese may be one of the lost tribes of Israel and that Jews sense this and can relax their strict dietary conventions when they enter a restaurant run by their lost compatriots. More prosaically, the historian Stanley Karnow thinks that Jewish-Americans, like all other Americans, consumed "exotic" dishes such as Chop Suey and Egg Foo Young without really knowing what they consisted of. Thus, whether the food was taboo or acceptable never arose. It tasted good, and "where ignorance is bliss . . ."

There are other factors beyond the culinary ones, of course. Chinese are potentially as racially or ethnically prejudiced as anyone else. After all, such pathologies have social-psychological, not genetic, roots. But, living as they did as newcomers and aliens, suffering deeply from racial prejudice, Chinese-Americans learned never to express their own prejudices and, in business, to treat all customers equally. It is no accident that the Chinese of the "diaspora" are known as "the Jews of Asia."

In short, Jews never experienced anti-Semitism in dealing with Chinese-Americans. Karnow recalls that, in his predominantly Jewish neighborhood in Brooklyn, Jews who would never have tolerated nonkosher meals at home flocked every Sunday evening to the local Chinese restaurant. The menu, he notes, translated "won ton" as "kreplach," a small dumpling similar in form to the wonton and, like it, served in soup. The only day the restaurant closed was on Yom Kippur. (As Karnow notes, the place would have closed during Ramadan had the clientele been Muslim.) It also helped that in those days Sunday was indeed "kept holy" by Christians and many restaurants were closed, so the Chinese restaurants had no real competition.

But the central fact is that Chinese food is popular universally, and that Chinese-American chefs readily adapted their style to the basic needs and demands of their American clientele of whatever ethnic or racial background, Jewish-Americans included.

In the great American ethnic and racial stew pot (definitely and happily not a "melting pot"), each cultural ingredient retains its own identity while contributing its own unique flavor to the special sauce we call American. Being savory, aromatic, and well seasoned is a hallmark of Chinese food, which may explain why it is popular among Jews—and everyone else. Eat in peace and concord, live in peace and concord, as one standard fortune cookie message puts it.

# Stir=Fried Beef with Broccoli

*Beef is an American favorite but, though the Chinese do eat meats, it has never been popular among us. Meats, in any case, are never the centerpiece of Chinese meals. A small quantity of meat or seafood serves to enliven and diversify the various dishes, which are dominated by vegetables and grains. In many Chinese dishes, vegetables overwhelm the meat.*

*This popular Chinese-American restaurant dish—beef with broccoli—illustrates the Chinese approach; it could as well be called "broccoli with beef." In America, however, rather more beef is used than would be customary in China.*

*The simple stir-fried dish is admirable for its freshness and completeness. Chinese-American chefs fairly quickly adopted the slightly sweet Western broccoli and paired it with the always popular American beef for a mouth-watering combination. Even George Bush would eat this broccoli.*

*Serves 4*

1 pound broccoli
1 pound flank steak
2 teaspoons light soy sauce
1 teaspoon Shaoxing rice wine or dry sherry
1 teaspoon Asian sesame oil
1/2 teaspoon baking soda
1 teaspoon cornstarch

3 tablespoons peanut oil
3 garlic cloves, peeled and lightly crushed
1 tablespoon fermented black beans
1/4 cup homemade chicken stock (page 60) or reduced-salt
  canned broth
1 tablespoon light soy sauce
2 teaspoons dark soy sauce
1 teaspoon Shaoxing rice wine or dry sherry
1 teaspoon sugar
3 tablespoons oyster sauce

Separate the broccoli florets, and peel and thinly slice the stems on the diagonal. Blanch the broccoli in a large pot of boiling salted water for 5 minutes. Drain, and plunge into cold water. Drain thoroughly.

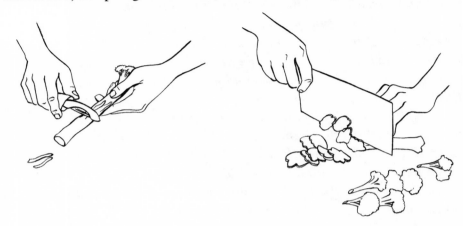

Cut steak in half lengthwise, then into thin slices, 2 inches wide by ¼ inch thick, cutting against the grain. Mix the beef with the light soy sauce, rice wine, sesame oil, baking soda, and cornstarch. Let sit for 20 minutes.

Heat a wok or deep pan until it is very hot. Swirl in the peanut oil, and when it is very hot and smoking, add the beef and stir-fry for 3 minutes. Remove the beef with a slotted spoon and drain off all but 1 tablespoon of oil.

Reheat the wok, toss in the garlic and black beans, and stir-fry for 1 minute. Then pour in the chicken stock, soy sauces, rice wine, and sugar and bring to a boil over a high heat. Dump in the broccoli and then the oyster sauce. Mix well, return the beef to the mixture, and continue to cook for another minute.

Transfer the contents to a large platter and serve at once.

# Traditional Pepper Beef

*This was among the most popular Chinese-American dishes served in the old-style restaurants. Its appeal was so great that even non-Chinese eating places featured it on their menus. I recall its being on the school cafeteria menu as well.*

*It is one of the few dishes that at once appealed to the American taste and yet followed the Cantonese Chinese preference for simple, clear, balanced dishes. The savory green sweet pepper pairs nicely with the hearty flavor of beef. A touch of oyster sauce, some onion slices, a clove or two of garlic, with rice on the side, and you had a delicious, well-balanced, complete meal. It was and is a very Chinese dish, except that in America the individual portions are much bigger!*

Serves 4

1 pound flank steak
2 teaspoons light soy sauce
1 teaspoon Shaoxing rice wine or dry sherry
1 teaspoon Asian sesame oil
1/2 teaspoon baking soda
1 teaspoon cornstarch

3 tablespoons peanut oil

3 garlic cloves, peeled and lightly crushed
1 red onion, thinly sliced
1 red pepper, seeded and cut into 1-inch pieces
1 green pepper, seeded and cut into 1-inch pieces
1 yellow pepper, seeded and cut into 1-inch pieces
1/2 cup homemade chicken stock (page 60) or reduced-salt
    canned broth
1 tablespoon Shaoxing rice wine or dry sherry
2 teaspoons light soy sauce
1 teaspoon sugar
1/2 teaspoon salt
1/4 teaspoon freshly ground black pepper
3 tablespoons oyster sauce
2 teaspoons Asian sesame oil

Cut steak in half lengthwise and then into thin slices, 2 inches wide by 1/4 inch thick, cutting against the grain. Mix the beef with the soy sauce, rice wine, sesame oil, baking soda, and cornstarch. Let it sit for 20 minutes.

Heat a wok or deep pan until it is very hot. Swirl in the peanut oil, and when it is very hot and smoking, add the beef and stir-fry for 3 minutes.

Remove the beef with a slotted spoon and drain off all but 1 tablespoon of oil.

Reheat the wok and oil, toss in the garlic and onions, and stir-fry for 3 minutes. Then toss in the peppers and add the chicken stock, rice wine, soy sauce, sugar, salt, and pepper and cook over high heat for 2 minutes. Pour in the oyster sauce and continue to cook for 2 minutes. Mix well, return the beef to the mixture, and continue to cook for another minute. Stir in the sesame oil, transfer the contents of the wok to a platter, and serve.

# Rich Braised Beef

*During my childhood, beef was rarely consumed by the Chinese-Americans in Chicago: in those days it was relatively expensive, and in any case the Chinese "red meat" is pork, compared with which beef has a strong flavor, too strong for most Chinese. However, cheaper cuts, such as oxtail, shank, or brisket, were both affordable and very popular among the Chinese. Not only was the price right, but, more important, these cuts could be infused with the spices that "naturalized" the beef and made it into a truly Chinese dish.*

*Star anise, cinnamon, cloves, and other powerful seasonings worked nicely with the strong flavor of beef. Dishes made this way could be prepared in advance and reheated with no loss of delectableness, an added bonus for homemakers who were often too tired to cook after a long day on the job.*

*My Chinese cousins in Oakland, California, prepare what I believe is the best version of this dish, better than anything I have experienced outside of Hong Kong. Their secret ingredient is fermented red bean curd (which can be found in Chinese markets), which gives the beef even more depth and flavor. This is my version of their recipe.*

*Serves 4*

3 pounds boneless beef shank or beef brisket
2 tablespoons peanut oil
4 slices ginger, 2 inches by ⅛ inch
4 garlic cloves, peeled and lightly crushed
4 scallions, cut into 3-inch segments
6 dried chilies, split in half
3 tablespoons fermented red bean curd (see recipe
    introduction)
3 tablespoons hoisin sauce
4 star anise

## Sauce

4 cups homemade chicken stock (page 60) or reduced-salt
    canned broth
3 tablespoons crushed Chinese rock sugar or granulated
    sugar
2 tablespoons light soy sauce
3 tablespoons dark soy sauce
¼ cup Shaoxing rice wine or dry sherry
1 teaspoon salt
½ teaspoon freshly ground black pepper

Cut the meat into 2-inch cubes and blanch them in a large pot of salted boiling water for 15 minutes. Remove the meat and drain well, discarding the water.

Heat a wok or large frying pan over high heat until it is hot. Swirl in the oil, and when it is very hot and slightly smoking, dump in the meat and stir-fry for 5 minutes, or until the meat is browned. Then toss in the ginger, garlic, scallions, and chilies and continue to stir-fry for 3 minutes. Now toss in the fermented bean curd and hoisin sauce, stirring to mix well, and the star anise. Pour in the sauce ingredients and bring the mixture to a boil. Lower the heat to a simmer, cover, and continue to cook for 2½ hours, or until the meat is tender.

Skim off any fat and serve. This dish can be made ahead of time; reheating is easy and actually improves the flavor.

# Chinese=American Food Today

Chinese cuisine is enjoying an extraordinary renaissance in America today. Because of changes in our immigration laws over the past twenty-five years, many more Chinese from every part of China have been allowed to enter the country. With them they have brought their own regional cuisines.

Remember that the vast majority of Chinese immigrants until 1965 came from one area in South China, the Guangxi-Guangdong (Canton) region. "Chinese-American" restaurants have hitherto almost always been Cantonese in cooking style, and all too often a bad parody of that style. Now restaurants in America specialize in all major and many minor regional cuisines.

*Chinese waitress showing American diners how to use chopsticks*

The four major regional styles of cooking may be grouped under the headings of South (Guangdong-Canton), East (e.g., Fujian, with Shanghai as a distinct minor regional style), West

(Sichuan, Yunnan, Hunan), and North (Beijing, Shanxi). But within these broad groupings there are many distinct subsets. Furthermore, when the communists took over in 1949, Hong Kong and Taiwan emerged as the centers of authentic Chinese cuisine, preserving and enhancing the glories of all regional styles.

Many authorities on Chinese cuisine believe that the South Chinese style, in particular the Cantonese, is the best of all, perhaps the best in the world. The scholar E. N. Anderson writes, "Cantonese cooking is unquestionably the one most often mentioned as the finest of all Chinese cuisines." He quotes an ancient Chinese proverb: "Live in Hangchow, marry in Suchou, dine in Canton, and die in Liuchou." (Those cities had, respectively, the most beautiful views, the loveliest women, the finest food, and the best coffin wood in the world.)

In much too brief a summary, Cantonese cooking can be characterized as subtle, fresh, understated, imaginative; Sichuan-Hunan cooking as hot and spicy; Northern or Beijing cooking as full-flavored and robust; Eastern-Shanghai cooking as sophisticated, complex, and cosmopolitan, incorporating elements from other regions and other parts of the world.

With these styles already well established in America, it is easy to find authentic dishes that were unavailable a generation ago: Shanghai specialties such as eels in sizzling oil with steamed bread; the very best Cantonese dim sum; spring rolls, shrimp dumplings, fried taro, steamed spareribs, steamed meat balls, and pork buns; or Cantonese steamed whole fish, sea bass especially, with ginger and scallions; Northern Mandarin-style Peking duck; Western-style crispy and spicy Sichuan beef; Northeastern-style dong so pork, a stew of pork steeped with vegetables that originated in the eleventh century to honor a Sung-dynasty poet.

These and countless other authentic dishes are available in the new "Chinese-American" restaurants. We have come a long way.

# My Mother's Savory Oxtail Stew

*This is among the most delicious dishes I remember from my child-hood. It remains one of my own standard home-cooked meals, and whenever I make it I am immediately transported back in time. My mother knew how to take cheap cuts of meat and coax every bit of flavor and texture from them. She infused oxtail stew with the most appropriate Chinese seasonings and spices, creating a succulent dish redolent of mouth-watering flavor and aroma. The stew has character enough to stand alone, and we usually enjoyed it simply with blanched lettuce leaves and rice.*

*Patience is required in making the stew. Oxtail is muscle meat and needs long, slow cooking to tenderize the tastiest part of the meat. The assertive seasonings balance the oxtail's strong beef flavor. This dish reheats nicely—it is perhaps even better the second day—and is perfect for a winter's evening.*

*Serves 4*

3 pounds oxtails
2 tablespoons peanut oil
1 cup coarsely chopped onions
6 garlic cloves, peeled and coarsely chopped
1 tablespoon salt
3 star anise
2 tablespoons hoisin sauce
2 tablespoons light soy sauce
1 tablespoon dark soy sauce
2 tablespoons Shaoxing rice wine or dry sherry
2 tablespoons Madras curry paste or powder
3 tablespoons crushed Chinese rock sugar or granulated
 sugar
2 teaspoons chili bean paste or sauce (see page 276)
1 teaspoon freshly ground black pepper
6 cups homemade chicken stock (page 60) or reduced-salt
 canned broth
1 pound potatoes, peeled and cut into eighths
1 pound carrots, peeled and roll-cut

### Garnish

1 head iceberg lettuce, leaves separated

Plunge the oxtails into salted boiling water and simmer them for 15 minutes. Remove them with a slotted spoon and drain well in a colander.

Heat a wok or large frying pan over high heat until it is hot. Swirl in the oil, and when it is very hot and slightly smoking, toss in the onions and garlic and stir-fry for 1 minute. Then dump in the oxtails and continue to stir-fry for 2 minutes. Toss in the salt, star anise, hoisin, soy sauces, rice wine, curry, sugar, chili bean paste, and pepper and continue to stir-fry for 2 minutes.

Transfer the contents of the wok to a large casserole and add the stock. Bring the mixture to a simmer and continue simmering gently for 20 minutes, uncovered, skimming frequently. Then cover tightly and continue to simmer for 3 hours. Check for doneness (the meat should literally come off of the bones) and skim off any excess fat from the surface.

Dump in the vegetables, cover, and continue to simmer gently for another 35 minutes, or until both the vegetables and oxtails are very tender.

Blanch iceberg lettuce leaves in a large pot of boiling salted water for 1 minute, just until they are barely wilted. Lay the lettuce on a large platter, ladle the oxtail stew over the leaves, and serve at once.

# Pickled Mustard Greens with Beef

*Talking with Chinese-American friends, I discovered commonality in our experiences of growing up with mothers who would make herbal medicinal wines and would sun-dry vegetables or, in my case, even chicken giblets. My mother prided herself also on pickling mustard greens that she would get at a bargain price when in season. In a large glass jar, she would combine the Chinese mustard greens with vinegar, sugar, and hot water, then hide the jar in a cool corner behind the sofa. The greens would be perfect in three months. Occasionally, when I yearned for a snack, I would sneak a bite. The sour shock would jolt my palate, a taste I can remember to this day. Her favorite method was to combine the pickled greens with beef in a simple stir-fry. Fortunately, one does not have to wait three months to experience this dish. You can easily buy freshly pickled mustard greens at Chinese groceries, either in a vacuum pack (the preferred method) or canned.*

Serves 4

1 pound flank steak
2 teaspoons light soy sauce
1½ teaspoons Shaoxing rice wine or dry sherry
1 teaspoon Asian sesame oil
1 teaspoon baking soda
1 teaspoon cornstarch

1¾ cups pickled mustard greens (see recipe introduction)

3 tablespoons peanut oil

3 garlic cloves, peeled and sliced
¼ cup homemade chicken stock (page 60) or reduced-salt
    canned broth
1 tablespoon light soy sauce
2 teaspoons dark soy sauce
2 teaspoons Shaoxing rice wine or dry sherry
2 teaspoons sugar

Cut steak in half lengthwise. Cut the beef into thin slices, 2 inches wide by ¼ inch thick, cutting against the grain. Mix the beef with the light soy sauce, rice wine, sesame oil, baking soda, and cornstarch. Let sit for 20 minutes.

Rinse the mustard greens well under cold running water. Drain thoroughly and slice them.

Heat a wok or deep pan until it is very hot. Pour in the peanut oil, and when it is very hot and smoking, add the beef and stir-fry for 3 minutes. Remove the beef with a slotted spoon and drain off all but 1 tablespoon of oil.

Reheat the wok and oil, add the garlic, and stir-fry for 30 seconds, then add the sliced mustard greens and stir-fry for 1 minute. Pour in the chicken stock, soy sauces, rice wine, and sugar and bring to a boil over high heat. Mix well, return the beef to the mixture, and continue to cook for another minute.

Transfer the contents of the wok to a large platter and serve at once.

# Stir-Fried Beef with Tomato and Egg

*My mother often made this quick and easy dish, using ingredients that were easily available and relatively inexpensive. Here she employed the inventive Chinese technique of combining seemingly disparate ingredients into a delectable blend. Although I don't know if the recipe is authentically Chinese, it certainly rests today deep in my taste memory. Mother often waited until I returned from school and then quickly stir-fried the ingredients together: savory, rich bits of beef with soft ripe tomatoes pulled together with strands of egg in a sauce.*

*Serves 4*

½ pound ground beef
2 teaspoons light soy sauce
1½ teaspoons Shaoxing rice wine or dry sherry
1 teaspoon Asian sesame oil
1 teaspoon cornstarch

4 beaten eggs
2 teaspoons Asian sesame oil
½ teaspoon salt

1½ tablespoons peanut oil
2 tablespoons finely chopped garlic
1 tablespoon finely chopped ginger
1 tablespoon coarsely chopped fermented black beans
3 tablespoons finely chopped scallions
1½ tablespoons light soy sauce
2 teaspoons dark soy sauce
1 tablespoon Shaoxing rice wine or dry sherry
1 teaspoon salt
1 teaspoon sugar
½ teaspoon freshly ground black pepper
¼ cup homemade chicken stock (page 60) or reduced-salt
   canned broth
3 medium-sized ripe tomatoes, quartered into wedges
2 teaspoons Asian sesame oil

Put the meat in a medium-sized bowl and mix it thoroughly with the light soy sauce, rice wine, sesame oil, and cornstarch. Set it aside and let it marinate for 15 minutes.

In a small bowl, lightly beat the eggs, then mix in the sesame oil and salt and set aside.

Heat a wok or large frying pan over high heat until it is hot. Swirl in the peanut oil, and when it is very hot and slightly smoking, quickly toss in the garlic, ginger, black beans, and scallions. Stir-fry this mixture for 30 seconds. Mix in the beef and continue to stir-fry, breaking up the meat, for 2 minutes, until it begins to lose its raw look. Pour in the soy sauces, rice wine, salt, sugar, and pepper. Give the mixture several good stirs, and then pour in the chicken stock. When the mixture comes to a boil, add the tomatoes. When it starts bubbling vigorously, drizzle in the egg mixture and stir it slowly. When the egg has set, pour in the sesame oil and give the mixture two more stirs.

Ladle the mixture into a bowl and serve at once.

# Classic Stir-Fried Beef with Oyster Sauce

*This was perhaps one of the most popular dishes served at our family restaurant. Oyster sauce made the mundane sliced beef appealingly exotic. Our patrons, of course, did not really know precisely what it was about oyster sauce that made it so appetizing and savory. Perhaps they thought is was a Chinese-American "surf and turf."*

*Oyster sauce is made from stewed oysters enlivened with various seasonings, such as garlic and chili, adding up to a taste that is meaty and not at all fishy. It goes extremely well with meats, especially beef. For many Americans, this dish was their first exposure to Chinese-American cuisine. When properly prepared and served, it always leads one satisfyingly deeper into authentic Chinese cookery.*

*Serves 4*

1 pound market or rib eye steak
1 tablespoon light soy sauce
2 teaspoons Shaoxing rice wine or dry sherry
2 teaspoons Asian sesame oil
2 teaspoons cornstarch

3 tablespoons peanut oil
3 garlic cloves, peeled and lightly crushed
2 medium-sized onions, sliced
1/4 cup homemade chicken stock (page 60) or reduced-salt canned broth
1 teaspoon Shaoxing rice wine or dry sherry
1 teaspoon sugar
3 tablespoons oyster sauce

Cut steak in half lengthwise, then into thin slices, 2 inches wide by ¼ inch thick, cutting against the grain. Mix the beef with the soy sauce, rice wine, sesame oil, and cornstarch. Let sit for 20 minutes.

Heat a wok or deep pan until it is very hot. Swirl in the peanut oil, and when it is very hot and smoking, add the beef and stir-fry for 3 minutes. Remove the beef with a slotted spoon and drain off all but 1 tablespoon of oil.

Reheat the wok, toss in the garlic and onions, and stir-fry for 3 minutes, or until the onions are wilted and lightly browned. Then pour in the chicken stock, rice wine, and sugar and bring to a boil over high heat. Pour in the oyster sauce. Mix well, return the beef to the wok, and continue to cook for another minute.

Transfer the contents to a large platter and serve at once.

Variation: This classic beef stir-fried dish could easily have asparagus, mushrooms, cucumbers, julienned zucchini, carrot batons, leeks, peas, or spinach added to it.

# The Tsai Family's Mongolian Beef

*Although I suspect that this recipe has little to do with Mongolian cooking—or with authentic Chinese cuisine, for that matter—it nevertheless appeared under this title in the Tsai family's Chinese-American restaurant. Ethnic Chinese know full well how different they are in so many ways from Mongolians—after all, the Mongols invaded and conquered the Chinese. But I am sure that the exotic name was invented to entice Americans to order this simple but delicious stir-fried beef dish.*

*The recipe illustrates the resourcefulness and good business sense of Chinese-American cooks, who are quick to adopt and adapt locally available foods and popular ingredients and use them to make very satisfying meals that beguile non-Chinese palates.*

Serves 4–6

1 pound finely shredded cabbage
1 tablespoon salt
1 pound lean ground beef
1 tablespoon Shaoxing rice wine or dry sherry
1 tablespoon light soy sauce
2 teaspoons Asian sesame oil
1/2 teaspoon freshly ground black pepper
1 tablespoon coarsely chopped garlic
2 teaspoons finely chopped ginger
2 teaspoons cornstarch

1 1/2 tablespoons peanut oil
1 1/2 tablespoons coarsely chopped garlic
2 tablespoons finely chopped shallots
2 medium-sized carrots, finely shredded
1 large red or green pepper, seeded and finely shredded
5 scallions, finely shredded

2 tablespoons hoisin sauce
3 tablespoons oyster sauce
1/2 teaspoon salt
1/4 teaspoon freshly ground black pepper
2 tablespoons Shaoxing rice wine or dry sherry

Put the cabbage and salt in a large bowl of cold water and let it sit for 1 hour. Then rinse and drain thoroughly.

Toss the ground beef in a bowl with the Shaoxing rice wine or dry sherry, soy sauce, sesame oil, pepper, garlic, ginger, and cornstarch, mix well, and let it marinate for about 20 minutes.

Heat a wok or large frying pan over high heat until it is hot. Swirl in the peanut oil, and when it is very hot and slightly smoking, dump in the garlic and shallots and stir-fry for 30 seconds. Then toss in the marinated beef and continue to stir-fry for 2 minutes, breaking up the meat. Now throw in the rest of the vegetables and continue to stir-fry until they have wilted, about 5 minutes. Pour in the hoisin sauce and oyster sauce, sprinkle on the salt and pepper, and continue to stir-fry over high heat for 3 minutes more. Then pour in the rice wine to finish glazing the dish.

Serve at once.

# Northern-Style Lamb with Garlic

*A Chinese poet once wrote, "There are seventy-two ways of cooking lamb; of these only eighteen or nineteen are palatable." These sentiments were widely shared by my family. Childhood memories of growing up at the Chinese-American table were notable for the absence of lamb. It is something we never ate. I discovered lamb when I ventured out into the American world and when I became friends with Chinese-Americans from Taiwan or North China. American lamb is especially delicious when it is stir-fried. This way of preparing it, with a lot of garlic and scallions to balance the lamb's robust flavor, is a popular one with Chinese.*

Serves 4

1 pound boneless loin or lean lamb chops
1 tablespoon Shaoxing rice wine or dry sherry
2 teaspoons dark soy sauce
1 teaspoon light soy sauce
2 teaspoons Asian sesame oil
2 teaspoons cornstarch
2 tablespoons peanut oil
6 tablespoons finely shredded scallions
6 garlic cloves, peeled and thinly sliced
2 teaspoons finely chopped fresh ginger
1 teaspoon ground roasted Sichuan peppercorns
   (see page 72)

Cut the lamb into thin slices 2 inches long by ¼ inch wide. Put the lamb in a bowl with the Shaoxing rice wine, soy sauces, sesame oil, and cornstarch. Let it stand for 20 minutes.

Heat a wok or large frying pan until it is hot. Add the peanut oil, and when the oil is very hot and slightly smoking, add the lamb and stir-fry for 2 minutes. Remove the lamb with a slotted spoon to a colander set in a bowl to drain. Reheat the wok, toss in the scallions, garlic, and ginger, and continue to stir-fry for another 4 minutes. Return the lamb to the wok and stir a few times to heat thoroughly. Sprinkle on the peppercorns and serve immediately.

# RICE and NOODLES

Familiar Beef and Tomato Lo Mein

Kai-Kai Coffee Shop's Barbecued Pork Chow Fun

Traditional Chow Mein

Steamed Rice

Tasty Pork Fried Rice

Savory Beef Chow Fun with Black Bean Sauce

East-West Spaghetti and Meatballs

Guo Bu Li's Hot Bean Sauce Noodles

The Tsai Family's Scallion Cakes

Soothing Rice Porridge

Mrs. Wing's Simple Stir-Fried Bean Thread Noodles

Subgum Chow Mein

Cantonese-Style Chow Mein

My Mother's Home-Style Savory Rice

Turkey "Shee Fan"

Savory Bean Thread Noodles

Tasty Vegetarian New Year Noodles

Heritage Chicken-Rice Casserole

Comforting Rice with Chinese Sausage

# Familiar Beef and Tomato Lo Mein

*"Mein" is Cantonese for "noodles," an everyday food eaten in South China. However, in America it has been transformed into a typical "Chinese-American" combination. In China itself beef is rarely eaten, and tomatoes were not a staple in Chinese cuisine until one hundred years ago. In America both foods are widely popular, and Cantonese restaurants, always alert to what the customers want, happily obliged by haphazardly mixing together much bigger portions than any Chinese would expect. The dish became a standard on the menu of every Chinese-American restaurant. Beef, tomatoes, and noodles are a wonderful com-bination, but they must be cooked properly to bring out their virtues. Frequently, the restaurant versions are greasy and over-cooked. I offer here a recipe that captures the best qualities of these enduringly popular and nutritious foods.*

*Serves 4*

1 pound flank steak
2 teaspoons light soy sauce
1 teaspoon Shaoxing rice wine or dry sherry
1 teaspoon Asian sesame oil
$1/2$ teaspoon baking soda
$1/2$ teaspoon salt
$1/4$ teaspoon freshly ground black pepper
1 teaspoon cornstarch

3 tablespoons peanut oil

3 garlic cloves, peeled and lightly crushed
$1/4$ cup homemade chicken stock (page 60) or reduced-salt
   canned broth
1 tablespoon light soy sauce
2 teaspoons Shaoxing rice wine or dry sherry
2 teaspoons sugar
3 tablespoons oyster sauce
3 medium-sized fresh tomatoes, cut into quarters

4 scallions, cut diagonally into 3-inch segments
3/4 pound fresh or dry Chinese noodles, blanched for
    2 minutes

Cut steak in half lengthwise. Cut the beef into thin slices, 2 inches wide by 1/4 inch thick, cutting against the grain. Mix the beef with the soy sauce, rice wine, sesame oil, baking soda, salt, pepper, and cornstarch. Let it sit for 20 minutes.

Heat a wok or deep pan until it is very hot. Swirl in the peanut oil, and when it is very hot and smoking, toss in the beef and stir-fry for 3 minutes. Remove the beef with a slotted spoon and drain off all but 1 tablespoon of oil.

Reheat the wok, toss in the garlic, and stir-fry for 1 minute. Then add the chicken stock, soy sauce, rice wine, sugar, and oyster sauce and bring the mixture to a boil over high heat. Dump in the tomatoes and the scallions. Now toss in the noodles, mix well, and cook for 2 minutes. Return the beef to the mixture and continue to cook for another minute.

Transfer the contents of the wok to a large platter and serve at once.

# Kai=Kai Coffee Shop's Barbecued Pork Chow Fun

*On hot humid evenings in Chicago, when my mother was too tired to cook, she would send me out to one of our local Chinese restaurants for a "take-home" meal. Our favorite place was the Kai-Kai, a small diner that specialized in Chinese-American standards but also prepared popular Chinese quick and easy dishes for those who knew what to order. The Kai-Kai's range of authentic Chinese foods was limited, but what they did they did well. We loved their barbecue. Actually, it was in my uncle's kitchen that the barbecue meats were roasted for the take-out service. The Kai-Kai Coffee Shop would then stir-fry the meat with soft, billowy fresh rice noodles. The outside of the meat was slightly crusty and crunchy, the inside tender and succulent. The combination of fresh Chinese bok choy, slices of barbecued pork, and rice noodles was delicious—comfort food at its best.*

Serves 4

1 pound pork shoulder

## Marinade

1½ teaspoons salt
1 teaspoon freshly ground black pepper
1 teaspoon five-spice powder
2 tablespoons light soy sauce
2 teaspoons Shaoxing rice wine or dry sherry
1 tablespoon hoisin sauce
1 tablespoon bean sauce (see page 276)
3 tablespoons sugar

3 tablespoons honey

1 pound bok choy or spinach
1½ tablespoons peanut oil
3 garlic cloves, peeled and crushed
1 teaspoon salt
1 pound fresh rice noodles*
½ cup homemade chicken stock (page 60) or
    reduced-salt canned broth
3 tablespoons oyster sauce

* Available from Chinese groceries or supermarkets.

Cut the pork shoulder into 3 strips. With a cleaver or sharp knife, make diagonal incisions into the meat without cutting through, about ⅛ inch deep, at intervals of 1 inch. This will allow the marinade to penetrate the meat. Rub the meat evenly with the salt, pepper, and five-spice powder, then toss in the rest of the marinade ingredients and mix well. Let it marinate in a cool place for several hours, or refrigerate overnight.

The next day, preheat the oven to 400° F.

Lay the pork on a wire rack in a shallow baking tray filled with ½ cup of water. Baste the pork with the marinade and roast for 30 minutes. Then baste the pork with honey and any leftover marinade, turn the temperature down to 325° F., and continue to roast for 25 minutes, or until the pork is cooked. Allow the pork to cool thoroughly. Cut into thin slices and set aside.

Trim the bok choy. Remove the stalks and cut them into 2-inch segments. Peel the stems and diagonally slice them. Wash well in several rinses of cold water. Blanch the bok choy in a large pot of boiling salted water for 1 minute, until it is slightly wilted. Remove and drain well.

Heat a wok or large frying pan over high heat until it is hot. Swirl in the oil, and when it is very hot and slightly smoking, add the garlic and salt and stir-fry for 10 seconds. Then add the rice noodles and stir-fry for 2 minutes, until they begin to brown slightly. Add the pork and bok choy and continue to stir-fry for 3 minutes. Finally, add the stock and oyster sauce and mix well. Transfer the mixture to a large platter and serve at once.

# Traditional Chow Mein

*Most Americans knew but two Chinese words: "chop suey" and "chow mein." Until very recently, these two foods sufficed to satisfy the interest in Chinese cookery. As I have indicated, this is no longer the case. However, chow mein and chop suey remain very prominent on the menus of hotel restaurants in certain areas of the country, cruise-ship restaurants, school cafeterias, and every inexpensive Chinese-American restaurant. They are even available commercially in the frozen-food section of the supermarket.*

*I am ambivalent about this promotion of second-rate dishes. Chow mein, literally meaning "stir-fried noodles," is popular in China, too. When the noodles are combined with meats, poultry, or seafood, and whatever vegetables may be in season, the dish provides a nutritious meal, balanced in tastes, textures, and colors. It is most popular in South China, and is a standard offering of street food stalls, cafés, and noodle shops. No dim-sum luncheon is complete without it.*

*In the American version, the noodles are deep-fried in*

*advance into crispy morsels, which are then allowed to dry. The simmering sauce, with whatever added meat and vegetables, is ladled over the noodles. This version bypasses the stir-frying stage, so that the dish can be served immediately. The first Chinese restaurateurs quickly learned that most Americans don't like to wait for their food, nor do they dawdle over it in conversation. The pioneer Chinese could not believe that, given a choice, people would actually eat that way, but, again, the customer is always right.*

*These early cooks did not mind tinkering with the authentic version of chow mein as long as the real thing remained available on the "secret menu." Here I offer two versions, the traditional stir-fried dish, and an updated version of the "classic" Chinese-American restaurant dish.*

# Traditional Chinese Stir-Fried Noodles

Serves 4

1/2 cup Chinese dried black mushrooms
3/4 pound boneless, skinless chicken breasts, cut into
  thin shreds
1 egg white
1/2 teaspoon salt
1/8 teaspoon freshly ground white pepper
1 teaspoon cornstarch

1 cup peanut oil, or 2 cups water (see variation) and
  2 tablespoons peanut oil
1 pound fresh thin Chinese egg noodles
3 scallions, finely shredded on the diagonal
1 tablespoon Shaoxing rice wine or dry sherry
2 tablespoons light soy sauce
2 tablespoons dark soy sauce
1 teaspoon salt
1/2 teaspoon freshly ground black pepper
2 tablespoons oyster sauce

Soak the mushrooms in warm water for 20 minutes. Then drain them and squeeze out the excess liquid. Remove and discard the stems, and finely shred the caps into thin strips.

In a small bowl, mix the chicken with the egg white, salt, pepper, and cornstarch and refrigerate for at least 20 minutes.

Heat a wok until it is very hot, and then swirl in the oil. When the oil is very hot, remove the wok from the heat and immediately add the chicken pieces, stirring vigorously to keep them from sticking. When the chicken pieces turn white, in about 2 minutes, quickly drain the chicken and all of the oil in a stainless-steel colander set in a bowl. Discard all the oil except 2 tablespoons.

Blanch the noodles in a large pot of salted boiling water for 3 minutes. Drain the noodles well and set aside.

Reheat the wok and the oil. (If you were using the water method, add 2 tablespoons of peanut oil.) Toss in the noodles, mushrooms, and scallions and pan-fry for 3 minutes. Then dump in the chicken, rice wine, soy sauces, salt, and pepper and continue to stir-fry for another 2 minutes. Pour in the oyster sauce and stir-fry for another 2 minutes. Place noodles on a platter and serve at once.

Variation: If you choose to use water instead of oil, bring it to a boil in a saucepan. Remove the saucepan from the heat and immediately add the chicken pieces, stirring vigorously to keep them from sticking. When the chicken pieces turn white, in about 2 minutes, quickly drain the chicken and all of the water in a stainless-steel colander set in a bowl. Discard the water.

# The Chinese=American Version    Serves 4

*This version tends to have more ingredients than the Chinese version.*

1/2 pound boneless, skinless chicken thighs, cut into shreds lengthwise
1 teaspoon light soy sauce
1 teaspoon Shaoxing rice wine or dry sherry
1/4 teaspoon salt
1/4 teaspoon freshly ground black pepper
1/2 teaspoon Asian sesame oil
1/2 teaspoon cornstarch
1/2 cup Chinese dried black mushrooms

3/4 pound fresh thin Chinese egg noodles
2 cups peanut oil
3 cloves garlic, thinly sliced
1/2 cup chopped celery
1/4 pound fresh water chestnuts, peeled and sliced, or
    4 canned water chestnuts, sliced
1/4 pound snow peas, trimmed
2 scallions, cut into 2-inch segments on the diagonal
1 tablespoon light soy sauce
2 teaspoons Shaoxing rice wine or dry sherry
1 teaspoon salt
1/2 teaspoon freshly ground black pepper
1 teaspoon sugar
1/2 cup homemade chicken stock (page 60) or
    reduced-salt canned broth
3 tablespoons oyster sauce
2 teaspoons cornstarch mixed with 1 tablespoon water
2 teaspoons Asian sesame oil

Mix the chicken with soy sauce, rice wine, salt, pepper, sesame oil, and cornstarch and let marinate for at least 20 minutes at room temperature.

Soak the mushrooms in warm water for 20 minutes. Then drain them and squeeze out the excess liquid. Remove and discard the stems, and finely shred the caps into thin strips.

Blanch the noodles in a pot of salted boiling water. Drain well, and separate the noodles on a tray to cool.

Heat a wok or large frying pan over high heat until it is hot. Swirl in the peanut oil, and when it is very hot and slightly smoking, deep-fry the noodles until they are brown and crispy. Remove with a slotted spoon and drain well on paper towels. Pour off all but 2 tablespoons of the oil.

Transfer the fried noodles to a large platter.

Reheat the wok with the oil, and when it is hot, add the garlic and stir-fry for 10 seconds. Dump in the chicken and stir-fry for another 2 minutes. Then toss in the celery, mushrooms, water chestnuts, snow peas, and scallions and stir-fry for 1 minute. Pour in the soy sauce, rice wine, salt, pepper, sugar, chicken stock, and oyster sauce. Bring the mixture to a simmer and cook for another minute. In a slow drizzle, add the cornstarch mixture, stirring all the while. When the sauce has slightly thickened, stir in the sesame oil. Pour this mixture over the noodles and serve at once.

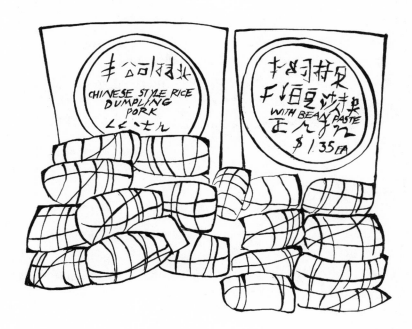

# Cooking Rice the Chinese Way

Steaming rice the Chinese way is simple, direct, and efficient. Although long-grain white rice is most often used, short-grain rice is also used on occasion.

The secret of preparing rice so that it is not sticky is to cook it first in an uncovered pot over high heat until most of the water has evaporated. Then the heat should be turned very low, the pot covered, and the rice cooked slowly in the remaining steam. As a child, I was instructed never to peek into the rice pot during this stage, or else precious steam would escape and the rice would not be cooked properly, thus bringing bad luck.

Here is a good trick that I learned from my mother: if you make sure to cover the rice with about an inch of water, it should always cook properly without sticking. Many box-top recipes for cooking rice call for too much water and result in a gluey mess. Cook it my mother's way and you will have perfect steamed rice, keeping in mind the following points:

◆ The water should be an inch above the surface of the rice; too much water will result in gummy rice.

◆ Never uncover the pot once the final simmering has begun; time the cooking and wait.

◆ Follow the directions for Steamed Rice and you are on your way to perfect rice.

# Fried Rice

Here are a few important points to remember when making authentic fried rice.

◆ The cooked rice should be thoroughly cool, preferably cold. Once it is cooled, much of the moisture in the rice evaporates, allowing the oil to coat the dry grains and keep them from

sticking. Store the cooked rice in the refrigerator until y~~~
ready to use it.

◆ Never put soy sauce in fried rice. This not only colors
the rice unnaturally but makes it too salty. Any moisture will make
the rice gummy. Fried rice should be quite dry.

◆ Always be sure the oil is hot enough to avoid saturating
the rice. Saturated rice is greasy and heavy. The finished fried rice
should have a wonderful smoky taste and flavor.

# Steamed Rice

Serves 4

1½ cups long-grain white rice
2½ cups water

Put the rice in a large bowl and wash it in several changes of water until
the water becomes clear. Drain the rice, put it in a heavy pot with the water,
and bring it to a boil. Continue boiling until most of the surface liquid has
evaporated, about 15 minutes. The surface of the rice should have small indentations, like a pitted crater. At this point, cover the pot with a very tight-
fitting lid, turn the heat as low as possible, and let the rice cook undisturbed
for 15 minutes. There is no need to "fluff" the rice; just let it rest for 5 minutes before serving it.

To make a smaller amount: Follow the directions above,
simply cutting the amount of rice to ¾ cup and the water to
1¼ cups.

# Tasty Pork Fried Rice

*Pork fried rice is another staple of Chinese-American restaurants, though it is rarely found in Chinese-American homes. As a combination of bits of marinated pork, stir-fried in a mixture of rice, eggs, and scallions, the dish has great appeal.*

*However, the Chinese-American restaurant version developed differently than the traditional Chinese version, in response to American preferences. That is, plenty of soy sauce was ladled over everything, including the rice—not something a Chinese would ever do. Even today, Americans generally prefer food on the salty side, and traditional soy sauce is quite salty. Chinese use soy sauce sparingly, so as to allow the original tastes of the various foods to come through. And never would it be poured on top of rice or used in fried rice, especially when one wants the clean, mild taste of rice made subtly smoky as it is stir-fried in the wok. In the Chinese recipe, therefore, soy sauce is avoided. We used to joke about this in the kitchen of my uncle's restaurant.*

*Another variation had to do with the proportion of pork to rice. For a number of reasons (including relative scarcity), Chinese cookery uses meat more as an additive, or flavoring, or contrast, than as a centerpiece. In bountiful America, however, we are accustomed to plenty of meat. After many complaints from American patrons, therefore, the amount of pork in proportion to the rice was tripled. I should note that the amount of rice was also increased, to satisfy the American appetite and customary expectations.*

*Here is my modern version of the Chinese-American staple, without all the soy sauce and with a more balanced portion of meat and rice.*

Serves 4

3 cups cold cooked long-grain rice

1/2 pound pork shoulder
2 teaspoons light soy sauce
1 teaspoon Shaoxing rice wine or dry sherry

1 teaspoon Asian sesame oil
1/2 teaspoon salt
1 teaspoon baking soda
1 teaspoon cornstarch

3 eggs
1 teaspoon Asian sesame oil
1 teaspoon salt

3 tablespoons peanut oil
3 tablespoons finely chopped scallions
1 cup shredded iceberg lettuce
1 cup bean sprouts
2 teaspoons salt
1/2 teaspoon freshly ground black
    pepper

Keep the rice in the refrigerator until you are ready to cook the fried rice.

Cut the pork into strips 1 inch long by 1/8 inch thick. Mix the pork with the soy sauce, rice wine, sesame oil, salt, baking soda, and cornstarch. In a small bowl, beat the eggs with the sesame oil and salt and set aside.

Heat a wok or deep frying pan until it is very hot. Swirl in 1 tablespoon of peanut oil, and when it is hot, toss in the pork and stir-fry for 1 minute. Remove the pork with a slotted spoon. Swirl in the remaining 2 tablespoons of oil, and when it is hot, pour in the egg and quickly stir-fry for 1 minute. Dump in the cold rice and stir-fry for 5 minutes over high heat. Finally, add the scallions, lettuce, bean sprouts, and the partially cooked pork. Continue to stir-fry for another 2 minutes. Salt and pepper to taste.

Turn the mixture onto a platter and serve at once.

# Savory Beef Chow Fun
# with Black Bean Sauce

*While the American diners ordered pork fried rice, chop suey, and chow mein to go, we Chinese-Americans preferred such dishes as this one, made with generous portions of soft rice noodles stir-fried with bits of beef in a black bean sauce. This "take-home" dish was one of our family's favorites, and is in fact a traditional and very popular South Chinese noodle classic. We would order it from a restaurant because, although we could cook this at home, a large quantity was hard to master in a home wok. We usually ordered two or three boxes, and the rice noodles were always smoky and fragrant. I always had the dubious task of calling in the order; my mother stood by my side to make sure I insisted on the very freshest noodles, and I would have to ask when the noodles were made, how long had they been sitting in the kitchen. The pungent aroma of black beans, the sauce redolent with garlic and ginger, the heartiness of the dish made for a very satisfying meal. I remember that my mother preferred this dish during a break in the mah-jongg games she played at home with her friends.*

*Serves 4*

1 pound flank steak
2 teaspoons light soy sauce
1 teaspoon Shaoxing rice wine or dry sherry
1 teaspoon Asian sesame oil
1/2 teaspoon baking soda
1 teaspoon cornstarch

3 tablespoons peanut oil

2 tablespoons finely chopped garlic
2 tablespoons fermented black beans
1 tablespoon finely chopped ginger
3 tablespoons finely chopped scallions
1 onion, finely sliced
1 tablespoon Shaoxing rice wine or dry sherry

2 teaspoons light soy sauce

2 teaspoons dark soy sauce

1/2 cup homemade chicken stock (page 60) or reduced-salt
   canned broth

1/2 pound separated fresh rice noodles*

2 tablespoons oyster sauce

* Available at Chinese groceries and supermarkets.

Cut the beef into thin slices, cutting against the grain. Mix the beef with the light soy sauce, rice wine, sesame oil, baking soda, and cornstarch. Let sit for 20 minutes.

Heat a wok or deep pan until it is very hot. Swirl in the peanut oil, and when it is very hot and smoking, quickly toss in the beef and stir-fry for 3 minutes. Remove the beef with a slotted spoon and drain off all but 1 1/2 tablespoons of oil.

Reheat the wok and oil. Toss in the garlic, black beans, ginger, scallions, and onion and stir-fry for 1 minute. Pour in the rice wine, soy sauces, and chicken stock and continue to cook for 3 minutes. Then add the rice noodles and stir-fry for 3 minutes. Finally, spoon in the oyster sauce. Mix well, return the beef to the mixture, and continue to cook for another minute.

Turn the mixture onto a large platter and serve at once.

# East=West Spaghetti and Meatballs

*That is not what my mother called this dish, of course. But she made the best-tasting version of spaghetti and meatballs I have ever enjoyed. I did not know what her recipe was until I first tasted the famous Shanghai dish called Lionhead Meatballs. Then I realized that she had simply substituted readily available American ingredients and blended things together perfectly. For example, she used beef instead of the original pork and mixed the traditional fresh water chestnuts, ginger, scallions, and onion into a spicy tomato sauce. She also used Italian pasta: a true Chinese-American-Italian creation. The Chinese have many forms of pasta, but the Italian semolina–durum wheat blends, which are not readily available in China, make the very best pastas. And, in true Italian fashion, my mother never overcooked her pasta, thus preserving its firmness and its clean, delicate, nut-like flavor. Paired with her East-West-Shanghai–inspired meatballs, this is a meal fit for pasta lovers of Chinese-Italian-American or any other ethnic mix.*

Serves 4

## Tomato Sauce

1 1/2 tablespoons olive oil
1 cup chopped red onions
4 garlic cloves, peeled and crushed
2 teaspoons finely chopped ginger
4 cups canned crushed tomatoes
2 teaspoons sugar
1 teaspoon salt
1/2 teaspoon freshly ground black pepper

## Meatballs

1 pound ground beef
1 egg white
2 tablespoons cold water
1/2 pound fresh water chestnuts, peeled and coarsely
    chopped, or 6 ounces canned, chopped
2 tablespoons light soy sauce
1 tablespoon dark soy sauce
2 tablespoons Shaoxing rice wine or dry sherry
1 teaspoon five-spice powder
2 teaspoons sugar
2 teaspoons salt
1/2 teaspoon freshly ground black pepper
Potato starch, for dusting
4 tablespoons peanut oil

1 pound Italian spaghetti

Heat a heavy saucepan and swirl in the olive oil. When it is hot, toss in the onions, garlic, and ginger and cook for 2 minutes over medium heat.

Then dump in the tomatoes, sugar, salt, and pepper, lower the heat, cover, simmer for 20 minutes, and set aside.

Put the beef in a food processor and mix with the egg white and cold water for 1 minute. The mixture should be light and fluffy. Do not use a blender, which would make the mixture too dense. Then toss in the water chestnuts, soy sauces, rice wine, five-spice powder, sugar, salt, and pepper and mix for another 30 seconds. The mixture should be slightly coarse, with bits of the water chestnuts adding texture.

Divide the mixture into 16 equal parts and roll each part into a large meatball. Dust each meatball with the potato starch. Heat a wok until it is hot, then swirl in 2 tablespoons of peanut oil. When the oil is hot and slightly smoking, drop in half of the meatballs, turn the heat down, and slowly brown the meatballs. Swirl in the additional 2 tablespoons of oil and fry the remaining meatballs. Drain them on paper towels.

Place the meatballs in the cooked tomato sauce, cover, and simmer for 15 minutes.

Meanwhile, cook the pasta according to the package instructions or according to your taste and drain well.

Arrange the pasta on a platter, lay the meatballs on top, pour the sauce over the dish, and serve at once.

# Guo Bu Li's Hot Bean Sauce Noodles

*The nature and scope of Chinese cooking available to Americans in restaurants were radically transformed during the 1970s and 1980s. The relaxing of American immigration laws allowed for increased emigration from all parts of China, especially Hong Kong and Taiwan. These newcomers brought with them their various regional cooking styles and preferences, which in many ways are quite different from the Chinese-American-Cantonese ways of doing things. And they are certainly different from the accommodating "Chinese-American" style that most Americans were familiar with. Spicy foods, rich braised soy sauce dishes,*

237

*aromatic rice wine sauces, chili pastes, and new techniques are but some of the innovations. Americans can now find Sichuan, Fukien, Hunan, and Beijing restaurants along with the familiar Cantonese establishments. A very happy result of this movement is that the Cantonese restaurants are now preparing the great authentic dishes of the classical Cantonese canon and demonstrating why in China itself Cantonese cooking has for centuries been accorded pride of place.*

*One non-Cantonese newcomer is the Guo Bu Li restaurant, a hole-in-the-wall place in Berkeley, California. Its clientele consists mainly of struggling students and knowing faculty who very much enjoy the Taiwanese style of cookery that has made the place so popular. There is no concession to the Cantonese approach, and there is a clear Northern and Beijing element in their recipes. In this dish, for example, the hot bean sauce is definitely of Beijing origin, and the addition of cucumbers and bean sprouts, with their crunchiness and contrasts, lightens what might otherwise be a heavy and unimaginative bowl of noodles. Some would consider it in many ways perhaps not so much a true Chinese as a "California-cuisine" dish.*

Serves 4

## Sauce

2 tablespoons peanut oil
2 tablespoons finely chopped garlic
2 teaspoons finely chopped ginger
3 tablespoons finely chopped scallions
1 pound lean ground pork
3 tablespoons bean sauce (see page 276)
2 tablespoons Shaoxing rice wine or dry sherry
1 tablespoon chili bean sauce or paste (see page 276)
1 tablespoon sesame paste* or peanut butter
2 tablespoons dark soy sauce
2 teaspoons light soy sauce
1/2 teaspoon salt
1/2 teaspoon freshly ground black pepper
2 teaspoons sugar
2 teaspoons chili oil

1 cup homemade chicken stock (page 60) or
   reduced-salt canned broth

1 cucumber, peeled, seeded, and shredded
1/2 pound bean sprouts
1 pound fresh Chinese noodles
1 1/2 tablespoons Asian sesame oil

### Garnish

3 tablespoons finely chopped scallions

\* Available at Chinese groceries or supermarkets.

Heat a wok or large frying pan over high heat until it is hot. Swirl in the peanut oil, and when it is very hot and slightly smoking, toss in the garlic, ginger, and scallions and stir-fry for 10 seconds. Dump in the pork, stirring to break up any large pieces, and continue to stir-fry for 2 minutes, or until the meat loses its pink color. Then pour in the rest of the sauce ingredients, stirring all the while. Bring the mixture to a boil and cook over high heat for 10 minutes. Then set the sauce aside.

In a large pot of salted boiling water, blanch the cucumber shreds for 2 minutes, remove with a slotted spoon, drain well, and arrange them on one side of a large serving platter. In the same water blanch the bean sprouts for 1 minute, remove them with a slotted spoon, drain, and arrange on the other side of the platter. Again in the same water, cook the noodles for 3 minutes; drain in a colander. Put the noodles in the center of the platter (with the cucumbers and bean sprouts on the sides) and toss noodles lightly with the sesame oil. Pour the hot bean sauce on top of the noodles. Scatter the scallions on top. Just before serving, toss the cucumbers and bean sprouts with the noodles and sauce.

# The Tsai Family's Scallion Cakes

*The family of my friend and fellow Chinese-American Ming
Tsai hails from North China, where wheat is eaten perhaps more
frequently than rice. This is a very popular treat in the*

*Northern regions, and one that Ming Tsai's family brought with them to America.*

*The recipe illustrates the Chinese penchant for enlivening the simplest foods with just salt and scallions; it is as unexpected as they are satisfying. These scallion cakes may be eaten as a breakfast food with rice porridge or soup noodles.*

Yields 4 large pancakes

2 cups all-purpose unbleached white flour
1 cup (approximately) very hot water
2 teaspoons salt
1/2 cup finely chopped scallions
5–6 tablespoons peanut oil

Stir the hot water into the flour a little at a time. Some types of flour require more water than others; add only enough to make a lumpy dough. The dough should just hold together when pressed into a ball. Knead the dough on a floured board until it is smooth (3 to 5 minutes). Put the ball of dough in a bowl and cover it with a damp cloth. Let it rest at least 30 minutes.

Knead the dough again for 20 to 30 seconds, just to make sure it is smooth. With your hands, divide the dough into 4 equal parts. Roll each dough piece into a ball between your palms. (1) Flatten it into a patty. Repeat with the remaining pieces of dough. (2) With a rolling pin,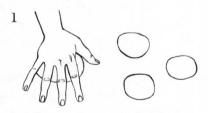
roll one piece of dough into a large pancake, about 8 or 9 inches across.
(3) Sprinkle with a quarter of the salt and chopped scallions.

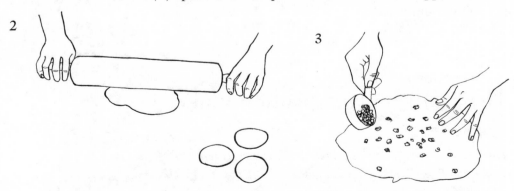

4

(6) Flatten each coil into a patty and roll it out again into a large pancake. Dust with flour if the pancake is sticking.

6

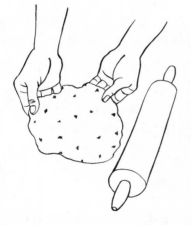

(4) Roll the pancake into a long roll. Then, with the rolling pin, flatten it. (5) Roll it into a coil, and let it rest for 20 minutes. Do the same with the rest of the dough.

5

Heat a wok or large frying pan over high heat until it is hot. Swirl in 1½ tablespoons of oil, and when it is very hot and slightly smoking, turn the heat down to moderate. Pan-fry 1 pancake until it is brown and crispy, flip it over, and brown the other side, adding more oil as necessary. Continue with the remaining dough until you have browned them all, keeping the cooked pancakes warm. Cut into segments and serve at once.

# Soothing Rice Porridge

*All my Chinese-American friends share with me the love of this comfort food, in which a small bit of rice is cooked with either plain water or broth into a soothing porridge. Once it is made, any type of food or flavoring you choose can be added to make this a filling light treat. For example, Amy Tan's mother added preserved vegetables. But perhaps the most Chinese-American and delicious variation is that of Gordon Wing's mother, who makes her porridge with leftover turkey bones. My mother made hers with preserved thousand-year-old eggs, which are still my favorite way of eating this porridge.*

*Serves 4*

12 cups water or homemade chicken stock (page 60) or
    reduced-salt canned broth
1/2 cup long-grain white rice
2 teaspoons salt
1 cup any flavoring of your choice, such as Sichuan preserved
    vegetables, or diced cooked chicken or duck, or leftover
    meats, fish, etc.
3 tablespoons finely chopped scallions
2 tablespoons finely chopped fresh coriander

Bring the water to a boil in a large pot and add the rice and salt. Let the rice come back to the boil and give it several good stirs. Then turn the heat down to low and partially cover the pot. Let the rice simmer for about 1 hour, stirring occasionally. The result will be a rather thick rice porridge, for most of the water will be absorbed in the cooking. Then add your chosen flavoring and simmer for a further 5 minutes uncovered. Just before serving, add the scallions and fresh coriander. Serve it at once. If you like, the porridge can be made in advance. In this case, reheat it slowly and simply add some more water if the porridge is too thick.

# Mrs. Wing's Simple Stir=Fried Bean Thread Noodles

This is a simple but very satisfying noodle dish that the mother of my colleague and good friend Gordon Wing often made, and which he himself is still delighted to serve and to enjoy.

*Gordon Wing with his parents*

Gordon's mother was very careful to get the right type of bean thread noodles so that the pasta would not turn too soft and mushy. Her favorite style is the Pagoda brand, imported from China. On her recommendation, I use that brand whenever it is available. This is typical home-style Chinese-American food. Of course, being frugal, Mrs. Wing was a bit less generous with the dried shrimp.

Serves 2—4

> 1/2 cup dried shrimp*
> 1/4 pound (about 2 2-ounce packages) bean thread noodles
> 1 tablespoon peanut oil
> 1 pound shredded Napa cabbage
> 1/2 teaspoon salt
> 1/2 teaspoon freshly ground black pepper
> 1 cup homemade chicken stock (page 60) or
>     reduced-salt canned broth
> 2 tablespoons light soy sauce
> 1 tablespoon Shaoxing rice wine or dry sherry
> 3 tablespoons finely chopped scallions

## Garnish

> 2 teaspoons coarsely chopped green scallions

* Available at Chinese groceries or supermarkets.

243

Soak the dried shrimp in warm water for 20 minutes, and when they are slightly soft, drain them and discard the water. Meanwhile, soak the noodles in a large bowl of warm water for 20 minutes. When they are soft, drain them and discard the water.

Heat a wok or large frying pan over high heat until it is hot. Swirl in the oil, and when it is very hot and slightly smoking, throw in the dried shrimp and stir-fry for 20 seconds. Add the cabbage, salt, and pepper and continue to stir-fry for 2 minutes. Now pour in the chicken stock, soy sauce, and rice wine. Toss in the scallions, dump in the drained noodles, and cook the mixture for a further 5 minutes, or until most of the liquid has evaporated. Ladle some noodles into individual bowls or into 1 large serving bowl, garnish with coarsely chopped scallions, and serve at once.

# Subgum Chow Mein

*"Mayonnaise" is the first French word most Americans learn; "chow mein" is their first Chinese word. In either case, one could do worse in terms of cookery.*

*This familiar and all-encompassing Chinese exotic appears on the menus of countless Chinese restaurants—I am tempted to say that every "Chinese-American" restaurant is required by culinary law at least to list the offering. Only "sweet-and-sour pork" matches it in popularity.*

*Chow mein entails a smart and very efficient marketing ploy on the part of Chinese restaurant owners. Simply take the same ingredients as for chicken subgum, stir-fry the mixture with noodles, and you have something completely different—or so it pleasingly seems.*

*Serves 4*

3/4 pound boneless, skinless chicken breasts
1 egg white
2 teaspoons cornstarch
1 teaspoon salt
1/4 teaspoon freshly ground white pepper

1 teaspoon Asian sesame oil, plus more to toss with noodles
1 pound chow mein noodles
1/2 cup peanut oil, or 1 cup water (see variation) and
   2 tablespoons peanut oil
3 garlic cloves, peeled and lightly crushed
1 small onion, peeled and sliced
4 ounces celery heart, sliced crosswise
1 cup 1/2-inch-thick-sliced small zucchini
2 red peppers, seeded and cut into 1-inch squares
1/2 cup peeled and sliced fresh water chestnuts, or canned
1 cup bok choy, washed and cut into 2-inch sections
5 scallions, cut into 2-inch segments
1 cup coarsely shredded Napa cabbage
1 tomato, cut into 8 wedges

## Sauce

4 tablespoons oyster sauce
2 tablespoons Shaoxing rice wine or dry sherry
4 tablespoons homemade chicken stock (page 60) or
   reduced-salt canned broth
1 teaspoon cornstarch mixed with 2 teaspoons water
1 teaspoon salt
1/4 teaspoon freshly ground black pepper
2 teaspoons Asian sesame oil

Cut the chicken into 1-inch cubes and mix it with the egg white, corn-starch, salt, pepper, and sesame oil. Refrigerate for at least 20 minutes.

Blanch the noodles in a pot of salted boiling water for 2 minutes. Drain, rinse under cold water, and toss immediately with sesame oil. Set aside.

Heat a wok until it is very hot, and then add the peanut oil. When the oil is very hot, remove the wok from the heat and immediately add the chicken pieces, stirring vigorously to keep them from sticking. As soon as the chicken pieces turn white, in about 2 minutes, quickly drain the chicken in a stainless-steel colander set in a bowl to catch the oil, reserving 2 table-spoons of the drained oil.

Reheat (or heat) the wok or a large frying pan over high heat until it is hot. Swirl in the reserved 2 tablespoons of oil (or add 2 tablespoons fresh peanut oil if you cooked chicken in water), and when it is very hot and slightly smoking, toss in the garlic and onion and stir-fry for 2 minutes. Then scatter in the celery, zucchini, peppers, and water chestnuts and continue to stir-fry for 2 minutes. Mix the bok choy, scallions, Napa cabbage, and tomato; toss this mixture into the wok, and continue to stir-fry for another 4 minutes, until the vegetables are just tender. Now pour in the sauce ingredients and bring it to a simmer. Add the blanched noodles and mix well. Return the chicken to the sauce with the noodles and give the mixture a few turns to mix well. Serve at once.

Variation: If you choose to use water instead of oil, bring it to a boil in a saucepan. Remove the saucepan from the heat and immediately add the chicken pieces, stirring vigorously to keep them from sticking. When the chicken pieces turn white, in about 2 minutes, quickly drain the chicken and all of the water in a stainless-steel colander set in a bowl. Discard the water.

# Cantonese-Style Chow Mein

*While Americans were ordering subgum chow mein, we were eating this more authentic version of chow mein. I say "authentic" because chow mein is not just an* ad hoc *throwing together of whatever foods are at hand. It is a traditional mainstay of the South Chinese diet, consisting of boiled and then stir-fried noodles (in Cantonese,* ch'ao min*), with added bamboo shoots, bean sprouts, slices of pork, or whatever other protein and vegetables are fresh and available. The recipe has been further refined by the imaginative chefs of Hong Kong.*

*In this version, thin egg noodles are blanched and then slowly browned until crispy; then the whole is flipped over to brown on the other side. The Chinese aptly call it "two-faced browned." The interior of this noodle cake remains soft and tender, giving the dish that contrast of texture that Chinese cookery so prizes. It is then topped with either stir-fried chicken or meats and vegetables. It is simply delicious.*

Serves 4

³/₄ pound boneless, skinless chicken breasts, finely shredded
¹/₂ tablespoon egg white
2 teaspoons cornstarch
1 teaspoon salt
¹/₂ teaspoon freshly ground white pepper

¹/₂ pound fresh thin Chinese egg noodles
3 tablespoons (approximately) peanut oil
¹/₂ cup peanut oil or water (see variation)
2 tablespoons Shaoxing rice wine or dry sherry
3 tablespoons oyster sauce
1 tablespoon light soy sauce
1 cup homemade chicken stock (page 60) or
   reduced-salt canned broth
1 teaspoon salt
¹/₂ teaspoon freshly ground black pepper
1 tablespoon cornstarch mixed with 1¹/₂ tablespoons
   stock or water

## Garnish

3 tablespoons finely shredded scallions

Combine the chicken, egg white, cornstarch, salt, and pepper in a small bowl. Mix well, and refrigerate for at least 20 minutes.

Blanch the noodles for 2 minutes in a large pot of salted boiling water. Drain them well.

Heat a frying pan until it is hot, then swirl in 1¹/₂ tablespoons of oil. Evenly spread the noodles over the surface, turn the heat to low, and allow the noodles to brown slowly. This should take about 5 minutes. When the noodles are brown, gently flip them over and brown the other side, adding more oil if needed. When both sides are browned, remove the noodles to a platter and keep warm in a turned-off oven.

Heat a wok until it is very hot, and then pour in the ¹/₂ cup of oil. When the oil is very hot, remove the wok from the heat, and immediately add the chicken shreds, stirring vigorously to keep them from sticking. As soon as the chicken pieces turn white, in about 2 minutes, quickly drain the chicken and all of the oil in a stainless-steel colander set in a bowl. Discard the oil.

Clean the wok and reheat it over high heat. Now pour in the rice wine, oyster sauce, soy sauce, chicken stock, salt, and pepper. Bring the mixture to a boil and add the cornstarch mixture. Bring it to a simmer again. Return the chicken to the sauce and give the mixture a few stirs. Pour this over the noodles, garnish with the scallions, and serve at once.

Variation: If you choose to use water instead of oil, bring it to a boil in a saucepan. Remove the saucepan from the heat and immediately add the chicken pieces, stirring vigorously to keep them from sticking. When the chicken pieces turn white, in about 2 minutes, quickly drain the chicken and all of the water in a stainless-steel colander set in a bowl. Discard the water.

# My Mother's Home=Style Savory Rice

*During winter school holidays, before my mother left for work, she would cook a special rice treat for my lunch at home. Her dish is a simple one to make but very satisfying. She would buy the dried bacon from the local Chinese store, chop it up, and cook it with a glutinous-rice mixture. She would then place this in a water bath over the radiator to keep it warm, and by noon the flavor of the bacon would have melded with the rice, creating a savory, mouth-watering treat. Although this home-style rice dish was typical of Southern or Cantonese cooking, her addition of peas would transform it into a true Chinese-American dish, a real hyphenated comfort food.*

Serves 4

2 cups glutinous rice (also known as sweet rice)
1/2 cup Chinese dried black mushrooms

2 tablespoons peanut oil
1/2 cup finely chopped scallions
1 tablespoon finely chopped fresh ginger
2 tablespoons coarsely chopped garlic

¹/₂ pound Chinese bacon* or Smithfield Virginia ham, sliced
¹/₂ pound fresh water chestnuts, peeled and coarsely
    chopped, or canned
2 cups homemade chicken stock (page 60) or reduced-salt
    canned broth
2 tablespoons light soy sauce
1 tablespoon Shaoxing rice wine or dry sherry
Salt and freshly ground black pepper to taste
1 cup frozen peas

* Available at Chinese groceries or supermarkets.

Put the glutinous rice in a large bowl, cover it with cold water, and soak overnight.

Soak the mushrooms in warm water for 20 minutes. Then drain them and squeeze out the excess liquid. Remove and discard the stems, and coarsely chop the caps.

Heat a wok or large frying pan over high heat until it is hot. Swirl in the oil, and when it is very hot and slightly smoking, toss in the scallions, ginger, and garlic and stir-fry for 1 minute. Now toss in the mushrooms, the Chinese bacon, the drained glutinous rice, and the water chestnuts and continue to stir-fry for 3 minutes, or until everything is thoroughly mixed. Pour in the chicken stock, soy sauce, and rice wine and mix well. Taste for salt and add several good grindings of freshly ground black pepper. Reduce the heat to low, cover, and cook for 15 minutes, stirring from time to time.

Remove from the heat, stir in the frozen peas, transfer the mixture to a heatproof bowl, and cover with plastic wrap.

Next set up a steamer, or put a rack into a wok or deep pan, and fill it with 2 inches of water. Bring the water to a boil over high heat. Carefully lower the bowl onto the rack. Turn the heat to low and cover the wok or pan tightly. Steam gently for 30 minutes, remove, and serve at once. This dish re-heats well.

# Chinese Bacon

Dried Chinese bacon is pork belly meat cured in a salt-and-spice mixture and then dry-smoked. Sold in Chinese stores by the piece or in vacuum-sealed plastic packs, it will keep for several months in the refrigerator. It is usually added to Chinese dishes for flavor. Chinese sausages or Smithfield Virginia ham may be used as a substitute.

# Turkey "Shee Fan"

*Whenever I talk with my Chinese-American friends—Amy Tan, Gordon Wing, Lillian Chou, and many others—about food, about family meals, about favorite dishes, we often sound like siblings recalling but one family's experiences.*

*I know that our sharing the same culinary traditions and customs is to be expected. Nevertheless, I still find it striking how closely the traditions and practices were followed in America, from Chicago to Boston, from Los Angeles to Seattle.*

*This soup is one of the shared Chinese-American practices. After every Thanksgiving meal, every Chinese-American mother would carefully save the carcass of the turkey. A broth would be made with these remains, and then a small amount of rice would be added. The result is Turkey "Shee Fan," or "broken rice in turkey broth."*

*A true Chinese-American concoction, the satisfying rice porridge would soak up the savory turkey flavors. There was something comforting about shee fan for Chinese-Americans, the way chicken soup is for Jewish-Americans.*

*Serves 4*

1 cooked turkey carcass
12 cups water, homemade chicken stock (page 60), or
     reduced-salt canned broth
¼ cup long-grain white rice
1 teaspoon salt

Bring the water and carcass to the boil in a large pot. Turn the heat to low and simmer for 2 hours. Remove the bones and carcass and toss in the rice and salt. Raise the heat and let the mixture come back to the boil and give it several good stirs. Then turn the heat down to low and partially cover the pot. Let the rice simmer for about 1 hour, stirring occasionally. Taste, and add more salt if necessary. It can be served immediately, or if you like, the shee fan can be made in advance. In this case, reheat it slowly and simply add some more water if the porridge is too thick.

# Savory Bean Thread Noodles

*Growing up Chinese-American, I was convinced very early in my life that Chinese mothers can quickly put together a delicious and satisfying dish with what seems to be a paltry amount of ingredients. In grade school, when I read the folktale "Stone Soup," it reminded me of the magic my mother appeared to work in our kitchen.*

*Later I learned that Chinese cuisine has a number of dry ingredients that need just a bit of soaking to create a substantial amount of food, with which a savory dish can be quickly concocted and stir-fried.*

*This is one of the many dishes my mother would make, especially when she was in a hurry. With a small amount of pork, she would create this mouth-watering dish that goes perfectly with rice.*

*Her secret ingredient was bean thread noodles, also popularly known in America as cellophane noodles. As with other noodles in general, when added to water they expand prodigiously. They*

*are delightfully light, finely white, almost transparent noodles.
Because they are dried, and therefore keep indefinitely, there
was always a supply of these noodles in our pantry.*

Serves 4

2 2-ounce packages dried bean thread (cellophane) noodles
1 tablespoon peanut oil
2 tablespoons coarsely chopped garlic
1/2 pound ground pork
1 cup homemade chicken stock (page 60)
  or reduced-salt canned broth
1 tablespoon Shaoxing rice wine or dry
  sherry
2 tablespoons oyster sauce
2 tablespoons light soy sauce
2 teaspoons dark soy sauce
1/2 teaspoon salt
1/2 teaspoon freshly ground black
  pepper
2 teaspoons Asian sesame oil

## Garnish

2 tablespoons coarsely chopped scallions

Soak the noodles in a large bowl of warm water for 15 minutes. When
they are soft, drain them and discard the water. Cut the noodles into 3-inch
lengths, using scissors or a knife.

Heat a wok or large frying pan over high heat until it is hot. Swirl in the
peanut oil, and when it is very hot and slightly smoking, add the garlic and
stir-fry quickly for 15 seconds. Then chuck in the meat and stir-fry, breaking
up the meat, for 3 minutes. Then pour in the stock, rice wine, oyster sauce,
soy sauces, salt, and pepper. Cook the mixture over a gentle heat for about
5 minutes. Now toss in the drained noodles and the sesame oil and cook for
a further 10 minutes, or until most of the liquid has evaporated. Ladle onto
a platter, sprinkle scallions on top, and serve at once with rice.

# Tasty Vegetarian New Year Noodles

*Growing up Chinese-American meant that I got to celebrate several extra holidays. After the Christmas holidays, I could always look forward to the Chinese New Year, usually a month or two later. Indeed, as the scholars Vera and Francis Hsu write, "Ask any Chinese born and raised in China what she or he liked best in the days of their childhood and 'Chinese New Year' is the most likely reply." So, within the Chinese-American community, it meant two weeks of hectic preparations followed by festive celebrations, including banquets, dinners, and red packets of money for the children. Red is an auspicious color in the Chinese tradition, always associated with happy occasions and good luck.*

*On the eve of Chinese New Year at home, we always dined*

*on vegetarian noodles. In Chinese culture, vegetables are a symbol of purification, and the long noodles symbolize a long life. I was constantly admonished not to cut the noodles, for if I did it would surely bring bad luck. In any case, this noodle dish is delectable and easy to make; it's a terrific side dish or snack.*

Serves 4

1/2 pound dried thin rice noodles*
1 tablespoon peanut oil
1/2 cup finely chopped Tianjin preserved cabbage†
2 tablespoons coarsely chopped garlic
2 teaspoons finely chopped ginger
2 tablespoons Shaoxing rice wine or dry sherry
1 tablespoon chili bean sauce (see page 276)
1 tablespoon dark soy sauce
2 teaspoons light soy sauce
1 tablespoon sugar
1/2 cup homemade chicken stock (page 60) or reduced-salt
    canned broth or water
1 tablespoon Asian sesame oil

## Garnish

3 tablespoons finely chopped scallions
2 tablespoons finely chopped fresh coriander

* Available at Chinese groceries or supermarkets.
† Available in ceramic crocks or glass jars at Chinese groceries or supermarkets.

Soak the rice noodles in warm water for 20 minutes. Drain well and set aside.

Heat a wok or large frying pan over high heat until it is hot. Swirl in the peanut oil, and when it is very hot and slightly smoking, toss in the preserved cabbage, garlic, and ginger and stir-fry for 1 minute. Then pour in the rice wine, spoon in the chili bean sauce, soy sauces, sugar, and stock. Chuck in the noodles, mix well, reduce the heat, and simmer for 3 minutes over low heat. Stir in the sesame oil.

Remove the noodles to a large bowl or platter. Scatter the scallions and coriander over them and serve at once.

# Heritage Chicken=Rice Casserole

*In 1989, when my mother and I returned to our ancestral village of Kaiping, China, we experienced many wonderful moments. Among the most memorable was when we were served this delightful home-style dish, one that recalled my own childhood. For Sunday lunch, if just my mother and I were at home, instead of making an elaborate meal, my mother would make this chicken-rice casserole. She could prepare it early in the morning and then go to the markets to shop.*

*I always found it deliciously satisfying. The rice would absorb all the chicken flavors, and we would finish with a broth thickened by the toasty rice scraps that clung to the bottom of the casserole.*

*It was simple home-style fare at its best.*

Serves 4

1¹/2 cups short-grain white rice
1 pound boneless, skinless chicken thighs
1 tablespoon light soy sauce
2 teaspoons dark soy sauce
2 teaspoons Shaoxing rice wine or dry sherry
1 teaspoon salt
¹/2 teaspoon freshly ground black pepper
2 teaspoons Asian sesame oil
2 teaspoons cornstarch
1¹/2 tablespoons peanut oil

## Garnish

1 tablespoon finely shredded fresh ginger
3 tablespoons finely shredded scallions

Put the rice in a heavy-bottomed medium-sized pot. Pour in enough water to cover the rice by about 1 inch. Bring the rice to a boil, and continue to cook until half of the water has evaporated. Reduce the heat to the lowest point possible and cover tightly. Cook for 5 minutes.

Chop the chicken into bite-size pieces and mix it with the soy sauces, rice wine, salt, pepper, sesame oil, and cornstarch.

Heat a wok or large frying pan over high heat until it is hot. Swirl in the peanut oil, and when it is very hot and slightly smoking, toss in the chicken and stir-fry for 5 minutes, or until the chicken is browned. Then pour the entire contents of the wok into a colander set in a bowl and drain well. Now toss all the chicken on top of the partially cooked rice, cover, and continue to cook for 20 minutes.

Garnish the chicken and rice with the ginger and scallions and serve at once.

# Comforting Rice with Chinese Sausage

*My working mother was a whirlwind of efficiency and skill in her kitchen. She would arrive home around 5:45 and by 7:00 that evening we would be enjoying a mini feast of at least four dishes. My mother was extremely organized and she moved artfully, combining and cooking various foods with each other.*

*This is one of those dishes. When the rice began to cook, she would lay two or three Chinese sausages on the surface of the rice. The rich sweet flavor and aroma of the sausages would slowly come together with the rice, dripping their savoriness into the rice to make it a special dish. It was simple to make and, to this day, when I am looking for a quick and very satisfying meal, I always make this dish.*

Serves 4

2 cups long-grain white rice
6 Chinese pork sausages (see page 168)

Put the rice in a heavy-bottomed medium-sized pot. Pour in enough water to cover the rice by about 1 inch. Bring the rice to a boil, and continue to cook until most of the water has evaporated. Reduce the heat to the lowest point possible, cover tightly, and cook for 2 minutes.

Cut the sausages diagonally into 2-inch slices. Put the sausages on top of the steaming rice, cover again tightly, and continue to cook for 15 minutes. The rice and sausage will cook slowly in the remaining steam. Turn off the heat and let it rest, still covered, for another 15 minutes before serving.

# VEGETABLES

# Earthly Spinach with Fermented Bean Curd

*From early childhood, I assumed that the Chinese were natural masters at preparing vegetables. Unlike the overcooked boiled vegetables I used to see at the school cafeteria or in restaurants, our dishes of vegetables were always vibrant, colorful, and bursting with mouth-watering aromas. We simply knew instinctively when to remove the vegetables from the heat so they wouldn't overcook, as well as how to season them properly. Even common vegetables, such as spinach, which many non-Chinese children despise, were heavenly on our table. Especially when they were paired with fermented bean curd, which always had a salty, unusual, strong flavor that seems to mellow when cooked. Even to this day, if I want the simplest of comfort food, I will have the fermented bean curd with plain rice—food that has a true Chinese soul.*

Serves 4

1¹⁄₂–2 pounds fresh spinach
1¹⁄₂ tablespoons peanut oil
3 cloves garlic, finely sliced
3 tablespoons chili fermented bean curd or plain fermented
   bean curd*
2 tablespoons Shaoxing rice wine or dry sherry
1 tablespoon sugar
3 tablespoons water

* Available at Chinese groceries or supermarkets.

Wash the spinach thoroughly several times, with at least 2 changes of cold water, and drain well. Trim any tough stems.

Heat a wok or large frying pan over high heat until it is hot. Swirl in the oil, and when it is very hot and slightly smoking, toss in the garlic and stir-fry for 10 seconds. Then quickly spoon in the fermented bean curd and crush it with a spatula, breaking it into small pieces. Throw in the spinach and stir-fry for 2 minutes. Pour in the rice wine, add the sugar and water, and continue to cook for another 3 minutes. Place on a serving platter and serve at once.

# A Recipe from the Garden— Stir-Fried Chinese Greens

*No meal in our home, whether it was a simple lunch or an after-noon snack, ever went without Chinese greens. My mother even managed to have them during hard Chicago winters. She would buy them when they were cheap in the summer and dry them on the iron fire escape, like bits of laundry. Unfortunately, living in an urban environment, we didn't have the luxury of a garden, as did my more fortunate friend Steve Wong. Living in Sacramento, California, where there was plenty of sunshine, his family were able to grow their greens. He remembers how delicious and earthy the vegetables smelled when his mother plucked them from the garden and simply stir-fried them in the same manner my mother used to prepare them. It is remarkable how two Chinese-Americans from such distant parts of the country still relish the memory of these modest stir-fried Chinese greens—cooked precisely the same way.*

*Serves 2–4*

1 tablespoon peanut oil
2 teaspoons Asian sesame oil
3 garlic cloves, peeled and finely sliced
2 teaspoons salt
1¹/₂ pounds (5 cups) Chinese greens, such as bok choy or Napa cabbage
2 tablespoons homemade chicken stock (page 60), reduced-salt canned broth, or water

Heat a wok or large frying pan over high heat until it is hot. Swirl in the two oils, and when they are very hot and slightly smoking, toss in the garlic and salt. Stir-fry the mixture for 15 seconds. Then quickly throw in the Chinese greens. Stir-fry for 3–4 minutes, until the greens have wilted a little. Then pour in the chicken stock or water and continue to stir-fry for a few more minutes, until the greens are done but still slightly crisp.

# Cantonese=Style Steamed Eggplant

*I am always surprised at how most Americans think Chinese steam our vegetables. In fact, we prefer either to blanch them quickly in hot, lightly salted water or to stir-fry them quickly in the wok. This is one of the few recipes in which eggplant is actually steamed instead of stir-fried. Steaming it whole and then covering it with a tasty sauce is not only easy but also a very nutritious way of enjoying the vegetable, and certainly less greasy.*

*It is worthwhile to try to get the Chinese variety if you can: you will find it slightly sweeter.*

Serves 2–4

1 pound Chinese eggplant or ordinary eggplant
1½ tablespoons finely chopped fresh ginger
3 tablespoons finely chopped scallions, white
    part only
2 tablespoons light soy sauce
1½ tablespoons peanut oil
1 tablespoon Asian sesame oil

## Garnish

Fresh coriander sprigs

If you are using Chinese eggplants, leave them whole. If you are using the regular, large variety, trim them, cut them in half lengthwise, and score them on the skin side by cutting diagonal crosswise indentations.

Next, set up a steamer, or put a rack into a wok or deep pan, and fill it with 2 inches of water. Bring the water to a boil over high heat. Put the egg-plant on a heatproof plate and carefully lower it into the steamer or onto the rack. Turn the heat to low and cover the wok or pan tightly. Steam gently for 30–40 minutes, or until the eggplants are very soft to the touch. Remove from the wok, and sprinkle the ginger and scallions evenly over the eggplant. Drizzle the soy sauce over all.

Clean out the wok and wipe it dry. Heat the wok or a large frying pan over high heat until it is hot. Swirl in the peanut and sesame oils, and when the oil is very hot and slightly smoking, drizzle it over the eggplant, garnish with the fresh coriander, and serve at once.

# Ming Tsai's Northern-Style Eggplant

*My Chinese-American friend Ming-Hao Clayton Tsai was born in Taiwan but grew up in Dayton, Ohio. Following one very common Chinese immigrant path, his parents, who are accomplished cooks, opened a Chinese restaurant, The Mandarin Kitchen. The restaurant's name is a marker. "Mandarin" refers to the members of the nine ranks of public servants of the imperial (Beijing) bureaucracy, each member's rank distinguishable by the particular button worn on one's official cap. But "Mandarin" is also the standard Chinese language and a northern Chinese dialect. The word thus implies North China and, therefore, Northern cuisine.*

*Thus, it should come as no surprise that Ming's parents were originally from the Beijing area and that in their restaurant they featured northern Chinese cuisine. At home, too, they emphasized the Northern style of cooking. Ming would take school lunches made up of such standard northern dishes as Red Roast Pork with potato bread. "Mongolian hot pots" were a favorite during the long Ohio winters. His grandmother made Beijing sauce noodles, and they all enjoyed Northern specialties like scallion cakes and Mongolian beef.*

*Here I offer a variation of one of the Ming family's recipes for eggplant—rich, spicy, and delectable. If possible, purchase the smaller, thin Chinese eggplants, which are sweeter; these can be found at most Chinese groceries or supermarkets as well as, on occasion, at your ordinary supermarket.*

Serves 4

1 pound Chinese eggplants

## Sauce

2 teaspoons peanut oil
2 tablespoons coarsely chopped garlic
2 teaspoons finely chopped ginger
3 tablespoons finely chopped scallions
2 teaspoons Shaoxing rice wine or dry sherry
2 tablespoons dark soy sauce
2 teaspoons chili bean sauce (see page 276)
2 teaspoons sugar
1/4 cup homemade chicken stock (page 60) or
    reduced-salt canned broth
1 tablespoon Asian sesame oil

Preheat the oven to 400° F. Lay the eggplants on an ovenproof tray and roast them for 20 minutes, or until they are soft and cooked through. Remove from the oven, and when they are cool enough to handle, peel them and cut into strips. Lay these on a warm platter.

Heat a wok or large frying pan over high heat until it is hot. Swirl in the peanut oil, and when it is hot and slightly smoking, toss in the garlic, ginger, and scallions and stir-fry for 15 seconds. Then pour in the rice wine, soy sauce, chili bean sauce, sugar, stock, and sesame oil. Bring the mixture to a simmer, pour this sauce over the eggplant, and serve.

# Stir=Fried Mustard Greens with Ginger

*Growing up in Chicago's very small Chinatown, I experienced life as a microcosm of a South Chinese village. In all practical matters, we were a self-contained community, with Chinese movies, shops, and all manner of authentic Chinese foods. Except in winter, there was available an assortment of fresh vegetables in all shades of color. In winter, we made do with dried, pickled, and canned vegetables.*

*As a child, I always enjoyed eating mustard greens, with their piquant bite. In our kitchen, the greens were simply stir-fried with salt and shreds of fresh ginger. The best part was the small tender stems.*

*Serves 4*

1¹/2 pounds Chinese mustard greens
1 tablespoon peanut oil
2 tablespoons finely shredded fresh ginger
1 teaspoon salt
2 tablespoons homemade chicken stock (page 60), reduced-
    salt canned broth, or water

Separate the leaves from the stems and cut them into slices. Peel the stems and cut them into thin diagonal slices.

Heat a wok or large frying pan over high heat until it is hot. Swirl in the oil, and when it is very hot and slightly smoking, toss in the ginger and salt. Stir-fry the mixture for 15 seconds. Then quickly throw in the Chinese mustard greens. Continue to stir-fry for 4 minutes, until the greens have wilted a little. Then pour in the chicken stock or water and continue to stir-fry for a few more minutes, until the greens are done but are still slightly crisp.

# Lettuce with Oyster Sauce

*Although my mother worked at a full-time job, leaving at seven
in the morning and returning around five-thirty in the afternoon, she always managed to put on a three- or four-dish Chinese
meal every night. At the time, I took it all for granted, as
children tend to do in regard to their parents' care. As an adult,
I learned to appreciate what she had been doing for the family all
of those years.*

*Many of the dishes she made were simple home-cooked recipes
that literally took minutes. Here is one of her standards—lettuce
prepared in a typically Chinese way, blanched and served with
oyster sauce. As is the Chinese custom, we rarely ate lettuce raw
in our home, but always as a cooked vegetable. Prepared in this
way, lettuce retains a crispy texture and its delicate flavor is
unimpaired by cooking. The combination makes a simple, quickly
prepared, tasty vegetable dish.*

Serves 2–4

1¹⁄₂ pounds iceberg lettuce
3 tablespoons oyster sauce
1 tablespoon peanut oil

Separate the lettuce leaves and blanch them in a pot of boiling salted
water for about 20 seconds, or until they have wilted slightly. Remove them
and drain immediately. Mix the oyster sauce with the oil. Arrange the lettuce
leaves on a serving dish, pour the oyster sauce mixture over it, and serve it
immediately.

# Stir-Fried Napa Cabbage with Dried Shrimp

*Napa cabbage was one of the most available Chinese vegetables in Chicago's Chinatown groceries. A hardy vegetable, it is easy to grow in large quantities on small plots. Most of my Chinese-American friends remember Napa cabbage as a regular part of their families' home cooking.*

*The cabbage has a mild but distinct taste, and a sweetness that is enhanced the more it is cooked. My mother often simply stir-fried it with dried shrimp, as in this recipe. I suggest soaking the dried shrimp in rice wine to give them an added dimension.*

Serves 2—4

2 pounds Napa cabbage
1/4 cup dried shrimp*
1/4 cup Shaoxing rice wine or dry sherry
1 1/2 tablespoons peanut oil
2 tablespoons coarsely chopped garlic
2 teaspoons salt
1/4 teaspoon freshly ground black pepper
3 tablespoons finely shredded scallions

* Available at Chinese groceries or supermarkets.

Cut the Napa cabbage into 1 1/2-inch strips and blanch them in a pot of boiling salted water for about 2 minutes. Drain thoroughly and set aside. Combine the shrimp and rice wine in a small bowl and let sit for 20 minutes. Drain the shrimp from the rice wine, retaining both.

Heat a wok or large frying pan over high heat until it is hot. Swirl in the oil, and when it is very hot and slightly smoking, toss in the garlic, then the shrimp, and stir-fry for 2 minutes. Dump in the blanched cabbage and the rice wine and continue to stir-fry for 5 minutes. Season the mixture with the salt and pepper. Finally, toss in the scallions and continue to stir-fry for 1 minute. Serve at once.

# Green Beans with Fermented Bean Curd

*Summertime in Chicago meant green beans fresh from the neighborhood gardens. And nothing is better than simply stir-frying the beans in a touch of fermented bean curd: it makes this classical vegetable dish piquant and savory while retaining the freshness and crunch of the beans. Fermented bean curd, available in jars, can easily be found at Chinese groceries and supermarkets.*

Serves 4

2 pounds fresh green beans
1¹/₂ tablespoons peanut oil
3 cloves garlic, finely sliced
3 tablespoons chili fermented bean curd or plain
     fermented bean curd (see above)
2 tablespoons Shaoxing rice wine or dry sherry
2 teaspoons sugar
6 tablespoons water

Trim the green beans.

Heat a wok or large frying pan over high heat until it is hot. Swirl in the oil, and when it is very hot and slightly smoking, toss in the garlic and stir-fry for 10 seconds. Then quickly spoon in the fermented bean curd and crush it with a spatula, breaking it into small pieces. Throw in the green beans and stir-fry for 2 minutes. Pour in the rice wine, add the sugar and water, cover, and continue to cook for another 3 minutes. Place on a serving platter and serve at once.

# Stir=Fried Jade Snow Peas and Crispy Water Chestnuts

*Ironically, this familiar Chinese restaurant dish never graced the family table at my home, or that of my Chinese-American friends. Snow peas were expensive and water chestnuts were used mainly in fillings, rather than by themselves. However, this very attractive and satisfying dish found its way onto the menus of almost every Chinese restaurant in the country.*

*It is not difficult to see why. Snow peas and water chestnuts are sweet and crunchy. Together they create a colorful and texturally contrasting combination that is very appealing. For Americans who knew only boiled vegetables, it was a revelation to experience the crunch and freshness of vegetables cooked in the Chinese way.*

*Serves 2–4*

1/2 pound (2 cups) fresh water chestnuts, or canned
1 tablespoon peanut oil
3 tablespoons finely diagonally sliced scallions, white and
    green parts
1 1/2 cups snow peas, trimmed
1 tablespoon light soy sauce
2 tablespoons water
1 teaspoon salt
1/2 teaspoon freshly ground black pepper
1 teaspoon sugar
2 teaspoons Asian sesame oil

Peel the fresh water chestnuts and thinly slice them.

Heat a wok or large frying pan over high heat until it is hot. Swirl in the peanut oil, and when it is very hot and slightly smoking, toss in the scallions. Stir-fry for 10 seconds, then add the snow peas and water chestnuts and stir-fry for 1 minute. Make sure you coat them thoroughly with the oil. Then toss in the rest of the ingredients except the sesame oil and continue to stir-fry for another 3 minutes. Stir in the sesame oil and serve at once.

# Oyster Sauce Bean Curd

*As I grew up, I became increasingly aware of my mother's enormous energy. She would come home from work and prepare every evening a fresh and delicious meal for us. She, of course, kept to very simple dishes, such as this bean curd with oyster sauce. It is easy to make, and typical of Chinese-American home cooking. Sometimes my mother would add carrots or tomatoes, but most of the time she made it this simple way. It is an appetizing and very satisfying home-style treat.*

*Incidentally, I remember how she used to complain about the quality of bean curd available in America, and how much better, silkier, and above all fresher the bean curd was in China. That was probably true in the 1950s and '60s but the quality of American bean curd has vastly improved over the years. I think that even my mother finds bean curd at the supermarket quite acceptable now.*

Serves 4

1 pound firm fresh bean curd
2 cups peanut oil
3 scallions (white and green parts), finely shredded
1 tablespoon coarsely chopped garlic
1 tablespoon light soy sauce
2 teaspoons dark soy sauce
1 tablespoon Shaoxing rice wine or dry sherry
2 teaspoons sugar
2 tablespoons oyster sauce
1/4 teaspoon freshly ground black pepper
1/4 cup homemade chicken stock (page 60), or reduced-salt
   canned broth, or water

Cut the bean curd into 1-inch cubes (see page 50). Drain them on paper towels for 10 minutes. Heat a wok or large frying pan over high heat until it is hot. Pour in the oil, and when it is very hot and slightly smoking, deep-fry the bean curd cubes. When they are crispy and brown, remove them and drain on paper towels. Drain off all the oil but 1 1/2 tablespoons.

Reheat the wok or large frying pan with the remaining oil over high heat until it is hot. When it is very hot and slightly smoking, toss in the scallions and garlic and stir-fry for 30 seconds. Then pour in the soy sauces, rice wine or dry sherry, sugar, oyster sauce, pepper, and stock or water. Toss in the bean curd and continue to cook for 4 minutes. Turn the heat back to high and continue to cook until most of the liquid has evaporated. Serve at once with rice.

# Braised Stuffed Bean Curd

*Big Number One Uncle, the chef, would occasionally make this special dish for our Monday-night dinners. Our family secret: the amount of shrimp he used depended on how much he had won at the racetrack the weekend before. His betting choices were what made this an "occasional" treat.*

*But it was one worth waiting for. He would first pan-fry the stuffed bean curd, then add a splash of rice wine, with stock and soy sauce to complete the recipe. The bean curd would absorb the sauce, and this turned a rather prosaic food into a mouth-watering, satisfying treat. The filling inside the bean curd was simple but truly tasty. Moreover, the occasion was always a joyful one, whether Uncle had beaten the ponies or not.*

*The dish can be made ahead of time, for it reheats quite well. Serve it with plain rice and other vegetables for a complete meal.*

*Serves 4*

1 pound firm bean curd

## Stuffing

1/4 pound fresh or frozen shrimp, peeled
1/4 pound ground pork
1/2 egg white
1/2 teaspoon cornstarch
1/2 teaspoon salt
1/4 teaspoon freshly ground black pepper
1/2 teaspoon Asian sesame oil
1 teaspoon Shaoxing rice wine or dry sherry
1/2 teaspoon sugar
1/2 teaspoon finely chopped fresh ginger
1 teaspoon finely chopped scallions

Cornstarch for dusting

## Sauce

3 tablespoons peanut oil
1/2 cup homemade chicken stock (page 60) or
    reduced-salt canned broth
2 tablespoons dark soy sauce
1 tablespoon Shaoxing rice wine or dry sherry
1/2 teaspoon salt
1/4 teaspoon freshly ground black pepper
2 teaspoons cornstarch mixed with 1 tablespoon water

## Garnish

2 tablespoons finely chopped scallions

Cut each bean curd square into quarters. With a paring knife and spoon, hollow out the squares, leaving a 1/4-inch wall all the way around. Save the extra bean curd you have scooped out, mash it with a fork, and set it aside for the stuffing. When you have prepared the bean curd squares, drain them on paper towels for 10 minutes.

Now prepare the stuffing. First, coarsely chop the shrimp. In a large bowl, mix the chopped shrimp with the remaining stuffing ingredients. Dust the inside of the hollowed-out bean curd lightly with cornstarch and gently fill each with a spoonful of the stuffing. The cornstarch will keep the filling from falling out. There should be some stuffing left over.

Heat a wok or large frying pan over high heat until it is hot. Swirl in the peanut oil, and when it is very hot and slightly smoking, turn the heat to low and add the stuffed bean curd, filling side down. Gently pan-fry, turning the bean curd when lightly browned and browning on the other side. Stir-fry the remaining stuffing mix over high heat for 1 minute. Pour off any excess oil and pour in all the sauce ingredients except the cornstarch mixture. Now return the stuffed bean curd squares to the wok or pan, layering them in gently, and bring to a simmer, cover, and cook for 3 minutes. Mix in the dissolved cornstarch and cook for another minute. Garnish with the scallions and serve at once.

# Stir=Fried Cabbage with Dried Shrimp

*Most first-generation Chinese-Americans like me grew up in relatively modest circumstances. Our parents had to keep a sharp eye on the budget. However, this parsimony never strictly applied to food.*

*Even for everyday eating, many of our parents could turn an inexpensive food like cabbage into an extremely tasty dish. Necessity is indeed one of the mothers of invention.*

*My friend Gordon Wing recalls that his mother used to add tiny bits of dried shrimp to an everyday food like cabbage, thus making it something really special. Because the dried shrimp were expensive, his mother very carefully apportioned them, but, after all, a little goes a long way. Extravagance was saved for special occasions, when budget considerations went out the window. I know that Gordon never complained about this dish.*

*Serves 4*

1/4 cup dried shrimp
1/3 cup Shaoxing rice wine or dry sherry
11/2 tablespoons salt
2 pounds shredded cabbage

2 tablespoons peanut oil
2 teaspoons salt
1/2 teaspoon freshly ground black pepper
2 tablespoons light soy sauce
1 tablespoon Asian sesame oil

Soak the dried shrimp in the rice wine for 1 hour or until they are slightly soft. Remove them from the rice wine with a slotted spoon and reserve both shrimp and wine.

Meanwhile, add the 11/2 tablespoons of salt to cold water and soak the cabbage in this for 1 hour. Drain the cabbage.

Heat a wok or large frying pan over high heat until it is hot. Swirl in the peanut oil, and when it is very hot and slightly smoking, toss in the dried shrimp and stir-fry for 1 minute, then add the cabbage, salt, and pepper and

*Ninetieth-birthday banquet for Gordon Wing's grandmother*

continue to stir-fry for 2 minutes. Now pour in the soy sauce and the rice wine that was set aside. Cook over high heat for 10 minutes, or until the cabbage is completely cooked. Swirl in the sesame oil and give the mixture several stirs. Serve at once.

# Simple Stir=Fried Tomatoes

*Fresh tomatoes, juicy and sweet, were a revelation to my mother. She had known about them in China but rarely encountered them in the traditional cuisine. Still, she made the most of their availability here in America. We would have them stir-fried with meats, eggs, even fish. For me, however, the most memorable dish was her simple stir-fried tomatoes. She would quarter fresh ripe tomatoes and then stir-fry them with garlic, salt, sugar, and pepper. Being a good Chinese cook, my mother valued the texture of the tomatoes, so they were cooked ever so briefly—never overcooked to a mush. The seasonings enhanced the flavor and taste of the tomatoes, making a delicious, colorful, and satisfying treat.*

*This dish takes but minutes and is a good vegetable side dish. Cherry tomatoes work just as well as the larger varieties.*

*Serves 4*

1 1/2 pounds fresh ripe tomatoes
1 tablespoon peanut oil
2 tablespoons finely sliced garlic
1 teaspoon salt
1 teaspoon sugar
1/2 teaspoon freshly ground black pepper

Quarter the tomatoes (if you are using cherry tomatoes, leave them whole). Heat a wok or large frying pan over high heat until it is hot. Swirl in the oil, and when it is very hot and slightly smoking, toss in the garlic and stir-fry for 10 seconds. Then chuck in the tomatoes, salt, sugar, and pepper and continue to stir-fry gently for 2 minutes. Remove and serve at once.

# Creamed Chinese Cabbage

*Here is a Chinese-American adaptation of a traditional Chinese dish. It typifies the ways in which overseas Chinese make use of local ingredients and techniques in order to prepare familiar foods in new ways. In China, this dish is normally braised for a long time in chicken stock; then chicken fat is added to the sauce, so that it is slightly rich. In America, where everyone is always hurried, Chinese-American cooks cut the cooking time and substitute a touch of heavy cream to give the sauce a unique milky texture.*

*Dairy foods are extremely rare in China except among certain minority groups in the North and in Southwestern China. But, growing up in America, I often drank a glass of milk with my meals. The Chinese are a very adaptable people, in culinary matters especially. This recipe is evidence of that.*

Serves 4

1 pound Napa cabbage
1 1/2 tablespoons peanut oil
3 garlic cloves, peeled and finely sliced
1 cup homemade chicken stock (page 60) or
    reduced-salt canned broth
1/4 cup finely chopped Smithfield ham
1/4 cup heavy cream
1 teaspoon salt
1/2 teaspoon freshly ground white pepper
2 teaspoons cornstarch mixed with 1 tablespoon water

Cut the cabbage into 2-inch-thick strips.

Heat a wok or large frying pan over high heat until it is hot. Swirl in the oil, and when it is very hot and slightly smoking, toss in the garlic and stir-fry for 15 seconds. Then chuck in the cabbage and stir-fry for 2 minutes. Next pour in the stock, ham, cream, salt, and pepper. Turn the heat to low, cover, and cook for 10 minutes, or until the cabbage is very tender. Remove the cabbage with a slotted spoon.

Pour in the cornstarch mixture and continue cooking, stirring, until the sauce is thick. Arrange the cabbage on a platter, pour the sauce over, and serve at once.

# Home=Style Braised Bean Curd with Pork

*A most satisfying and comforting dish is this savory concoction made with bean curd, which went extremely well with just plain rice. My mother used soft silky bean curd which gave the dish a custardlike texture. Unlike my mother, I have always loved hot spices, so she would make it quite hot for me. If I was home for a school holiday, she would prepare this in the morning so I could simply reheat it for my lunch.*

Serves 4

1 pound fresh soft bean curd
2 tablespoons peanut oil
2 tablespoons coarsely chopped garlic
1/2 pound ground pork
2 tablespoons whole bean sauce (see page 276)
2 tablespoons dark soy sauce
1 tablespoon Shaoxing rice wine or dry sherry
1/2 teaspoon salt
1 tablespoon chili bean sauce (see page 276)
1/2 cup homemade chicken stock (page 60) or reduced-salt
   canned broth
2 teaspoons cornstarch mixed with 1 tablespoon water

Carefully cut the bean curd into 1-inch pieces.

Heat a wok or large frying pan over high heat until it is hot. Swirl in the oil, and when it is very hot and slightly smoking, toss in the garlic and stir-fry for 20 seconds. Then chuck in the pork and stir-fry for 8 minutes. Now add the whole bean sauce, soy sauce, rice wine, and salt, and continue to stir-fry 1 minute. Spoon in the chili bean sauce and continue to stir-fry for 30 seconds. Finally, pour in the stock, gently slide in the bean curd, turn the heat to low, and cook gently for 3 minutes. Stir in the cornstarch mixture to thicken slightly and cook for another minute. Ladle the mixture into a serving bowl and serve at once.

# Bean Sauce

Seasonings made from fermented soybeans are one of the oldest forms of food flavoring in China. Before 200 B.C., the ancient Chinese used a form of salted and fermented soybeans, as well as another type of thin, salty sauce. These were precursors of the bean sauce of today made from yellow or black dried soybeans, which are partially decomposed by adding a mold culture, then salted, dried, or mixed with brine. Strongly flavored and salty, they are used to enhance and intensify the taste of Chinese dishes. Today, you can find bean sauce made with yellow beans, flour, and salt fermented together—thick, spicy, and aromatic. Correctly blended, it is quite salty but provides a distinctive flavor to Chinese sauces and is used often. The traditional bean sauce follows the ancient recipe for pickled yellow soybeans in a salty liquid. There are two forms: whole beans in a thick sauce; and mashed or pureed beans (sold as crushed or yellow bean sauce). My mother frequently used the whole bean sauce, as in Home-Style Braised Bean Curd with Pork (page 275). When combined with garlic and chili, it becomes chili bean sauce. Bean sauces in all forms are available in glass jars at Chinese groceries or supermarkets. Kept in the refrigerator, it will last indefinitely.

# Joyce Wing's Curried Potatoes

*This is a true Chinese-American dish, combining basic ingredients—potatoes and curry—that are unusual in traditional Chinese cuisine. But, in a typical Chinese way, Joyce Wing would put together foods and seasonings that were at hand and create a substantial and inexpensive dish to be enjoyed by the whole family.*

*My friend Gordon Wing tells me that his mother did not add carrots or any other vegetables, because she wanted the basic curry-potato blend to shine through. And she usually made the dish with beef or chicken, stir-fried separately and mixed in just before serving. In fact, the curry powder, potatoes, and onions are all prepared sequentially, the point being to preserve their individuality and thus to enhance the varied tastes of the final ensemble.*

*Joyce Wing prefers to cook the potatoes until they begin to dissolve, so as to thicken the dish. And if the curry has lost some of its zest, her trick is to add some diced chili pepper, a step she sometimes has to take.*

*Gordon and I argue about whether his hometown, Boston, has colder winters than my Chicago. But we do agree that this dish is perfect for a cold winter's evening in any place.*

*Serves 4*

1 1/2 pounds russet potatoes
1 pound yellow onions
3 tablespoons peanut oil
2 tablespoons coarsely chopped garlic
3 tablespoons Madras curry powder
2 cups homemade chicken stock (page 60) or reduced-salt
    canned broth
2 tablespoons plus 2 teaspoons light soy sauce
2 teaspoons salt
2 teaspoons sugar
1/2 pound ground beef
1 teaspoon Shaoxing rice wine or dry sherry
1 teaspoon Asian sesame oil
1 teaspoon cornstarch

Peel and cut the potatoes into 1-inch pieces. Cut the onions into slices.

Heat a wok or large frying pan over high heat until it is hot. Swirl in 1 tablespoon of the peanut oil, and when it is very hot and slightly smoking, toss in the garlic and half of the curry powder and stir-fry for 30 seconds. Then chuck in the potatoes and stir-fry for 2 minutes. Remove them and set aside. Reheat the wok over high heat, and when it is hot, add another tablespoon of oil, toss in the onions and the rest of the curry powder, and stir-fry until the onions are caramelized, about 3 minutes. Return the potatoes to the wok, pour in the chicken stock and 2 tablespoons of soy sauce, and sprinkle in the salt and sugar. Transfer the mixture to a heavy casserole, cover, turn the heat to low, and simmer gently for 1½ hours, or until the potatoes are thoroughly cooked and have begun to dissolve.

Meanwhile, mix the beef with the remaining 2 teaspoons of soy sauce, the rice wine, sesame oil, and cornstarch. Heat a wok or large frying pan over high heat until it is hot. Swirl in the remaining 1 tablespoon of oil, and when it is very hot and slightly smoking, add the ground beef and stir-fry for 5 minutes, breaking it up.

When the potatoes are cooked, stir in the beef and serve at once.

Variation:  Substitute ½ pound of chopped boneless, skinless chicken thighs or ground turkey meat or pork for the beef.

# My Mother's Stir=Fried Pumpkin in Black Bean Sauce

*Nowhere does the principle that necessity is the mother of invention apply more than in this dish, in which my mother combines sweet pumpkin with a savory black bean sauce. In China, a variety of squashes and melons are available and enjoyed. However, in Chicago's Chinatown, with its long, cold Midwestern winters, we were limited to a much narrower range of Chinese vegetables. Out of necessity, we learned to adopt local American vegetables and adapt them to our taste.*

*My mother stir-fried and then braised pumpkin until it was tender, as in this simple recipe. Sometimes she would add a small amount of fried ground beef, but often it arrived at the table as a tasty vegetarian dish. While my American schoolmates were using pumpkins for their Halloween jack-o'-lanterns, at home we were enjoying this treat. It was like having their pumpkins and eating mine, too.*

*Serves 4*

1½ pounds pumpkin (weighed whole)
1½ tablespoons peanut oil
3 tablespoons chopped shallots
2 tablespoons coarsely chopped fermented black beans
2 tablespoons coarsely chopped garlic
1 tablespoon finely chopped fresh ginger
1 teaspoon salt
Freshly ground black pepper to taste
2 tablespoons Shaoxing rice wine or dry sherry
1 tablespoon chili bean sauce (see page 276)
1 tablespoon light soy sauce
2 tablespoons dark soy sauce
2 teaspoons sugar
1 cup homemade chicken stock (page 60) or
   reduced-salt canned broth
2 teaspoons Asian sesame oil

Remove and discard the hard skin of the pumpkin, as well as the pulp and seeds. Cut the pumpkin into 2-inch pieces.

Heat a wok or large frying pan over high heat until it is hot. Swirl in the peanut oil, and when it is very hot and slightly smoking, toss in the shallots, black beans, garlic, ginger, salt, and pepper and stir-fry for 1 minute. Then toss in the pumpkin pieces and stir-fry for 2 minutes. Finally, add the rice wine, chili bean sauce, soy sauces, sugar, and chicken stock. Reduce the heat, cover, and simmer for 25 minutes, or until the pumpkin is soft. Turn the heat back to high and cook for 2 minutes, then stir in the sesame oil and give the mixture several good stirs to mix well. Serve at once with another meat dish.

# Chinatown Stir-Fried Asparagus with Oyster Sauce

*Perusing menus from hundreds of Chinese restaurants in America, I was struck by the number that feature this simple stir-fried asparagus dish. It is truly a Chinese-American dish, for asparagus is a relatively recent arrival in Chinese cooking. The ever-pragmatic Chinese cooks instantly realized the appeal of this popular vegetable in America and learned to combine it with a tasteful and very Chinese treat—oyster sauce. The result quickly became a popular standard item that every American diner in Chinese restaurants throughout the country could count on. Thick asparagus, with its meaty stem, was preferred, because it married well with the savory oyster sauce. This easy stir-fried dish nevertheless had the hint of exotic China. It makes a nice vegetable accompaniment to any meal.*

Serves 4

1¹/₂ pounds fresh thick asparagus
1¹/₂ tablespoons peanut oil
1 teaspoon salt
Freshly ground black pepper to taste
2 tablespoons finely sliced garlic
¹/₂ cup homemade chicken stock (page 60) or
    reduced-salt canned broth
2 teaspoons Shaoxing rice wine or dry sherry
3 tablespoons oyster sauce
2 teaspoons Asian sesame oil

Remove the hard ends of the asparagus, then cut the vegetable into thick diagonal slices.

Heat a wok or large frying pan over high heat until it is hot. Swirl in the peanut oil, and when it is hot and slightly smoking, toss in the salt, pepper, and garlic and stir-fry for 30 seconds. Now toss in the asparagus and continue to stir-fry for 1 minute. Pour in the chicken stock, rice wine, and oyster sauce and continue to cook over high heat for 3 minutes, or until the asparagus is tender. Stir in the sesame oil and serve at once.

# My Mother's New Year Dish

*The Chinese New Year celebration was always the biggest holiday in my family. We would pay the traditional homage to our ancestors by burning incense at the small family altar that stood at one end of the living room. My job was to rub some honey over the kitchen-god poster on the kitchen wall so that he could report only sweet and good things to the Jade Emperor in heaven.*

*Then the New Year's food preparation would begin. Certain foods were always served at the New Year table, because they symbolized particular good and noteworthy aspirations. Fish, which represent abundance and good fortune, were an essential item. Likewise noodles, a symbol of longevity—what good is abundance and good fortune without the time to enjoy them?*

*My mother, being a good and faithful Buddhist, always made her vegetarian dish, a savory vegetable casserole that I remember to this day. I have altered my mother's recipe by using chicken stock; she used water, though a vegetarian stock could be substituted. The bonus is that this dish reheats well.*

Serves 4

1 pound firm bean curd
1/2 cup Chinese dried black mushrooms
1/4 pound (2 2-ounce packages) bean thread noodles
1/2 cup soaked hair vegetable (1 ounce dried); see box,
   page 282
1 pound Napa cabbage
1 1/2 cups peanut oil
1 teaspoon salt
1/2 teaspoon freshly ground black pepper
2 tablespoons Shaoxing rice wine or dry sherry
1 1/2 cups homemade chicken stock (page 60) or
   reduced-salt canned broth
2 tablespoons light soy sauce
1 tablespoon dark soy sauce
2 tablespoons whole yellow bean sauce (see page 276)
3 tablespoons oyster sauce
1 tablespoon Asian sesame oil

Cut the bean curd into 1-inch cubes. Drain it on paper towels. Soak the mushrooms in warm water for 20 minutes, then drain them and squeeze out the excess liquid. Remove and discard the stems, and finely shred the caps into thin strips. Soak the bean thread noodles in warm water for 20 minutes and drain well. Soak the hair vegetable in warm water for 20 minutes and drain well.

Cut the Napa cabbage into 1-inch pieces.

Heat a wok or large frying pan over high heat until it is hot. Pour in the peanut oil, and when it is very hot and slightly smoking, deep-fry the bean curd cubes in 2 batches. Drain each batch well on paper towels.

Drain off all but 1½ tablespoons of oil and reheat the wok. Toss in the mushrooms, Napa cabbage, salt, and pepper and stir-fry for 4 minutes. The mixture will be rather dry. Then toss in the bean thread noodles, hair vegetable, rice wine, stock, soy sauces, bean sauce, and oyster sauce. Bring the mixture to a simmer, toss in the fried bean curd, cover, and cook for 15 minutes.

Finally, swirl in the sesame oil and serve at once with plain rice.

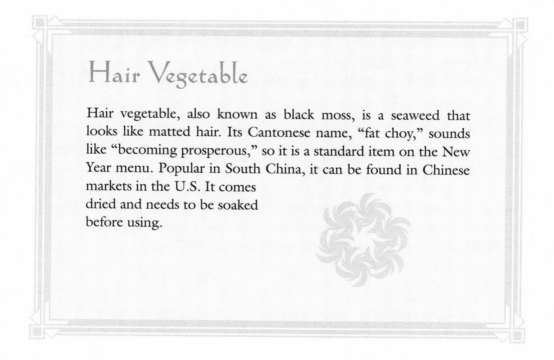

## Hair Vegetable

Hair vegetable, also known as black moss, is a seaweed that looks like matted hair. Its Cantonese name, "fat choy," sounds like "becoming prosperous," so it is a standard item on the New Year menu. Popular in South China, it can be found in Chinese markets in the U.S. It comes dried and needs to be soaked before using.

# Simple Stir=Fried Celery with Shrimp Paste

*Celery has unfortunately and undeservedly acquired a bad repu-
tation in Chinese-American cooking, because it is used simply as a
filler in so many dishes. For restaurant owners it was a cheap way
to bulk up a dish, but the vegetable has better uses. We ate Chinese
celery at home as a dish by itself. My mother often stir-fried the
small, intensely flavored celery with shrimp paste. This simple,
aromatic vegetable dish literally took minutes to make.*

Serves 4

1½ pounds Chinese celery or ordinary celery
2 tablespoons peanut oil
2 teaspoons coarsely chopped garlic
2 tablespoons finely chopped scallions
1 tablespoon Shaoxing rice wine or dry sherry
2 teaspoons shrimp paste or sauce*
2 teaspoons sugar
3 tablespoons homemade chicken stock (page 60), reduced-
    salt canned broth, or water
1 teaspoon Asian sesame oil

* Available at Chinese groceries or supermarkets.

Trim the base of the celery and all the top leaves. Separate the stalks.
With a small sharp knife, remove strings as needed from the tough stalks.
Chop the celery stalks into 1-inch pieces.

Heat a wok or large frying pan over high heat until it is hot. Swirl in the
peanut oil, and when it is hot and slightly smoking, toss in the garlic and scallions and stir-fry for 10 seconds. Then toss in the celery and continue to stir-
fry for 1 minute. Drizzle in the rice wine, spoon in the shrimp paste and
sugar, and continue to stir-fry for 1 minute. Finally, drizzle in the stock or
water and continue to cook over high heat for 3–4 minutes, until just tender.
Then drizzle in the sesame oil, mix well, pour onto a platter, and serve at once
as a vegetable side dish.

# Chinese Celery

Chinese celery is virtually identical in form to European celery but differs in size. The bunches are less compact and the individual stalks are thin. Apparently they are the same species and represent divergent development over fifteen hundred years. Both have the same aromatic flavor and crispy, externally fibrous texture. The Chinese celery probably evolved from a wild form of Asian celery. In China, celery has a long history of use as a flavoring herb and vegetable. Today, it is one of the most widely grown vegetables in China.

# Festive Stuffed Cucumber

*It was always a festive occasion when there was a stuffed vegetable on the dinner table, for this meant my mother had had the time to make a complicated dish. One of my favorite dishes from my childhood is stuffed bitter melon. When it was not in season, my mother would substitute cucumbers. They lend themselves to stuffing, because their tender, succulent flesh complements so many savory fillings. Thick cucumber slices are stuffed and then shallow-fried; this seals in the flavors of the stuffing. Then the cucumbers are simmered with seasonings to create the sauce. I think you will agree that this dish would enhance any table on a festive occasion.*

*Serves 4*

1½ pounds cucumbers
2 tablespoons cornstarch

## Stuffing Mixture

½ pound fatty ground pork
¼ cup peeled, finely chopped fresh water chestnuts, or
   canned
1 egg white
2 tablespoons finely chopped scallions
2 teaspoons finely chopped fresh ginger
2 teaspoons Shaoxing rice wine or dry sherry
2 teaspoons light soy sauce
2 teaspoons sugar
1 teaspoon salt
1 teaspoon freshly ground black pepper
1 teaspoon Asian sesame oil

3 tablespoons peanut oil

## Sauce

1 cup homemade chicken stock (page 60) or
   reduced-salt canned broth
2 tablespoons Shaoxing rice wine or dry sherry
2 tablespoons oyster sauce
1 tablespoon light soy sauce
1 teaspoon dark soy sauce
2 teaspoons sugar
1 teaspoon cornstarch mixed with 1 tablespoon
   water

## Garnish

2 teaspoons Asian sesame oil
2 tablespoons finely chopped fresh coriander

Cut the cucumbers into 1-inch slices without peeling them. Remove the
seeds and pulp from the center of each cucumber slice, using a small sharp
knife. Hollow out the cucumber, leaving at least ¼ inch of shell. Lightly dust
the hollow interior of the cucumber slices with a little cornstarch. Mix all the

stuffing ingredients together in a large bowl. Then fill each cucumber ring with this stuffing.

Heat a wok or large frying pan over high heat until it is hot. Swirl in 1 tablespoon of the peanut oil, and when it is moderately hot and slightly smoking, gently layer in the stuffed cucumber rings and cook them slowly until they are slightly browned. Turn them over and brown the other side, adding more oil if necessary. You may have to do this in several batches. When the cucumber rings are brown, remove them from the oil and drain them on paper towels. When you have fried all the cucumber rings, wipe the wok or pan clean.

Mix the stock, rice wine, oyster sauce, soy sauces, and sugar and pour them into the reheated wok or pan. Bring the liquid to a simmer, and then layer in all the stuffed cucumber rings. Cover the pan with a lid and simmer slowly for 7 minutes, or until the cucumbers are completely cooked. Transfer them to a serving platter, lifting them out of the sauce with a slotted spoon.

Pour in the cornstarch mixture and simmer until slightly thickened, then reduce the sauce by a third over a high heat. Swirl in the sesame oil and sprinkle in the fresh coriander. Pour the sauce over the stuffed cucumbers and serve at once.

*My mother and I with our immediate family in Kaiping. Family pictures in the background, including my childhood photos*

# Stir=Fried Cabbage with Garlic

*Green cabbage was rarely eaten in our Cantonese home. My Chinese-American friends like Lillian Robyn, who was originally from Beijing, often ate cabbage. She would simply stir-fry it with meat or by itself, as in this tasty vegetable dish. Salted water draws out the moisture and gives the cabbage a crispy texture. This easy-to-make dish is a fine accompaniment to any meat or fish dish.*

Serves 2—4

1¹/₂ pounds green cabbage
1 tablespoon salt

1¹/₂ tablespoons peanut oil
1 teaspoon salt
¹/₄ teaspoon freshly ground black pepper
3 tablespoons coarsely chopped garlic
1 teaspoon sugar
2 teaspoons Shaoxing rice wine or dry sherry
2 teaspoons Asian sesame oil

Trim the cabbage by removing any tough outer leaves. Core and discard the center stem. Finely shred the cabbage leaves. In a large bowl, toss the cabbage shreds with salt, then cover with cold water and leave to sit for 1 hour. Rinse well in fresh cold water and drain.

Heat a wok or large frying pan over high heat until it is hot. Swirl in the peanut oil, and when it is very hot and slightly smoking, sprinkle with salt and pepper, toss in the garlic, and stir-fry for 1 minute. Then toss in the cabbage, sugar, and rice wine and continue to stir-fry over high heat for 5 minutes. Drizzle in the sesame oil and give the mixture a few good stirs. It is now ready to be served.

# Hong Kong—Style Broccoli

*Chinese-American cooking has taken a turn toward Hong Kong in recent years as chefs and new arrivals from there have brought with them their creative innovations in food. A lighter, fresher spirit with a touch of traditional Chinese seasonings and flavorings is now the current rage in Chinese restaurants throughout America. Instead of Chinese broccoli, which has a slightly mustardlike taste, American broccoli, with its sweet taste and crispy texture, is a great favorite in Hong Kong as well as America.*

Serves 4

1 pound fresh broccoli
1/2 cup Chinese dried black mushrooms
1 1/2 tablespoons peanut oil
1 teaspoon salt
1/2 teaspoon freshly ground black pepper
1 teaspoon sugar
1 tablespoon Shaoxing rice wine or dry sherry
1 tablespoon light soy sauce
3 tablespoons oyster sauce
2 teaspoons Asian sesame oil

Separate the broccoli heads into small florets; then peel and slice the stems. Blanch the broccoli pieces in a large pot of boiling salted water for 3 minutes, and then immerse them in cold water. Drain thoroughly.

Soak the mushrooms in warm water for 20 minutes. Drain them and squeeze out the excess liquid. Remove and discard the stems, and finely shred the caps into thin strips.

Heat a wok or large frying pan over high heat until it is hot. Swirl in the peanut oil, and when it is very hot and slightly smoking, toss in the broccoli, mushrooms, salt, pepper, and sugar. Stir-fry for 3 minutes, and then pour in the rice wine, soy sauce, and oyster sauce. If the mixture seems a bit dry, ladle in 2 tablespoons of water and continue to stir-fry at moderate to high heat for 2 minutes, until the vegetables are thoroughly heated through. Drizzle in the sesame oil, and continue to stir-fry for 30 seconds. The vegetables are ready to be served.

# Simple Stir=Fried Mushrooms

*Brown mushrooms were a revelation when I first sampled them at the school cafeteria. I had grown up with thick black mushrooms that were rehydrated and then cooked until they were plump and full of flavor. The ones I had at school were watery and tasteless. However, I have since learned how they should be cooked. Stir-frying them in a wok leaves them slightly firm with a wonderful texture: nothing mushy about them. When sliced, they make a quick and easy vegetable side dish. This dish literally takes minutes to assemble and cook.*

Serves 2—4

1¹/₂ tablespoons peanut oil
1 teaspoon salt
2 tablespoons coarsely chopped garlic
1 teaspoon finely chopped ginger
1 pound thinly sliced fresh brown mushrooms
2 teaspoons Shaoxing rice wine or dry sherry
2 teaspoons light soy sauce
1 teaspoon sugar
2 teaspoons Asian sesame oil

Heat a wok or large frying pan over high heat until it is hot. Swirl in the peanut oil, and when it is very hot and slightly smoking, toss in the salt, garlic, and ginger and stir-fry them for 1 minute, or until the garlic begins to brown. Quickly dump in the mushroom slices, and continue to stir-fry for 2 minutes. Now pour in the rice wine, soy sauce, and sugar and continue stir-frying for 5 minutes, or until any liquid has been reabsorbed by the mushrooms. Finally, drizzle in the sesame oil, give the mushrooms a few stirs, and serve at once.

# Stir=Fried Bean Sprouts

*A dish that many of my Chinese-American friends talked about was a simple stir-fry of soybean sprouts. Soybean sprouts are larger and crunchier than the more commonly available mung bean sprouts. Unfortunately, soybean sprouts are available only season-ally, and even then may be found only in Chinese groceries. Mung bean sprouts, however, are readily available, and they are the ones most commonly found in supermarkets. Chinese-Americans use mung bean sprouts as an acceptable substitute. We always blanch or stir-fry them—never eat them raw. Once stir-fried, this rather bland and simple vegetable is turned into a tasty treat, the heat of the wok infusing the sprouts with a zesty, slightly smoky flavor. This recipe makes a nice vegetable side dish.*

Serves 4, as a side dish

1 pound fresh bean sprouts
2 tablespoons peanut oil
1 teaspoon salt
2 tablespoons finely shredded fresh red chili, seeded
2 tablespoons finely chopped scallions
1 teaspoon light soy sauce
1 teaspoon Shaoxing rice wine or dry sherry
2 teaspoons Asian sesame oil

Pick over the bean sprouts, discarding any brown ones.

Heat a wok or large frying pan over high heat until it is hot. Swirl in the peanut oil, and when it is very hot and slightly smoking, toss in the salt and chilies and stir-fry for 30 seconds. Then dump in the bean sprouts and scal-lions and stir-fry another minute. Now drizzle in the soy sauce and rice wine or dry sherry and continue to stir-fry for 1 minute. Finally, drizzle in the sesame oil and continue to stir-fry for 1 minute. Turn the mixture onto a plat-ter and serve at once, or allow it to cool and serve at room temperature.

# A FEW DESSERTS

*Almond Cookies*

*Steamed Sponge Cake*

*Home-Style Almond Jelly with Fresh Fruit*

# Almond Cookies

*An authentic Chinese-American invention, these popular cookies are found in almost every Chinese restaurant, as well as food shops in Chinatown. In China, real almonds are rare and expensive, thus little used. The Chinese use apricot kernels, cooked to eliminate their toxicity, as the Western world uses almonds.*

*The origins of these almond cookies in America are rather murky, but, given the availability and pleasing qualities of the almonds, they were soon incorporated in the cuisine by Chinese-American chefs. They are a delicious treat, and not overly sweet. The original calls for lard, but I have used butter instead, for a richer flavor and more satisfying texture.*

Makes 16

8 tablespoons (1 stick) unsalted butter at room
   temperature
1 cup sugar
1 egg
1 teaspoon almond extract
1/2 cup ground almonds
2 cups all-purpose unbleached white flour
1 teaspoon baking powder
pinch of salt
Egg wash: 1 egg beaten with 2 tablespoons of water

Preheat the oven to 375° F.

Using an electric mixer or a hand beater in a large bowl, mix the butter and sugar until pale yellow. Then toss in the egg, almond extract, and ground almonds. Mix thoroughly.

Combine the flour and baking powder and sift this into the butter-sugar mixture. Toss in the salt and mix. Do not overmix.

Roll the dough into a log about 12 inches long and cut into 16 even pieces. Roll each piece into a ball and flatten slightly. Place on a baking tray, brush the tops of all the cookies with the egg wash, and bake for 15 minutes, or until golden brown.

# Steamed Sponge Cake

*Our Sunday table always included two reassuring foods, what I
call our standard "comfort foods": fresh chicken (which my mother
most often dispatched, plucked, and prepared herself), and sponge
cake, which was central to the almost ritual afternoon tea with
the neighbors. "Chicken every Sunday" is as Chinese-American as
sponge cake. (But rice remains the king of South Chinese comfort
foods.)*

*The chicken was usually either steeped or steamed, these being
my mother's favorite ways to ensure that the delicate chicken taste
was at once preserved and yet enhanced by the added seasonings.*

*Early in the morning, before she left for the Chinatown
live-poultry market to select the chicken, my mother would steam
the sponge cake in the wok. She would then rest the cake on top of
the refrigerator until teatime, in the late afternoon. One of our
neighbors, Mrs. Tsai, would sometimes make a sweet almond puree
to go with the cake. Tea was an event I always looked forward to
and enjoyed. We need such pleasant rituals of friendship and
community.*

*Serves 4–6*

1½ cups all-purpose unbleached white flour
2 teaspoons baking powder
½ teaspoon baking soda
Pinch of salt
6 eggs, separated
1¼ cups sugar
½ cup milk

Sift the flour, baking powder, baking soda, and salt together.

In a bowl, beat the egg yolks with the sugar for 5 minutes, until they are
well blended. Pour in the milk. Mix well, and add the sifted ingredients. Continue mixing well until you have a smooth batter. In a separate bowl, beat the
egg whites until they form soft peaks. Fold the egg whites into the cake batter. Generously butter an 8-inch cake pan. Pour the batter into the pan.

Next, set up a steamer, or put a rack into a wok or deep pan, and fill it
with 2 inches of water. Bring the water to a boil over high heat. Put the cake

into the steamer or onto the rack. Turn the heat to low and cover the wok or pan tightly. Steam over medium heat for 25 minutes, or until a toothpick inserted into the cake comes out clean. Remove the cake from the steamer. The cake should be light and springy to the touch. Unmold the cake onto a platter, slice, and serve.

## Agar=agar

Agar-agar is a sparkling, pure form of gelatin processed from a type of seaweed. In Chinese cooking, it is generally used for sweets and confections in the same manner as gelatin. It differs from gelatin in that it begins to set at a higher temperature. However, for best results— a firmer texture—it needs refrigeration. Its texture is more delicate than that of gelatin. Agar-agar comes in stick and powdered forms.

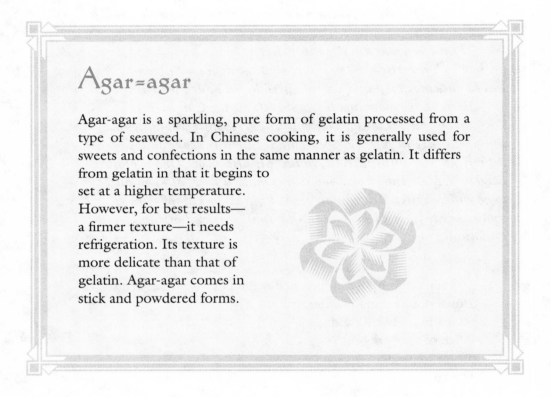

# Home=Style Almond Jelly
# with Fresh Fruit

*Growing up Chinese-American meant, among other things, that
we rarely enjoyed the sugary-sweet desserts so popular in American cooking. Instead, slices of fresh oranges were the standard
dessert. On special occasions we would enjoy almond jelly, an
almond-flavored gelatin sweet. This Chinese Jell-O is made with
agar-agar, which can be found in Chinese markets as well as
Japanese food stores. On hot, humid Chicago summer evenings,
we especially enjoyed this cooling almond jelly. Served with fresh
orange segments, it was a lovely, refreshing dessert.*

*Serves 4*

4 cups hot water
1 cup blanched almonds
1 stick (5 grams) agar-agar (see box opposite)
1 cup sugar
1 cup milk
1 teaspoon almond extract
2 oranges

Pour 2 cups of hot water over the almonds, and let them sit for at least
2 hours. Soak the agar-agar in cold water for at least 1 hour. Puree the
almonds and water in a blender and strain through a fine sieve. Reserve the
liquid. Remove and drain the agar-agar.

In a medium-sized pan, combine the remaining 2 cups of hot water with
the sugar and the drained agar-agar. Simmer for at least 30 minutes, or until
the agar-agar has dissolved completely. Add the reserved almond liquid, milk,
and almond extract. Strain this mixture through a fine sieve into a 9-inch
square baking dish. Allow it to cool at room temperature, then refrigerate for
several hours, until firm.

Peel the oranges and remove all the white pith. Separate them into segments. When the almond jelly is ready, cut it into 1-inch cubes. In individual
bowls put some orange segments and some almond jelly cubes.

# Fortune Cookies

It was once said that fortune cookies were invented in China about a thousand years ago, but that the times were so bad—floods; famines; no ginger, garlic, or soy sauce; droughts; wars—and all of the predictions and sayings that appeared in the cookies were so gloomy that the bakers stopped making them.

A nice story but not true. Fortune cookies were invented in 1916, in Los Angeles, by a Chinese-American noodle manufacturer, David Jung. He got the idea of making sweet, thin, crispy cookies with a message folded up inside from Chinese rebels, who would hide their communications with each other inside of buns and other foods. The cookies were an immediate success. Chinese restaurants are not famous for their desserts; fruits and vanilla ice cream were about all they served. So the fortune cookies appealed to both the sweet tooth and the imagination of the customers.

The earliest messages in the cookies were indeed limited to predictions, almost always couched in Charlie Chan–Confucius language, foretelling good things to come or ambiguously cautious about the future. No sense upsetting the customers. I am convinced that every American who ate in Chinese restaurants, until very recently, enjoyed fortune cookie messages and felt there just *might* be something to them.

However, the world grows old and cynical. In the past twenty years or so, the Delphic pronouncements in the fortune cookies have given way to standard one-liners, ethnic and erotic references, and black humor, such as: "Pay your bill immediately! You are about to have a heart attack!"

I have discovered that these fortune cookies are invariably folded by hand, in factories that resemble those my mother worked in fifty years ago; the workers are usually recent immigrants, nonunionized, who work very hard, for low wages. Such conditions remind me of a message a comedian claimed he found in his cookie: "Help! I'm a prisoner in a Chinese bakery!"

Nonetheless, except in the most upscale establishments, fortune cookies are still part of the Chinese-American dining experience. And recently a Brooklyn noodle company contracted with a state-owned company in Canton to build and run a fortune cookie factory there. The messages will be printed in Chinese and English around the general
theme "You will be rich and famous."
Like chop suey, it worked in America,
so why not in China?

# Selected Bibliography

*American Section: Special Recipe Cook Book of the Woman's Society of Christian Services of the St. Mark's Methodist Church*. Stockton, Calif.: St. Mark's United Methodist Church, 1966.

*The Art of Chinese Cooking*. Rutland, Vt.: Charles E. Tuttle, 1956.

Chan, Anthony B. *Gold Mountain: The Chinese in the New World*. Vancouver: New Star Books, 1983.

Chan, Sou. *The House of Chan Cookbook*. Garden City, N.Y.: Doubleday, 1952.

Chan, Sucheng. *This Bitter-Sweet Soil: The Chinese in California Agriculture, 1860–1910*. Berkeley: University of California Press, 1986.

Chang, Isabelle. *What's Cooking at Chang's: The Key to Chinese Cooking*. New York: Liveright, 1959.

Chao, Buwei Yang. *How to Cook and Eat in Chinese*. New York: John Day, 1945.

Chao, Buwei Yang, and Yuenren Chao. *Autobiography of a Chinese Woman*. Westport, Conn.: Greenwood Press, 1970; original ed. New York: John Day, 1947.

Chen, Jack. *The Chinese of America*. San Francisco: Harper & Row, 1981.

Cheng, F. T. *Musings of a Chinese Gourmet*. London: Hutchinson, 1954.

Chiang, Cecelia Sun Yun. *The Mandarin Way*. Boston: Little, Brown, 1974.

*Chinatown Handy Guide: San Francisco*. Edited and published by John T. C. Fang. San Francisco: Chinese Publishing House, 1959.

*The Chinese Cook Book: Covering the Entire Field of Chinese Cookery in the Chinese Order of Serving, from Nuts to Soup*. Edited by Mr. M. Sing Au. Reading, Pa.: Culinary Arts Press, 1936.

Chu, Grace Zia. *The Pleasures of Chinese Cooking*. New York: Simon & Schuster, 1962.

*Cooking with Square & Circle*. San Francisco: Square & Circle Club, 1977.

Daniel, Roger. *Chinese and Japanese in the United States Since 1850*. Seattle: University of Washington Press, 1988.

De Barry Nee, Victor G., and Brett De Barry Nee. *Longtime Californ': A Docu-*

*mentary Study of an American Chinatown.* Stanford, Calif.: Stanford University Press, 1972.

*Eating Out in Chinese Restaurants: A Guide to Ordering Chinese Food.* Singapore: Asia Pacific Press, 1972.

Feng, Doreen Yen Hung. *The Joy of Chinese Cooking.* New York: Greenberg, n.d.

Froud, Nina. *Cooking the Chinese Way.* London: Spring Books, 1960.

Glick, Clarence E. *Sojourners and Settlers: Chinese Migrants in Hawaii.* Honolulu: University Press of Hawaii, 1980.

Grossman, Ruth, and Bob Grossman. *The Chinese-Kosher Cookbook.* New York: Paul S. Eriksson, 1963.

Hee, Yep Yung. *Chinese Recipes for Home Cooking.* Sydney: Associated General Publications, 1951.

Hodgson, Moira. *Chinese Cooking with American Meals.* Garden City, N.Y.: Doubleday, 1970.

Hom, Ken. *Chinese Technique.* New York: Simon & Schuster, 1981.

———. *Ken Hom's Chinese Cookery.* New York: Harper & Row, 1986.

———. *Ken Hom's East Meets West Cuisine.* New York: Simon & Schuster, 1987.

———. *Asian Vegetarian Feast.* New York: William Morrow, 1988.

———. *Fragrant Harbor Taste: The New Chinese Cooking of Hong Kong.* New York: Simon & Schuster, 1989.

———. *Ken Hom's Quick & Easy Chinese Cooking.* San Francisco: Chronicle Books, 1990.

———. *The Taste of China.* New York: Simon & Schuster, 1990.

———. *Sainsbury's Cooking of China.* London: Martin Books, 1993.

———. *Ken Hom's Chinese Kitchen.* New York: Hyperion, 1995.

———. *Ken Hom Cooks Chinese.* London: BBC Books, 1996.

———. *Ken Hom's Asian Ingredients.* Berkeley, Calif.: Ten Speed Press, 1996.

———. *Ken Hom's Hot Wok.* London: BBC Books, 1996.

Hong, Maria, ed. *Growing Up Asian American: An Anthology.* New York: William Morrow, 1993.

Hoobler, Dorothy, and Thomas Hoobler. *The Chinese American Family Album.* New York: Oxford University Press, 1994.

Hsuan Chen, Julia I. "The Chinese Community in New York: A Study in Their Cultural Adjustment, 1920–1940." Unpublished Ph.D. dissertation, American University, 1941.

SOLON PUBLIC LIBRARY
SOLON, IOWA

Jan, Dr. Lee Su. *The Fine Art of Chinese Cooking*. New York: Gramercy, 1962.

Kan, Johnny, and Charles L. Leong. *Eight Immortal Flavors*. Berkeley: Howell-North Books, 1963.

Kao, George. *Cathay by the Bay: San Francisco Chinatown in 1950*. Hong Kong: Chinese University Press, 1988.

Karnow, Stanley. "Year In, Year Out, Those Eateries Keep Eggrolling Along." *Smithsonian Magazine,* January 1994.

Kim, Bok-Lim C. *The Asian Americans: Changing Patterns, Changing Needs*. Montclair, N.J.: Association of Korean Christian Scholars in North America, 1978.

Kinkead, Gwen. "A Reporter at Large: Chinatown—I." *New Yorker,* June 10, 1991.

———. "A Reporter at Large: Chinatown—II." *New Yorker,* June 17, 1991.

Knoll, Tricia. *Becoming Americans: Asian Sojourners, Immigrants, and Refugees in the Western United States*. Portland, Ore.: Coast to Coast Books, 1982.

Kuo, Chia-ling. *Social and Political Change in New York's Chinatown: The Role of Voluntary Associations*. New York: Praeger, 1977.

La Lande, Jeffrey M. " 'Celestials' in Oregon Siskyous: Diet, Dress and Drug Use of the Chinese Miners in Jackson County, CA, 1860–1900." *Northwest Anthropological Research Notes,* vol. 16, no. 1 (Spring 1982), pp. 31–39.

Lapidus, Dorothy Farris. *The Scrutable Feast: A Guide to Eating Authentically in Chinese Restaurants*. New York: Dodd, Mead, 1977.

Lee, Beverly. *The Easy Way to Chinese Cooking*. Garden City, N.Y.: Doubleday, 1963.

Lee, Jim. *Jim Lee's Chinese Cook Book*. New York: Harper & Row, 1968.

Lin, Tsuifeng, and Hsiangju Lin. *Cooking with the Chinese Flavor*. Englewood Cliffs, N.J.: Prentice-Hall, 1956.

———. *Secrets of Chinese Cooking*. New York: Bonanza Books, 1960.

Ling, Mei-Mei. *Chop Suey: A Collection of Simple Chinese Recipes Adapted for the American Home*. Honolulu: Chop Suey, 1953.

Liu, Catherine. *Chinese Cooking the American Way*. Dallas: Chinese Cooking Institute, 1976.

Liu, Dolly. *"Chow": Secrets of Chinese Cooking*. Shanghai: Kelly & Walsh, 1939.

Loewen, James W. *The Mississippi Chinese: Between Black and White*. Prospect Heights, Ill.: Waveland Press, 1971.

Lovegren, Sylvia. *Fashionable Food: Seven Decades of Food Fads*. New York: Macmillan, 1995.

Low, Henry. *Cook at Home in Chinese*. Hong Kong: Pacific Printing & Mfg. Co., n.d.

Lyman, Stanford M. *Chinese Americans*. New York: Random House, 1974.

McCawley, James D. *The Eater's Guide to Chinese Characters*. Chicago: University of Chicago Press, 1984.

McCunn, Ruthanne Lum. *Thousand Pieces of Gold*. San Francisco: Design Enterprises of San Francisco, 1981.

———. *Chinese American Portraits: Personal Histories 1828–1988*. San Francisco: Chronicle Books, 1988.

McHale, Lucy Chee, and Joyce Goldberg. *The All-American Chinese Cookbook: Fine Chinese Cooking with Common American Ingredients*. Maplewood, N.J.: Hammond, 1980.

Mei, Yu Wen, and Charlotte Adams. *100 Most Honorable Chinese Restaurants*. New York: Avenel Books, 1963.

Melendy, H. Brett. *Chinese and Japanese Americans*. New York: Hippocrene Books, 1972.

*Oriental Cookbook*. Edited by Alice Miller Mitchell. New York: Rand McNally, 1950.

Pan, Lynn. *Sons of the Yellow Emperor: The Story of the Overseas Chinese*. London: Secker & Warburg, 1990.

Reichl, Ruth. "Dining in New York." *New York Times,* March 8, 1994.

*San Francisco Chinatown on Parade*. Edited by H. K. Wong. San Francisco: Chinese Chamber of Commerce, 1961.

Siu, Paul C. P. *The Chinese Laundryman: A Study of Social Isolation*. New York: New York University Press, 1987.

Stern, Jane, and Michael Stern. *Square Meals*. New York: Alfred A. Knopf, 1985.

Stockard, Janice E. *Daughters of the Canton Delta: Marriage Patterns and Economic Strategies in South China, 1860–1930*. Stanford, Calif.: Stanford University Press, 1989.

Sung, Betty Lee. *Mountain of Gold: The Story of the Chinese in America*. New York: Macmillan, 1967.

———. "Chop Suey and Chow Mein." In *Chinese in America*. New York: Macmillan, 1972.

Tan, Amy. *The Kitchen God's Wife*. New York: G. P. Putnam's Sons, 1991.

Tan, Thomas Tsu-wee. *Your Chinese Roots: The Overseas Chinese Story*. Union City, Calif.: Heian International, 1987; original ed. Singapore: Times Books International, 1986.

Tsai, Shih-Shan Henry. *The Chinese Experience in America*. Bloomington: Indiana University Press, 1986.

Wing, Fred. *New Chinese Recipes*. New York: Edelmuth, 1942.

Wong, Nellie C. *Chinese Dishes for Foreign Homes*. Shanghai: Kelly & Walsh, 1935.

*Yee Fow—the Chinese Community in Sacramento*. Published by John T.C. Fang. Sacramento: Chinese Publishing House, 1961.

Yu, Renqui. "Chop Suey: From Chinese Food to Chinese American Food." In *Chinese America: History and Perspectives 1987*. San Francisco: Chinese Historical Society of America, 1987.

# Index

slicing, 22
  diagonal, 23
  horizontal or flat, 22–3
Smithfield ham, 55
snow peas
  chicken and
    chow mein, 228–9
    with water chestnuts and bean
      sprouts, 127–8
  chop suey, 177–8
  moo goo gai pan, 140–1
  shrimp with, 81–2
  stir-fried, with water chestnuts, 267
soups, 41–62
  abalone and squab, 47–9
  bean curd, 50–1
  chicken
    with cucumber, 57–8
    stock, 60–2
    subgum, 54–5
  lettuce-egg drop, 42–3
  mustard greens, 52–3
  Napa cabbage, 51–2
  oxtail, 43–4
  sizzling rice, 58–60
  squab and ham, 55–6
  watercress, 45
  wonton, 45–7
*Sour Sweet* (Mo), 19
soy bean sprouts, *see* bean sprouts
soy sauce, 29
Soy Superior Sauce, 29
spaghetti and meatballs, 235–7
spareribs, barbecued, 186
spinach
  with fermented bean curd, 258
  stir-fried
    with beef and oyster sauce,
      218
    with pork, 202
sponge cake, steamed, 293–4
spring rolls, 164–5

squab
  banquet-style crispy, 149–50
  minced, in lettuce leaves, 150–1
  soup
    with abalone, 47–9
    with ham, 55–6
squash, pork liver stir-fried with,
  188–9
squid, aromatic garlic, 99–100
star anise, 33
steamer, use of wok as, 27
stew, oxtail, 212–13
stir-frying, preparing wok for, 28
stock, chicken, 60–2
subgum, chicken, 108–9
  chow mein, 244–6
  soup, 54–5
suckling pig, roast, 5
sugar, 40
sugar snap peas, shrimp with, 82
Superior Soy, 29
sweet rice vinegar, 35
sweet-and-sour
  chicken, 120–2
  dipping sauce, for egg rolls, 162
  pig's feet, 199
  pork, 184–5
  shrimp, 78
Swiss chard, pork stir-fried with, 202

Taiwan, 9, 51, 211
  emigration from, 237
  lamb in, 220
  sesame oil from, 30
Tan, Amy, 9, 101–5, 242, 250
techniques, 22–8, 179
  chopping, 25
  dicing, 24
  mincing, 24–5
  roll-cutting, 23
  scoring, 25

# Knopf Cooks American

The series of cookbooks that celebrates the culinary heritage of America, telling different aspects of our story through recipes interspersed with historical lore, personal reflections, and the recollections of old-timers.

"Our food tells us where we came from and who we are . . ."